# UNDERSTANDING AND COPING WITH FAILURE

Failure is a theme of great importance in most clinical conditions and in everyday life, from birth until death. Its impact can be destabilizing, even disastrous. In spite of these facts, there has been no comprehensive psychoanalytic exploration of this topic. *Understanding and Coping with Failure: Psychoanalytic perspectives* fills this gap by examining failure from many perspectives. It goes a long way toward increasing understanding of the numerous issues involved and provides many valuable insights into ways of coping with these challenging experiences, and several chapters discuss positive aspects of failure – what can be learned from what would otherwise simply be regrettable experiences.

Brent Willock, Rebecca Coleman Curtis and Lori C. Bohm bring together a rich diversity of topics explored in thoughtful ways by an international group of authors from the United Kingdom, Canada and the United States. Failed therapies (which have been examined in the literature) are but one element freshly explored in this comprehensive exploration of the topic. The book is divided into sections covering the following topics: Failing and forgiving; Society-wide failure; Failure in the family; Therapeutic failure; Professional failure in the consulting room and on the career path; Integrity vs despair: facing failure in the final phase of the life cycle; Metaphoric bridges and creativity and The long shadow of childhood relational trauma.

*Understanding and Coping with Failure* will be eagerly welcomed by all those trying to increase their awareness, understanding and capacity to work with the many ramifications of this important issue. Because of the uniqueness of this broad, detailed exploration of the complexities of the failure experience, it will be essential reading for psychoanalysts, psychotherapists, psychologists, psychiatrists, social workers, counselors and students in these disciplines. It will also appeal to a wider audience interested in the psychoanalytic perspective.

**Brent Willock** is President of the Toronto Institute for Contemporary Psychoanalysis, Board Member of the Canadian Institute for Child and Adolescent Psychoanalytic Psychotherapy and on the faculty of the Institute for the Advancement of Self Psychology. He is the editor with Lori C. Bohm and

Rebecca Coleman Curtis of *Comparative-Integrative Psychoanalysis* (Analytic Press, 2007), *On Deaths and Endings: Psychoanalysts' reflections on finality, transformations and new beginnings* (Routledge, 2007) and *Loneliness and Longing: Conscious and unconscious aspects* (Routledge, 2011).

**Rebecca Coleman Curtis** is Professor of Psychology at Adelphi University and Faculty and Supervisor at the William Alanson White Institute and Supervisor at the National Institute for the Psychotherapies, New York.

**Lori C. Bohm** is Supervising Analyst, Faculty and Director at the Center for Applied Psychoanalysis and Intensive Psychoanalytic Psychotherapy programs at the William Alanson White Institute. She is Psychotherapy Supervisor in the Clinical Psychology Doctoral Program at City College of the City University of New York.

# UNDERSTANDING AND COPING WITH FAILURE

## PSYCHOANALYTIC PERSPECTIVES

*Edited by Brent Willock,*
*Rebecca Coleman Curtis and*
*Lori C. Bohm*

Routledge
Taylor & Francis Group

LONDON AND NEW YORK

First published 2014
by Routledge
27 Church Road, Hove, East Sussex BN3 2FA

and by Routledge
711 Third Avenue, New York, NY 10017

*Routledge is an imprint of the Taylor & Francis Group, an informa business*

© 2014 Brent Willock, Rebecca Coleman Curtis, and Lori C. Bohm

*British Library Cataloguing in Publication Data*
A catalogue record for this book is available from the British Library

*Library of Congress Cataloging-in-Publication Data*
Understanding and coping with failure : psychoanalytic perspectives / Brent Willock, Rebecca Coleman Curtis and Lori C. Bohm (eds).
pages cm
1. Failure (Psychology) 2. Adjustment (Psychology) I. Willock, Brent. II. Curtis, Rebecca C. III. Bohm, Lori C.
BF575.F14U544 2014
155.2'4–dc23
2013047532

ISBN: 978-0-415-85852-6 (hbk)
ISBN: 978-0-415-85853-3 (pbk)
ISBN: 978-1-315-77319-3 (ebk)

Typeset in Times New Roman
by Cenveo Publisher Services

MIX
Paper from
responsible sources
FSC
www.fsc.org    FSC® C013056

Printed and bound in Great Britain by
TJ International Ltd, Padstow, Cornwall

# CONTENTS

CONTENTS

# CONTRIBUTORS

**Elizabeth Allured**, Faculty, Derner Institute of Advanced Psychological Studies, Adelphi University and Suffolk Institute for Psychoanalysis and Psychotherapy.

**Ann Baranowski**, Faculty, Toronto Institute for Contemporary Psychoanalysis and Wilfrid Laurier University.

**Janet G. Benton**, Supervisor/Faculty, William Alanson White Institute, Institute for Contemporary Psychotherapy, Teachers College, Columbia University, City University of New York and Metropolitan Center for Mental Health.

**Linda S. Bergman**, Former Assistant Director of Clinical Services, Postdoctoral Psychotherapy Center, Adelphi University and private practice, Centerport, Long Island and New York City.

**Lori C. Bohm**, Supervising Analyst, Faculty member and Director at the Center for Applied Psychoanalysis and Intensive Psychoanalytic Psychotherapy, William Alanson White Institute, Psychotherapy Supervisor, Clinical Psychology Doctoral Program at City College of the City University of New York.

**Mark B. Borg, Jr**, Supervisor, William Alanson White Institute, Senior Partner, Community Consulting Group and Owner, Human Anti-Depressant Project.

**Frances M. Clark**, Training Therapist and Supervisor, Scottish Training in Psychoanalytic Psychotherapy and Adult Psychotherapist, NHS, Glasgow.

**Rebecca Coleman Curtis**, Professor of Psychology, Adelphi University and Faculty, William Alanson White Institute.

**Michelle Flax**, Supervising Analyst and Faculty, Toronto Institute for Contemporary Psychoanalysis.

**Tiffany L. Frank**, Postdoctoral Psychology Fellow at the Jewish Board of Family and Children's Services, Pride of Judea, Douglaston, NY.

**Marsha A. Hewitt**, Professor, Social Ethics and Religion, Trinity College and Department of Religion, University of Toronto and Faculty, Toronto Institute for Contemporary Psychoanalysis, and Institute for the Advancement of Self-Psychology.

**Richard Holloway**, Writer and broadcaster. Former Gresham Professor of Divinity in the City of London and Bishop of Edinburgh and Primus (Archbishop) of the Scottish Episcopal Church.

**Stephen Hyman**, Director, Adelphi University Postgraduate Program in Psychodynamic School Psychology and Supervisor, Adelphi University Postgraduate Programs in Psychoanalysis and Psychotherapy.

**Robert Langan**, Training and Supervising Analyst, William Alanson White Institute.

**Judith E. Levene**, Supervising Analyst and Faculty, Toronto Institute for Contemporary Psychoanalysis; Faculty, Toronto Institute of Psychoanalysis; Associate Professor Emeritus, Wilfrid Laurier University and Faculty, Department of Psychiatry, University of Toronto.

**Karl Loszak**, Faculty, Supervisor and Board member, Toronto Institute for Contemporary Psychoanalysis.

**Molly Ludlam**, Couples psychoanalytic psychotherapist and Editor of *Couple and Family Psychoanalysis*.

**Christopher A. McIntosh**, Assistant Professor, Department of Psychiatry, University of Toronto and Head, Gender Identity Clinic, Centre for Addiction and Mental Health.

**Robert Mendelsohn**, Professor, Gordon F. Derner Institute of Advanced Psychological Studies, Adelphi University.

**John V. O'Leary**, Faculty and Supervisor, William Alanson White Institute and Staff Psychologist, Columbia Presbyterian Hospital.

**Ionas Sapountzis**, Faculty and Supervisor, Derner Institute of Advanced Psychological Studies, Adelphi University.

**Henry M. Seiden**, Adjunct Faculty and Clinical Supervisor, Pace and Yeshiva Universities; Clinical Instructor, Mount Sinai Psychiatry Department, Queens Hospital Center; Faculty, New School for Social Research and several independent training institutes.

**Amira Simha-Alpern**, Adjunct Professor and Supervisor, Derner Institute of Advanced Psychological Studies, Adelphi University; Faculty, Suffolk Institute for Psychotherapy and Psychoanalysis and Director, Potential Space for Continuing Education in Psychology and Psychotherapy.

**John A. Sloane**, Assistant Professor, Department of Psychiatry, University of Toronto and Faculty, Institute for the Advancement of Self Psychology and Toronto Institute for Contemporary Psychoanalysis.

**Michael Stern**, Clinical Supervisor, Institute for Contemporary Psychotherapy and formerly Adjunct Associate Professor, Teachers' College, Columbia University.

**J. Gail White**, Faculty and Supervisor, Toronto Institute for Contemporary Psychoanalysis and formerly Lecturer, York University and University of Toronto.

**Brent Willock**, President, Toronto Institute for Contemporary Psychoanalysis; Faculty, Toronto Child Psychoanalytic Program and Institute for the Advancement of Self Psychology.

# ACKNOWLEDGEMENTS

For brainstorming that led to this book, many thanks to Dr. Michael Stern (New York University's Postdoctoral Program in Psychotherapy and Psychoanalysis), Professor Rebecca Coleman Curtis and Dr. Lori C. Bohm (William Alanson White Psychoanalytic Society), Professors Michael O'Loughlin and Ionas Sapountzis (Adelphi Society for Psychoanalysis and Psychotherapy), Frances Clark and Amanda Cornish (Scottish Institute for Human Relations), and Dr. Brent Willock (Toronto Institute and Society for Contemporary Psychoanalysis). Thanks also to Kate Hawes and her outstanding team at Routledge for welcoming this manuscript into their publishing home.

Finally we would like to thank the following:
Excerpt from "Home Is So Sad" from *The Complete Poems of Philip Larkin* by Philip Larkin, edited by Archie Burnett. Copyright © 2012 by The Estate of Philip Larkin. Introduction copyright © 2012 by Archie Burnett. Reprinted by permission of Farrar, Straus and Giroux, LLC.

Excerpt from *Worstward Ho*, copyright © 1983 by Samuel Beckett. Used by permission of Grove/Atlantic, Inc. Any third party use of this material, outside of this publication, is prohibited.

Excerpt from "The Wandering Wingless" from *Failure: Poems by Philip Schultz*. Copyright © 2007 by Philip Schultz. Reprinted by permission of Houghton Mifflin Harcourt Publishing Company. All rights reserved.

"A Hermit Thrush" from *Collected Poems of Amy Clampitt* by Amy Clampitt, copyright © 1997 by the Estate of Amy Clampitt. Used by permission of Alfred A. Knopf, a division of Random House, Inc.

# VINCENT VAN GOGH AND THE PARADOX OF FAILURE

During his lifetime, Van Gogh sold only one painting – *Red Vineyard at Arles*. At the time of his death, his career, friendships, romantic life, and mental health all seemed like failures. His more than 900 paintings remained unsold and relatively unknown. Afterwards, he came to be regarded as one of the best painters of all time.

In July 1890, from Auvers-sur-Oise, he wrote to his brother and sister: "I too still felt very saddened, and had continued to feel the storm that threatens you also weighing upon me. What can be done – you see I usually try to be quite good-humoured, but my life, too, is attacked at the very root, my step also is faltering … I've painted another three large canvases since then. They're immense stretches of wheat fields under turbulent skies, and I made a point of trying to express sadness, extreme loneliness" (www.vangoghletters.org). By July 29, 1890, Van Gogh was dead, believed by most to be a suicide.

On December 23, 1888, the famous incident in which he severed a portion of his ear lobe took place, after which Van Gogh was found at home, unconscious. He lapsed into an acute psychotic state and spent three days in solitary confinement, bandaged about the ear. He had no memory of his attacks on Paul Gauguin, his self-mutilation, or his early stay at the hospital. Although many think he suffered from bipolar disorder, others believe this episode was due to temporal lobe epilepsy (Stafford & Webb, 2004). Apparently potassium bromide helped him recover from the psychotic state and within days he painted *Self-Portrait with Bandaged Ear and Pipe*.

As editors, we resonated when Brent Willock suggested *Wheatfields with Crows*, generally considered Van Gogh's final painting, as the cover for this book. I loved the idea, having hung Van Gogh's *Bedroom at Arles* in my college room, traveled out of my way to see the village of Auvers-sur-Oise and Van Gogh's paintings at the Kroller-Muller Museum in eastern Holland, and having just visited the hospital at Arles where he painted the gardens. Thinking there is something more appealing about a human face, we settled on *Self-Portrait with Bandaged Ear and Pipe* for our cover. We all considered Van Gogh a good representation of the paradox of failure.

Rebecca Coleman Curtis

# References

Stafford, T. & Webb, M. (2004). *Mind Hacks: Tips and Tricks for Using Your Brain.* Sebastopol, CA: O'Reilly Media.
www.vangoghletters.org. August 23, 2013.

# INTRODUCTION

## Fail up! Analyzing failures and using them to our advantage

*Rebecca Coleman Curtis and Tiffany L. Frank*

> What was I doing here / in this public pain? / Everything I loved I feared. / Was this what failure was – / endless fear?
>
> Philip Schultz, *Failure*

Schultz wrote these words from a psychiatric ward in San Francisco. After writing them, he published two more books of poetry and won a Pulitzer Prize, while continuing his work as director of the Writers' Center in New York. While reading his poetry, I (Curtis) heard advice about how to handle failure on radio and television from an advertising agency (the Grey Group), an athlete (Diana Nyad) and her support team, a celebrity (Tavis Smiley), and research projects (Ohio State Leadership Center).

Failure – one word that can so quickly cause panic, anxiety, fear, and a flood of other emotions in all of us. Whether it be thinking about a previous mishap, a possible future failure, or a task in which we may be currently not living up to our potential, the result is the same. Very few want to think about it, or discuss our insufficiencies.

Many suggestions for coping with failure have appeared in the popular literature. The idea of rewarding failure was the subject of an article in the *Wall Street Journal* called "Better Ideas through Failure – Companies Reward Employee Mistakes to Spur Innovation, Get Back Their Edge" (Shellenbarger, 2011). Gary Shapiro of Consumer Electronics Association, co-author of a book on innovation, *Mistakes are OK—Hiding Them is Not*, talks openly about his own screw-ups, Shellenbarger reported. The Grey Group, the advertising firm responsible for the talking-baby ads, hands out "Heroic Failure" awards because management is concerned about getting ideas that are "edgier or riskier, or new and totally unproven" (p. D1). Similarly, Sure Payroll in Glenview, Illinois, has a "Best New Mistake" award. "The most successful people tend to be those with the most failures" (p. D1), stated Dean Keith Simonton, a psychologist studying creativity and innovation.

Diana Nyad tried to swim from Cuba to Florida in August 2011, at age 61. Having to stop due to asthma, she decided to turn disappointment into advantage. She stated she would get out "to analyze the problem." To CNN's Sanjay Gupta (2011), she reported, "I had never been more confident – never, never – never a moment of doubt … Getting out: What a shame … a real bitter pill to swallow." While she was deciding to get out, her supporter said, "This is going to be painful, no doubt about it," and, later, "This was a success. You sure did inspire everyone who knows you." And many of us who don't know her! In September 2011, Nyad made another attempt at the Cuba to Florida swim, but had to stop because of jellyfish and Portuguese-man-of-war stings. She completed the swim in September 2012, on her fifth attempt. Gupta said her plan is "audacious and maybe impossible."

Failure is often a fear of taking risks. Without them, life may feel deadened. "Happiness comes from facing challenges and going out on a limb and taking risks. If you're not willing to take a risk for something you really care about, you might as well be dead," stated Frolov and Schneider (1993), screenwriters for *Northern Exposure* and *The Sopranos*. There can be costs to action, but greater ones to inaction.

In "What If the Secret to Success is Failure?" (Tough, 2011), Dominic Randolf, headmaster of Riverdale Country School in New York City, says, "This push on tests is missing out on some serious parts of what it means to be a successful human" (p. 40). With psychologists Duckworth, Peterson, Seligman, and Levin of the KIPP network of charter schools in New York City, Randolf put together a list of character traits to predict achievement and happiness in life, including zest, curiosity, self-control, social intelligence, gratitude, grit, and optimism. The opposite traits predict failure to be resilient in difficult times – giving up, pessimism, lack of social and emotional intelligence, etc.

These educators and psychologists were influenced greatly by Seligman and Peterson, leading cognitive behavioral psychologists. The educators refer to teaching children skills to control their tempers and be resilient as part of their education at Riverdale and the KIPP schools. "Cognitive behavioral therapy (CBT), involves using the conscious mind to understand and overcome unconscious fears and self-destructive habits, using techniques like 'self-talk'—putting an immediate crisis in perspective by reminding yourself of the larger context" (Tough, 2011, p. 48). Although cognitive behavioral approaches can be useful, many times these "common-sense," often rather simplistic strategies, are not enough. The present book not only focuses on ways to overcome such fears and habits, but also on what some of these unconscious fears may be – the province, traditionally, of psychoanalysis.

Another psychologist, Levine (2006), recently argued that lack of real suffering is leading many American youth, especially the affluent, to be "at risk." They have been so protected from difficulty and so confident of a relatively secure life that they are not prepared to cope with failures, losses, disappointments and traumas. My children (Curtis) at Hunter Elementary School in New York City had insoluble problems mixed in with their soluble math problems. At first glance, this seemed needlessly frustrating, but then I saw the wisdom. The children would learn not to spend time on problems that were too difficult when they could be solving others. They would become desensitized to failure. It would be expected when engaged in difficult work.

Social support is another factor known to help people deal with setbacks. For many individuals, psychotherapists provide such support. These therapeutic relationships are the subject of many chapters in this book.

Often adults want to push personal, professional, and other failures from their minds, locking them away from consciousness, never to be thought of again. Every child is told to learn from his or her mistakes, but how often does anyone look deeply enough to learn? More often than not, people want to share and discuss their successes rather than failures. They want to celebrate achievements, not dwell on mishaps and fumbles. And rightfully so, as there is much pride in sharing achievements and successes. There can, however, be just as much, and possibly more, to learn from failures. That is the beauty of the contributions in this book. They take a look at "failures" and, rather than locking them away, examine them for learning, development, and enrichment. In so doing, they give space for what is so often a source of shame, sadness, and other difficult emotions to become, instead, a place for understanding and growth.

Tavis Smiley, the acclaimed broadcaster, author, journalist, and publisher, grappled with the topic of failure in his recent book, *Fail Up: 20 Lessons on Building Success from Failure*. In it, he chronicled his failures, how he got past them, and how he was able to turn them into successes, or opportunities for development and enhancement of character. From major life decisions, like moving to another city and wondering about whether or not he could make it, to career-related slip-ups, like someone recording him cursing in a radio station, Smiley shows how he changed his attitude and learned lessons from each "failure."

A change in attitude or perspective goes a long way when understanding or recovering from failure or disappointment. Many great people have picked themselves up this way; "Failure is only the opportunity more intelligently to begin again," Henry Ford stated (Ford & Crowther, 1923, p. 273).

With all these role models who were able to change their perspectives and grow from defeat, it seems perplexing that many of us are still so scared to fail and feel ashamed when we do. It is therefore helpful to read, in this current book, in-depth studies about how failures have often not destroyed, but rather have provided, substance and enriched individuals. These careful explorations can help allay our fears and concerns.

This volume explores failure in many different contexts. Each chapter offers a unique viewpoint and opens up space for continuing conversation on the subject. A good balance of theory and clinical examples makes this book easily readable. In addition to its appeal for clinicians, it raises areas of possible interest for researchers, and provides examples of coping with failure that may prove useful to a wider readership.

One word not so often associated with failure is "forgiveness." This is a contribution of the opening chapters by Holloway and Loszak. Discussing forgiveness through the lens of the child/parent relationship and seeing it as a template for learning how to repair, Loszak shows how it is healthy and necessary to fail and forgive. Holloway examines why there is so much shame and toxicity associated with failing. Exploring athletic and military failures and poetry, he discusses how we might be more forgiving of ourselves and others. Forgiving oneself may occur in psychoanalysis as patients come to feel safe enough to be fully known. The importance of this experience in a human relationship has been implicit in psychoanalytic relationships, but these authors make it explicit.

Cultural values can lead to perceptions of failure. Even seeking treatment can be seen as failure. Benton discusses how United States culture, emphasizing quick fixes, with goals being more important than process, and desires to be special, created difficulties for her patient. Although this individual wanted to use a self-help book, it was ultimately the intimacy of her vulnerability with her therapist that led to change.

Institutions, communities, and systems can fail individuals. For Borg's patient, this was all too true. His case study shows how one analyst used patient and system failures as a productive part of the treatment. Allured discusses a common blind spot in the psychological community. Through her child patients, she cued into the overwhelming anxieties related to our planet's uncertain future. Detailing how these manifested in her patients, she focuses on our need to better understand the impact of the non-human environment.

Another aspect of failure explored is family context. With a case that began as a struggle about homework, Hyman examines how parental failure in attunement impacts child development. Ludlam looks at the dynamic in a couple possibly needing to split up and how that outcome may or may not constitute failure. She identifies common misconceptions of couples' therapy and discusses how "failure" may be the only way to start anew and grow. Mendelsohn uses the Icarus myth and two case examples of adult men who struggled with success and failure in relation to their fathers to show the depths of the unconscious hold of this theme. Here we see the fear of crashing and what happens if one begins to act on internalized hopes and goals. Seiden explores the concept of home and the inevitable longing for it, which can never be fulfilled. He looks at how a friend from Taiwan living in New York and a patient from an Italian section of Brooklyn managed their struggles in light of failing to feel at home.

The section of the book on therapeutic failure starts with one of the most well known cases in psychoanalytic history – Dora. It seeks to elucidate one pitfall that Freud himself may have stumbled into during this analysis – shame. Simha-Alpern draws a parallel between Dora and a patient of hers who also fled treatment. Ways in which both analyst and patient contributed to this flight are examined.

Hewitt presents a patient who, for many therapists, is the most difficult and frightening, namely the suicidal individual. Approximately 30,000 people in the

United States alone commit suicide each year. Coping with suicidal patients is extremely difficult for any analyst. Hewitt's patient demands a letter from her to intercede with a project from which he has been rejected or else he will kill himself. The analyst manages to negotiate this difficult situation and to help this man with his depression and make progress, but his ultimate situation in life remains mysterious.

Professional mistakes and failures in one's career spoken about openly and honestly comprise the next few chapters. Clark shares specific moments when she failed to maintain the analytic frame. Bergman discusses a treatment failure related to her inability to contain her patient's rage. Using this patient's email communications subsequent to this enactment, she elucidates the relationship rupture and repair. Sloane shares his experience of a painful personal failure related to his attempt to become a training analyst and his journey after this rejection. This section also visits a more theoretical side of failure, asking how we can look at it differently in hopes of reducing its pain. To begin answering this question, O'Leary provides a balanced attribution theory, highlighting the role of chance in failure.

One failure common to the human condition, well described and delineated in this book, relates to aging and mortality. Stern introduces us to some elderly patients and the struggles they are facing. He talks about feeling obsolete, and the narcissistic and realistic injuries and challenges of the elderly. White and Flax continue with three elderly patients struggling with bodily deterioration. They show how creativity, especially poetry and art, can be helpful when facing physical failures. Langan discusses the nature of analytic work and the human experience of finding meaning through one another against the backdrop of the fact that one day we shall all cease to exist. His case underscores the importance of discussing shameful memories before death.

The creativity that proved to be an important vehicle in work with the elderly is also a concept that pervades much of psychoanalytic thought. Baranowski revisits Otto Rank's notion of the neurotic as failed artist. She demonstrates the value that a new relationship provides as a playground for self-creation. McIntosh discusses a patient who experienced a great deal of failure in life, beginning with a bodily injury. He shows us how his patient's metaphors and dreams concerning his body and his work in a Japanese martial art intertwined with the analytic work to promote progress. Sapountzis examines ways in which failures in understanding can contribute to therapeutic process if they are viewed within the framework of transitional space. Illustrating his point with various cases, including one of gender identity confusion, he shows the value of play as his patient grows from saying only sounds like "pherma pherma" to communicating with meaningful sentences.

Towards the end of this book, Levene and Willock talk about how adult difficulties are often re-creations of childhood traumas or failures. In both their contributions, profound emotional experiences become reactivated in adulthood – one through illness, the other through an act of perversion. Their detailed studies clearly demonstrate how failures can stay with individuals throughout a lifetime and can be worked through therapeutically.

This book begins to desensitize us to the word "failure," reducing some of the shame and anxiety associated with it. Hopefully this volume will also stimulate many conversations and lines of inquiry as to how people can look at, think about, understand, and learn from what may at first be perceived only as failure. While self-help books and web sites provide some useful ideas about how to handle failure, this current contribution helps us to understand what may be useful when those techniques do not work and a more in depth analysis is required and beneficial.

This volume also provides glimpses of the intricate, close relationships in psychoanalytic treatments that give rise to expressions of vulnerability, art, poetry, memories, myths, and meanings. Each chapter makes it clear that there is a wealth of knowledge to be gained from "failure." Rather than brushing them under the rug, the authors aim to help us to "fail up" by providing a sense of the growth-producing potential in many failures.

# References

Ford, H. & Crowther, S. (1923). *My Life and Work*. Garden City, NY: Doubleday, Page & Company.

Frolov, D. & Schneider, A. (1993). *Northern exposure, Northern lights*. www.imdb.com/title/tt0662375/.

Gupta, S. (2011) Jellyfish, currents cut short Cuba-to-Florida swim. CNN, September 17.

Levine, M. (2006). *The Price of Privilege: How Parental Pressure and Material Advantage Are Creating a Generation of Disconnected and Unhappy Kids*. New York: Harper Collins.

Schultz, P. (2009). *Failure*. New York: Harcourt.

Shellenbarger, S. (2011). Better ideas through failure. *Wall Street Journal*, September 27, D1, D4.

Smiley, T. (2011). *Fail Up! 20 Lessons on Building Success from Failure*. New York: Smiley Books.

Tough, P. (2011). What if the secret to success is failure? *New York Times Magazine*, September 18 (pp. 38–44, 48, 85).

# Part I

# FAILING AND FORGIVING

# 1

# FAIL BETTER

## Richard Holloway

When I was asked to write this chapter, the reason given for the invitation was a short broadcast I had done for the BBC some time before on the theme of failure. It is one thing to pull off a snappy two-minute radio talk, quite another to extend it to chapter length; but I am glad the invitation was issued not only because of the honour you have done me in inviting me, but because it has given me an opportunity to think a bit more systematically about such a profound topic. I want to begin by repeating the central thought in the broadcast referred to.

It concerned one of the greatest tragedies in the history of baseball. It occurred on October 25, 1986, when the Boston Red Sox had a comfortable two-run lead against the Mets, in what the Americans modestly call the World Series. The Mets were batting and a Red Sox veteran, Bill Buckner, was fielding at first base. Inexplicably, he let a lightly tapped ball roll between his legs into outfield, enabling the Mets to get a home run and victory. Buckner was a baseball hero who had won thousands of games for the Red Sox over the years with his line drives and brilliant fielding. All that was forgotten, and he is now famous for the day he lost the Red Sox the World Series.

This incident led Stephen Jay Gould (2002, p. 63), the great scientist and baseball fan, to observe that triumph's pleasures are intense but brief, while failure remains with us for ever. He suggested that this was a good thing because failure expresses our common humanity. When people in public life fail in some way, as they all invariably do from time to time, fair-minded people will always forgive them, provided they admit what happened. 'Sorry, folks, I guess I dropped the ball.'

I suspect Bill Buckner would have found little comfort in Gould's dismissal of what to him was an enduring shame. Gould was right to say failure expresses our humanity, but why do we so often associate it with shame? And why are we so anxious to hide our failures? Why is failure such a toxic word? All I can do in this short chapter is offer a few preliminary thoughts – three themes on the topic – each followed by a suggestion.

## First theme: why this fear of failure?

One of the most interesting books I have read on this or any other subject is Norman F. Dixon's (1988) *On the Psychology of Military Incompetence*. Dixon was fascinated by those snafus or cock-ups that riddle military history at all times, in all places. Before seeking an explanation for the failures, he offered many examples. Here are two of them (pp. 36ff., 112).

In 1854, during the Crimean War, Lord Raglan ordered a cavalry regiment, the Light Brigade, to charge the Russian cannons. Tennyson's famous poem described what happened.

> Forward the Light Brigade!
> Was there a man dismay'd
> Not though the soldiers knew
> Someone had blundered:
> Theirs not to make reply,
> Theirs not to reason why,
> Theirs but to do and die:
> Into the Valley of Death
> Rode the six hundred.

Of the 673 cavalrymen who charged the Russian guns, 100 rode back.

In 1893, the Royal Navy was on manoeuvres in the South Atlantic with the elderly, short-sighted Admiral Tryon in charge. He ordered two parallel columns of battleships to reverse direction by turning inwards. The other officers on the brig could see that the combined turning circle required for the manoeuvre was greater than the actual distance between the ships, but they dared not question the order. HMS *Camperdown* rammed HMS *Victoria* with great loss of life.

At the risk of greatly oversimplifying his thesis, Dixon discovered that at the heart of all the examples of military incompetence he explored there was a human type he called the authoritarian personality. It had four characteristics, the fourth being the really significant one.

1    There was an anal-retentive neatness and fear of mess and confusion in this type of person. They craved an ordered universe and ran their lives on the fixed tramlines of duty and routine.
2    They were emotionally frigid and afraid to let go of control.
3    They were deferential to those above them in the pecking order and contemptuous of those below. It could be said of them what was said of a recent US Ambassador to the UN: he kissed up and kicked down.
4    The most powerful motive in the authoritarian personality was fear of failure. Keeping out of trouble was more important than any hope of success. Everything was done by the book. When the book did not have the answer to a particular situation, they were incapable of improvising.

Dixon said the authoritarian personality was the result of conditional loving in childhood. Potty-training was the metaphor he used. Approval was only achieved and affection experienced if the child performed on time and into the appropriate vessel. This created a personality for whom keeping out of trouble and doing everything by the book were their dominant purposes. Fear of failure became their main motive.

## First consequential suggestion

At the root of our fear of failure lies belief in an implicit or explicit metaphysic of surveillance. For me, this metaphysic is symbolically expressed in a Victorian wall plate a friend mischievously left me in his will. It shows a large, staring eye, with this motto underneath: 'Thou God see'st me'. For the person living under this threat, life is not an experiment in being, a process of discovery; it is a search for approval through avoidance of what is disapproved of. You may well ask why on the scales of judgement a single feather of failure can psychologically outweigh a prodigious record of achievement, but this is the mindset created by the surveillance metaphysic. It is also why a prohibitionist ethics of avoidance is more stultifying to our humanity than an ethics of excellence and achievement. Excellence and achievement are the result of the constant experience of failure, not the frightened flight from it that is characteristic of the craven personality. Failure is a necessary concomitant of an ethic of achievement.

## Second theme: we are not as free as we think we are

The illusion of free will is another element we must consider in any useful exegesis of failure. We are not as free, any of us, as we think we are. We are determined in a *general* way by the story of the universe and its accumulated expression in our own individual being. Each of us has a new brain floating above a sea of old passions, all of which come from our species' deep history. And we are determined in *particular* by our own family history, which none of us chose. No one can edit their past, though it can help to understand how it made us what we became. The English poet Philip Larkin (2003, p. 142) understood this. In his poem 'This be the Verse', he claimed parents mess up their offspring, even if they do not mean to. Having been 'fucked up' by their parents, they pass their faults and misery on to their offspring.

The same idea was expressed more philosophically by the English ethicist Mary Warnock:

> If we think about the nature of human choice we must recognize that, though what people want and choose may in some sense be explicable, it cannot be completely predictable because of the innumerable contingencies within the context of which a choice is made. If everything were

known and if I lived in laboratory conditions where the contingencies and chance happenings could be kept on record from the moment of my birth, then my choices might appear foregone conclusions if anyone could be bothered to draw them. But we do not live in such conditions and never could. We could never know all that happened in the past to influence me, nor what was even now happening to limit or guide my choices. We feel free because we act against a background of ignorance, including ignorance of our own genetic system and of the input of circumstances and environment on the computer that is our own brain. Spinoza said that freedom was the ignorance of necessity.

(1992, p. 1045)

## Second consequential suggestion

We need an anthropology based on compassionate realism about the human condition. We are morally hybrid creatures who are not wholly in control of ourselves. How should we respond to our predicament? A philosopher who is a helpful guide here is Hannah Arendt (2000), who writes:

Though we don't know what we are doing when we are acting, we have no possibility ever to undo what we have done. Action processes are not only unpredictable, they are also irreversible; there is no author or maker who can undo, destroy, what he has done if he does not like it or when the consequences are disastrous. The possible redemption from the predicament of irreversibility is the faculty of forgiving, and the remedy for unpredictability is contained in the faculty to make and keep promises. The two remedies belong together: forgiving relates to the past and serves to undo its deeds, while binding oneself through promises serves to set up in the ocean of future uncertainty islands of security without which not even continuity, let alone durability of any kind, would ever be possible in the relationships between men. Without being forgiven, released from the consequences of what we have done, our capacity to act would, as it were, be confined to one single deed from which we could never recover; we would remain the victim of its consequences for ever ... Without being bound to the fulfillment of promises, we would never be able to achieve that amount of identity and continuity which together produce the 'person' about whom a story can be told; each of us would be condemned to wander helplessly and without direction in the darkness of his own lonely heart, caught in its ever changing moods, contradictions, and equivocalities. In this respect, forgiving and making promises are like control mechanisms built into the very faculty to start new and unending processes.

(2000, pp. 180–181)

So the remedy for our predicament is the twofold strategy of promising and forgiving.

## Third theme: how do we recover a culture of promising and forgiving?

Before offering some suggestions, let me first publish a health warning. We should rid ourselves of the hope of perfection either in ourselves or in our institutions (e.g. if only we could find the right structure, programme, guru, religion, leader, psychoanalytic theory, therapeutic approach or manual of military tactics). Perfectionist abstractions only become other modalities of our imperfection, but their seductive power makes them particularly dangerous. In *The Chestnut Casts His Flambeaux*, poet A.E. Housman (1922) got it right: 'The troubles of our proud and angry dust /Are from eternity, and shall not fail'.

Nevertheless, there are things we can do to manage the muddle better, and a good way to begin is to understand the power of the promise in helping us manage the unruly reality of human nature. Implicit in the promise is moral realism, aimed at arming the subject against the unpredictability of circumstance, including the unpredictability of their own nature. Self-knowledge is an important part of this process. Acknowledge from the choices you have made the kind of person you have revealed yourself to be. Only radical self-knowledge will enable you to modify your character.

Just as important, if we are to learn from our failures, is the faculty of forgiving. One of the paradoxes of forgiveness is that it is the remedy for those who have broken their promises, so its very possibility makes us more likely to acknowledge the mistakes we have made and even benefit from them. Forgiveness is as important to stable institutions as is the pledged or promised life. This is the element in the human contract that is particularly weak in our culture at the moment. For whatever reason, we seem to be living through a particularly vengeful time, and the surveillance capacity of the media, amplified by its insatiable appetite for disclosures and revelation, adds to the sense of pressure public figures live under. Nietzsche had an interesting thing to say on this subject. In an early essay on the *Use and Abuse of History* he writes:

> In order to determine the extent and thereby the boundary point at which past things must be forgotten if they are not to become the grave diggers of the present, one has to know the exact extent of the plastic energy of a person, of a people, of a culture; that is, the power to grow uniquely from within, to transform and incorporate the past and the unknown, to heal wounds, to replace what is lost, and to duplicate shattered structures from within ... There are people so lacking this energy that they bleed to death, as if from a tiny scratch, after a single incident, a single pain, and often in particular a single minor injustice.

> (1997, p. 62)

How are we to recover the capacity for forgiveness in a vengeful culture that has destroyed the distance that used to cloak our mistakes from the public gaze? Let me, in conclusion, offer my:

## Third Consequential Suggestion

To his most famous novel, *Howard's End*, E.M. Forster appended the epigraph 'ONLY CONNECT'. The novel's theme was the sexual hypocrisy of Edwardian England. In particular, Henry Wilcox's hypocrisy is revealed when he refuses to help the needy Leonard Bast because he is afraid that assisting him might uncover the affair he had had with his wife.

Our moral and personal failures are great teachers of compassion and forgiveness; but only if we learn to connect them to others' failures. In *She Teaches Lear*, the Scottish poet Iain Crichton Smith (1985) wisely reminded us that 'From our own weakness only are we kind' (p. 54). In 'Old Woman', his poem about one who failed to connect, Smith described a harsh, cold woman who forgave no one. Not even when alone and ageing did 'she forgive our poor journey and our common grave' (p. 18). Nothing is more calculated to entrench our fear of failure than our own failure to forgive. The bewitching paradox of the moral life is that it is our failures that teach us the greatest lesson, forgiveness. *Only connect ...*

The other paradox worth noting is the spiritual danger our moral successes place us in. It was Yehuda Amichai (1996), the greatest Israeli poet of the twentieth century, who taught me that lesson, so I'll give him the last word. He noted in 'The Place Where We Are Right', flowers will never grow, no more than they would in a hard, thoroughly trampled yard. In contrast, doubts and love dig up the soil, like a plough or mole. In this aerated zone, 'a whisper will be heard' (p. 34). What does the whisper say to us? So you failed? Fail again. Fail better.

## References

Amichai, Y. (1996). *The Selected Poetry of Yehuda Amichai*, trans. Chana Bloch and Stephen Mitchell. Berkeley: University of California Press.

Arendt, H. (2000) Labor, work, action. In *The Portable Hannah Arendt*. London: Penguin.

Dixon, N.F. (1988). *On the Psychology of Military Incompetence*. London: Futura.

Gould, S.J. (2002). *I Have Landed*. London: Jonathan Cape.

Housman, A.E. (1922). *Last Poems*. London: G. Richards.

Larkin, P. (2003). *Collected Poems*. London: Faber & Faber.

Nietzsche, F. (1997). The use and abuse of history. In *Untimely Meditations*. Cambridge: Cambridge University Press.

Smith, I. C. (1985). *Selected Poems*. Manchester: Carcanet.

Warnock, M. (1992). Ethical challenges in embryo manipulation. *British Medical Journal*, 304: 1045–1049.

# 2

# FAILING WITH GRACE

## How a golden thread of forgiveness
## runs through psychoanalysis

### *Karl Loszak*

'Forgive us our failures, as we forgive those whose failures torment us.' If psychoanalysis had a prayer, this might be it. Many will shudder at the oxymoron of a psychoanalytic prayer. As a group, we have taken to heart Freud's insistent eschewal of religion. Until recently, forgiveness was rarely mentioned in psychoanalytic writing. Yet those in the Judeo-Christian tradition have long sought forgiveness for their failures: by yearly atonement, weekly confession, or in prayer.

In this chapter I argue that themes of forgiveness and reconciliation run as a thread through foundational psychoanalytic writings, and that forgiveness rests at the very heart of psychoanalytic endeavor. After an attempt to corral some of its essential features, my focus will be on forgiveness in the relationship between children and their parents. This line of thought leads us to recognize the internalized otherness within each of us – of the other lurking within the 'I' – thus blurring the traditional dichotomy between intrapsychic and intersubjective. Through a brief examination of seminal contributions from Klein, Winnicott, Ogden, Green, Freud, Kohut, and Kristeva, I encourage the reader to consider the value of holding forgiveness close at hand during your clinical hours.

## Forgiveness undefined: what is forgiveness?

Forgiveness is protean; it strenuously resists definition. What follows is my attempt to distill – from an idiosyncratic sampling of psychoanalysis, philosophy, theology, and popular culture – some essential elements of a family resemblance. I refer to this account as 'the usual story' – a kind of virtual centre, around which diverse perspectives can be seen to cluster.

The bare bones account of ordinary forgiveness runs as follows. One person wrongs another; I call them the 'offender' and the 'aggrieved'. I prefer these terms to the more usual 'perpetrator' and 'victim' because of the prejudgment entailed by such legalistic terminology (used, for example, by McWilliams & Lependorf,

1990, p. 432). Offences run the gamut. One may be aggrieved in response to the 'perpetration' of a minimal offence. Or one may be the object of the most grievous offence without being reduced to a 'victim'.

The evil act symbolically elevates the offender and diminishes the aggrieved; it signals the offender's contempt for the other. Talion law dictates that equality be restored (Exodus 21: 12–27). Talion law is usually thought of as recommending harsh punishment – at least an eye for an eye. More accurately, it implies measured punishment: neither too little nor too much. The word's etymology entails the notion of keeping score by means of notches on a stick; hence, keeping a 'tally'.

The offender must recognize both wrongdoing and harm caused. He must inform the aggrieved, preferably in public, that he knows these things. Popular culture is rife with laughable 'apologies' that fall far short of this ideal; e.g. 'If I caused any oversensitive soul to take offence … then I regret their hurt feelings.' The offender must atone: that is, he must place himself at one – on a level – with the aggrieved, usually accomplished by lowering himself through sacrifice or elevating the aggrieved by means of compensation. Finally, he must forbear: having recognized the error of his ways, he promises never again to commit a similar offence.

On an interpersonal plane, we might conceive of failure and forgiveness as a social analogue of the biological process of rupture and repair. Notice, however, that it also demands of both participants significant intrapsychic work. The 'usual story' ends happily. The relationship is repaired; social order is re-established.

Real life is not so simple. Indeed, much writing on forgiveness consists in exploration of the innumerable ways that experience deviates from this ideal. If the offender fails to recognize harm done, the process is stillborn. If the offender is narcissistic – or the aggrieved masochistic – forgiveness may founder. If the offence is murder, the apology falls on deaf ears. Akhtar (2002) has offered an exhaustive discussion of the variations on forgiveness encountered in clinical practice. Truth and reconciliation may be achieved in the absence of forgiveness. Often forgiveness is impossible … even then, it may be possible. Like celibacy or abstinence, forgiveness is not a state permanently achieved; rather it is an ideal, repeatedly approached.

One deviation I wish to highlight is this: without mutual desire for a continuing relationship, there cannot be reconciliation. This crucial difference was recognized by the Greeks in their distinction between two kinds of war. In battle among Greek city-states, it was recognized by both parties that social harmony might one day be restored; such conflict the Greeks labeled 'civil war'. In the case of barbarians with whom there was no expectation of reconciliation, the Greeks engaged in 'savage war'. In modern times savagery continues to be justified on the basis of the otherness of supposedly subhuman 'barbarians', such as that inflicted on the 'Huns' in Dresden, 'Japs' in Hiroshima, or 'gooks' in Mai Lai.

## A parent forgives her child; a child forgives his parent

Most of us can easily call to mind estranged couples who have chosen to be civil – or savage. It has been said that one sign of a good marriage is the ability to fight well; silently implied, of course, is the capacity for forgiveness and reconciliation. Other opportunities for rupture and repair abound – in friendships, business dealings, the workplace, and in everyday interaction. But the forgivenesses I wish to examine are those bestowed first on children by their parents and, reciprocally, on parents by their children. Any parent can testify to the pattern of forgiveness and reconciliation embedded in the raising of a child. Any child can enumerate parental failures which may – or may not – be forgiven. A parallel obtains in the therapeutic dyad: on one hand, the analytic attitude turns on forgiveness; and on the other, we analysts inevitably afford our patients many opportunities to forgive us.

If my spouse betrays me, I have options. But if my parent betrays me? I may choose to disown the person of my parent; but I *cannot* disown the internal parental imago. My parent lives on within me in a way that no one else ever can. For this reason, the capacity for forgiveness is essential to growth and development. When a parent fails a child, the child sustains a loss: not a loss of the object per se, but a loss of the ideal object, or even the 'good enough' object. Where there is loss, there may be mourning. It is here, in the loss and mourning inherent in children's coping with parental failures, that we can centre the theme of forgiveness within psychoanalysis.

## Forgiveness in psychoanalysis

With the foregoing outline in mind, I propose now briefly to trace a few threads of the trajectory of forgiveness within psychoanalysis (cf. Doyle, 1999; Hunter, 1978; Wangh, 2005). The betrayal of children by their parents constitutes one of Freud's early discoveries. Tragically, it was no sooner considered than denied. When Freud abandoned the seduction theory, there followed a long period of neglect. Nevertheless, whether in reality or in fantasy, the failings of parents vis-à-vis their children has remained a central theme in psychoanalysis since the beginning.

One searches in vain for much forgiveness in Freud – the work *or* the man. Freud was notoriously *unforgiving*, as attested by a pantheon of estranged former associates: Brucke, Breuer, Fliess, Stekel, Adler, Jung, Rank, Sadger, and Ferenczi, to name but a few (Breger, 2000; Sadger, 2005). One sympathetic, yet chilling, witness is Khan, who tells us:

> Freud outgrew Fliess … We have now arrived at an era where we have to face the fact that human beings with rare gifts, where they use the other as a catalyst towards the fruition of their self-experiences, have to face the responsibility of destroying the agent into the bargain. Freud did that with a courage that is unmatched and unparalleled in the history of human relationships as I know it.
>
> (1947, p. 111)

In spite of this rather bleak picture, there are hints of forgiveness in the open receptivity that forms the core of the talking cure and in Freud's thoughts on object loss in 'Mourning and melancholia' (1917, p. 237), to which we shall return presently.

Melanie Klein's implicit attention to failure and forgiveness reveals itself in her statement: 'People who have been able to establish the primal good object with relative security are *capable of retaining their love for it in spite of its shortcomings*' (1975, p. 193, my emphasis). Among parental failings, one can easily discern a spectrum. No one who is subject to ordinary human frailty can live up to an idealized parental imago. Minor failures of empathy or attunement abound in times of stress or fatigue. Blind spots due to character surely lead us all to fail our children in pervasive and consistent fashion. One is reminded here of the apocryphal story of the analyst whose fondest wish for her children is that they be analysable. And this leads us to the other end of the spectrum: parents whose children might justly accuse them of abuse or deprivation, of 'soul murder' (Shengold, 1989), and who struggle mightily to forgive. Child forgives parent.

But Klein complicates the relation between inner and outer, between offender and aggrieved. Klein is known for her emphasis on the intrapsychic, on innate inner drives. Yet, arguably, the core of her genius resides in her analysis of the dialectic between introjection and projection: between the otherness within and the sameness without. To be sure, the infant is frustrated by the *actual* failures of the breast, of the mmm-other. But, Klein (1975) reminds us, 'When the infant reaches the depressive position... he also feels that the object's badness is largely due to his own aggressiveness and the ensuing projection' (p. 196). In the Kleinian view, a mother protects her infant from his projected aggression by disconfirming his fantasy. That is, she forbears from expressing aggression, thus allowing the infant to organize an experience of ambivalently held whole objects. To the child's aggressiveness, any parent might add ill temper, disobedience, greed, pigheadedness, reckless behaviour, and a list of other 'offences'. Parent forgives child.

Forgiveness is central also to the thinking of Donald Winnicott. In his view, a prime element of the mother's role is to allow herself to be *used* by her ruthless and cannibalistic infant (Winnicott, 1945, p. 142; 1949, p. 73). Note that the word *ruth* is an archaic form meaning 'pity'; it is related to *rue*, which carries the connotation of sorrow, regret, compassion, contrition; and also related to Old Norse *hryggja* or *hryggva*, meaning 'distress or grieve' (Onions, 1966). If the mother succeeds, there ensue cycles of use (destruction) and refinding, through which the infant gains an experience of a (m)other who can forgive him his destructiveness. In this way, the infant himself develops a 'capacity for concern' (Winnicott, 1978, p. 206). Mother forgives infant. Infant develops capacity for forgiveness.

Moving from development to treatment, let us listen to Heinz Kohut (1984): 'Each time an analyst's interpretations are wrong, inaccurate, or otherwise faulty, there is the anxious question of whether the selfobject analyst ... will be able *to recognize his mistake* and thus transform a potential trauma into a development-enhancing, structure-building optimal frustration' (p. 207, my emphasis). Kohut's conception of how analysis cures – through empathic failure, optimal frustration, and transmuting internalization – is essentially a process of forgiveness, of patient forgiving analyst. The small failures of optimal frustration are non-traumatic *only* against a background of success; a baseline of attunement renders tolerable repeated minor misattunements. In the language of forgiveness, the baseline of trust and the wish for relational continuity make possible the repeated skirmishes of a civil war ending in atonement and reconciliation. Patient forgives analyst.

## Forgiveness and mourning in psychoanalysis

I would now like to focus more closely on the relationship between forgiveness and mourning. Forgiving our parents their failures frees us to live life – precisely because we *are* our parents, partially but inescapably. In a Heideggerian sense, we are 'thrown' into a life profoundly determined by our biological and cultural inheritance. It is largely due to parental identifications that we become who we are. The impossibility of escape is captured perfectly in the story of the adolescent patient who confidently assures his analyst, 'My father has absolutely no influence over me; whatever he stands for, I do the opposite.'

I have suggested that parental failures constitute losses. To examine the mourning process, let us return to Freud via Ogden's (2002) re-examination of 'Mourning and melancholia'. Freud proposed that loss of an object entails impoverishment of the self. In mourning, the loss is repaired as cathexis is gradually withdrawn from the missing object and returned to the 'I'. In melancholia, mourning is averted; cathexis is *not* withdrawn from the lost object, and the deficit in the self remains. The depressive pays a steep price for fending off the pain of loss. He loses a relationship with a disappointing, but vital, object; instead he settles for a 'shadow of the object' and thus for an emotionally constricted life. In the words of André Green (2005), the melancholic settles into 'a sort of interminable torpid mourning, the subject never having succeeded in accepting or overcoming this or that loss' (p. 152).

The hard work of mourning has a parallel in the labor of forgiveness. Dietrich Bonhoeffer (2003) warned against 'cheap grace' or 'cut-rate forgiveness' (pp. 43–44), by which he means facile reconciliation. A true state of grace is not easily won. Before reconciliation is possible, forgiveness requires recognition of harm done, reparation, and atonement. How does one achieve this in the representational world vis-à-vis a parental imago which has failed? One negotiates with oneself, so to speak. Easy excuses or denial of harm will not suffice. Indeed, the urge to destroy the object must be experienced and acknowledged. If the process falters, then the parental imago remains, inert; it becomes the 'dead mother' (Green, 2001, pp. 170–200). An uneasy peace is made. Life may carry on around this bloodless zone, but sequestering the unresolved complex sucks energy.

Instead, war is called for. The unacknowledged loss – or failure – must be brought to life, and experienced with all its attendant grief and rage. Only then can the undigested lump be attacked and metabolized, freeing for salvage what positive identifications may remain, and releasing energy for life. Ogden (2002) puts it bluntly: 'In order to grieve the loss of an object, one must first kill it, that is, one must do the psychological work of allowing the object to be irrevocably dead, both in one's own mind and in the external world' (p. 779). Although Ogden is describing object loss per se, I suggest that a parallel occurs in the loss experienced through parental failure, though in this case the loss is virtual. The disappointed child has not lost his parent – but he has lost the parent he hoped for, and perhaps even the parent he might reasonably have expected. The process of mourning such loss, of forgiving the failure, entails recognizing the offence (shortcoming, lack, absence), grieving the loss, forgiving the object, and finally forgiving the 'ego-identified-with-the-object'. It is in this sense that forgiving our parents their failures frees us to live life. Kristeva (1989) eloquently captures the imperative: 'Reconciliation with a loving mother, though she might be unfaithful or even a prostitute, beyond and in spite of her "lapses", thus appears as a condition for reconciliation with one's self' (p. 199).

## Conclusion

Contemporary psychoanalysis endeavors to embrace the fundamental social embeddedness of the human mind. Thus, the time seems ripe to rehabilitate the essentially relational process of forgiveness by recognizing its presence within psychoanalytic theory and practice. I have suggested that forgiveness can be seen as a route to intersubjective – and intrapsychic – repair in response to failure and, as such, is essential to healthy development.

In psychoanalysis people seek to be known, and to know themselves. Ultimately, forgiveness renders it safe to be known. If we would have our patients bracket their censorship and follow the fundamental rule of free association, then *we* must commit to forgive them whatever failures may thus be revealed (Kristeva, 2002, p. 12). Forgiveness – both in the acceptance inherent in the analytic attitude and in our patient's forgiveness of our failings as analysts – opens a pathway to the future (Holloway, 2002, p. 13). Recognizing the essentially relational nature of forgiveness, Hanna Arendt (1958) argues that 'only love has the power to forgive' (p. 242). This act of love called forgiveness is the *sine qua non* of psychoanalysis.

## References

Akhtar, S. (2002). Forgiveness: origins, dynamics, psychopathology, and technical relevance. *Psychoanalytic Quarterly*, 71: 175–212.

Arendt, H. (1958). *The Human Condition*. Chicago: University of Chicago Press.

Bonhoeffer, D. (2003). *Discipleship: Dietrich Bonhoeffer Works*, vol. 4. Minneapolis: Fortress Press.

Breger, L. (2000). *Freud: Darkness in the Midst of Vision*. New York: John Wiley and Sons.

Doyle, G. (1999). Forgiveness as an intrapsychic process. *Psychotherapy* 36(2): 190–198.

Freud, S. (1917). Mourning and melancholia. *Standard Edition*, vol. 14, pp. 237–260. London: Hogarth Press.

Green, A. (2001). *Life Narcissism, Death Narcissism*, trans. A. Weller. London: Free Association Books.

Green, A. (2005). *Key Ideas for a Contemporary Psychoanalysis: Misrecognition and Recognition of the Unconscious*. London: Routledge.

Holloway, R. (2002). *On Forgiveness*. Edinburgh: Canongate.

Hunter, R.C.A. (1978). Forgiveness, retaliation and paranoid reactions. *Canadian Psychiatric Association Journal*, 23: 167–173.

Khan, M. (1974). Montaigne, Rousseau and Freud. In *The Privacy of the Self: Papers on Psychoanalytic Theory and Technique*. New York: International Universities Press.

Klein, M. (1975). *Envy and Gratitude & Other Works*. New York: Dell.

Kohut, H. (1984). *How Does Analysis Cure?* ed. Arnold Goldberg, with the collaboration of Paul Stepansky. Chicago: University of Chicago Press.

Kristeva, J. (1989). *Black Sun: Depression and Melancholia*, trans. L.S. Roudiez. New York: Columbia University Press.

Kristeva, J. (2002). *Intimate Revolt: The Powers and Limits of Psychoanalysis*, vol. 2, trans. J. Herman. New York: Columbia University Press.

McWilliams, N. & Lependorf, S. (1990). Narcissistic pathology of everyday life: the denial of remorse and gratitude. *Contemporary Psychoanalysis*, 26(3): 430–451.

Ogden, T.H. (2002). A new reading of the origins of object-relations theory. *International Journal of Psycho-Analysis*, 83: 767–782.

Onions, C.T. (ed.) (1966). *The Oxford Dictionary of English Etymology*. Oxford: Oxford University Press.

Sadger, I. (2005). *Recollecting Freud*, trans. J.M. Jacobson & A. Dundes. Madison: University of Wisconsin Press.

Shengold, L. (1989). *Soul Murder: The Effects of Childhood Abuse and Deprivation*. New York: Fawcett.

Wangh, S. (2005). Revenge and forgiveness in Laramie, Wyoming. *Psychoanalytic Dialogues*, 15: 1–16.

Winnicott, D.W.W. (1945). Primitive emotional development. *International Journal of Psychoanalysis*, 26: 137–143.

Winnicott, D.W.W. (1949). Hate in the countertransference. *International Journal of Psychoanalysis*, 30: 69–74.

Winnicott, D.W.W. (1978). *Through Paediatrics to Psycho-Analysis*. London: Hogarth Press.

# Part II

# SOCIETY-WIDE FAILURE

# 3

# SUCCESS AND FAILURE

## Cultural and psychoanalytic perspectives

### *Janet G. Benton*

'I don't want to have this problem anymore, and I don't want to spend any time on it. Just fix me.' A new patient in her early twenties started her first treatment session with this statement. She spoke sincerely and earnestly. The pressure was on to come up with change, fast! We spent many months focusing on issues embedded in this statement: her preoccupation with goals over process (no problems, please); her belief that someone else could and should cure her (just fix me); her insistence that the fixing be quick (got no time).

How you set a goal and implement a task, who does what work, how much time is needed and can be allotted – these are but some of the issues integral to achieving success or suffering failure. The quickness of efficiency must be weighed against the slowness of experiencing. There also are other issues, such as: meeting standards versus being perfectionistic; expressing personal individuality versus needing to always be special. Flexibility, especially about revising expectations about all these issues, is a key factor. These concerns, including the tendency to think of them as dichotomous – either/or, right/wrong or, in psychoanalytic terms, as 'split' – instead of on a continuum, are both cultural and specific to individuals' psyches.

In American culture, many parents expect their children will be high achievers, and many therapists privilege the idea that their patients should succeed in living. A failed life is probably anathema by everyone's standards. More nuanced, subtly hued, personally felt experiences are often overlooked or disregarded, as people scramble through polarized lives. Decision-making is often determined by cultural norms, with insufficient input from genuine, personal feelings.

For instance, persons who unwittingly marry for convenience or political gain without having paid attention to, or valued, feelings of dislike or disrespect for their partner may eventually face divorce. Another example would be recent college graduates who do not sufficiently value their passion for a specific field and, instead, head in another direction because of financial or status rewards. Some time during their adult lives, people such as these often report a sense of having lost themselves, or never even having had a chance to find themselves in the first place. Too constrained by conventional definitions of success and failure, they have not honored their feelings when making important life decisions. If they seek therapy, they often discover that many mundane decisions have also not been adequately informed by genuine feelings. (Ken Eisold explores this theme from the perspective of what is conscious or unconscious in *What You Don't Know You Know;* Eisold, 2010).

I, like all therapists, have witnessed patients' struggles with what they and others perceive as success and failure, struggles that lead often to anxiety, then depression, and a loss of *joie de vivre*, of liveliness. Sometimes I have wondered if I see this particular constellation of difficulties more often, or the patterns are more evident, because I work with a number of artists, many of whom face lack of recognition and/or rejection on a regular basis. Success and failure are always on their minds. Not being paid for their efforts easily exacerbates the pain they feel around these issues. I think, however, that these difficulties reveal themselves across a wide realm of work and love experiences and are not more specific to artists.

Couples, for instance, wrangle with their individual and spouses' expectations of success. What does a couple's version of 'the good life' look like? Should they have children? If so, when, and what, is the right way to raise them? Whatever their criteria (smart kids, well-mannered kids, financially successful kids, famous kids, and sometimes just happy kids), parents want success, not failure. The stakes are high.

The workplace also is rampant with issues about success and failure, usually measured by money and prestige. Who gets more for doing what kind of job? Who gets recognized and how? What is 'fair' and should be fought for versus sometimes just recognizing the truth of the old adage, 'Life isn't fair'? Suck it up. Get over it. How does one do this, however, without feeling that one has failed?

In the following pages, I will explore several issues raised above from cultural and psychoanalytic points of view. In particular, I will discuss how perfectionism and being special relate to goals and process. I will draw upon Winnicott's (1975) and Kohut's (1984) ideas, respectively, about the need for omnipotence and the search for the ideal. I also ask what psychoanalysts/psychotherapists can do to constructively address these issues in therapy. I focus on shame, a source of significant distress in issues involving success and failure.

## Goals and process

Technological advances have contributed greatly to changes in our culture and values, including ideas about success and failure. Tremendous enhancements brought about by computerization and internet use have shifted our expectations about speed of access, reduction of tedious tasks, breadth and depth of knowledge, questioning hierarchy and elitism, while also including new and diverse voices, many of which have no filters. These expectations have, in turn, shifted other expectations about how we do things. One changed expectation is that goals now often supersede process. Immediate effects supersede thoughtfulness. Getting the job done is often more important than *considering what the job is* and *how it gets done*, often because we don't actually have to *do the job* in today's instantly accessible world. My young patient's demand, 'I don't want to have this problem anymore, and I don't want to spend any time on it. Just fix me', exemplifies this attitude.

Ideas about who has what kind of agency are shifting (Frie, 2008). Changes in our interface with technology are contributing to deep change – I would say disconnection – with what we have traditionally called our sense of 'self'. Hayles (1999) refers to this phenomenon as becoming posthuman, machine-like. Lippmann adds that, 'Inner life is a burden, the very opposite of a machine. That's the point – a machine is programmed. Inner life is not. And beware to those who express an effort to think and feel about, to support, to care for that inner world' (2009, p. 24).

Also embedded in the example of my patient are other changes in expectations that, I think, have been influenced by quick connections in daily life and the ease with which we can solve certain problems. Frustration tolerance and resiliency, important for managing success and failure, are not exercised as often in routine tasks of daily living as they once were. Early in treatment, this patient and I encountered an impasse about my therapeutic approach, i.e., asking questions, exploring, see what might be impeding her from achieving goals, including her goal of being 'fixed'. She told me my method was too slow. I was not inspirational enough. (She was reading a self-help book that advised, 'Look to the future. Forget the past. Rewrite your narrative in positive terms'). Therapy was too frustrating. She had no resiliency about how to solve this problem, i.e., she just wanted to quit. I remarked testily about her difficulties working on things. She was surprised at my tone. We muddled through the rest of the session, not sure what had gone on between us.

The next time we met, we got through this impasse, for several reasons, I think. My own frustration tolerance had been stretched to the limit. I was, however, able to recognize and constructively use anger that had been accumulating for some time as my patient's contempt for me and for the therapy had become increasingly apparent. I had been feeling muzzled. With modulated anger, I told her emotional work is just that – work. It sometimes is frustrating and requires lots of curiosity and willingness to try new ideas, i.e. requires resiliency. I spoke passionately. She heard me and was able to say later that it was the passion, the affect, not so much the content of what I said, that penetrated her strong defense about this issue. (She already knew the content – people had been telling her for years she could never stick to anything.)

I had decided that if she seemed open, I would tell her the following emotional and cognitive *process* that I had observed in myself in trying to figure out what had happened. I told her I realized I had not only disappointed her as a therapist, but also thought I had empathically failed her the week *before* our impasse. She had asked me at that time to read the self-help book she loved. I had declined, with the excuse of being short on time. (This excuse reflects my own valuation of efficiency.) I said that, in addition to declining, I should have asked what it would have meant to her for me to read the book and how she felt about my refusal. I asked if, in rejecting her request, I had shamed her by not acknowledging what she felt was important and whether she, in turn, had wanted to retaliate and shame me by telling me I was an inferior therapist. When each of us was shamed, each of us grew angry. (This is an example of mutual shaming that can occur in therapy; see Jacobs, 1996; Orange, 2008.) She agreed that I had annoyed her with what she thought was rigidity, but she had not been aware of her humiliation, of wanting to shame me, or even that that had happened. This was a surprise to her. She just knew I was angry. She remarked insightfully that she often gets a similar reaction with other people, i.e. she elicits anger, but never understands why.

I decided to talk to this patient about my process for several reasons. First, I felt safe enough with her to have such a conversation. I thought the time had come for her to know how I felt when I did not acquiesce to her ideas about how I should do my job. I was tired of the self-help book. I was modeling that the so-called 'failure' in our communication had been laden with meaning and could be understood as a therapeutic 'success' because we were talking about the failure. I was also modeling the *process* of taking time to go back to an incident, of feeling my feelings, of analyzing why I felt the way I did and what in my past made me shame-prone to my patient's remarks about therapy being too slow. This patient had limited experience with this psychoanalytic process of self-reflection.

An unanticipated outcome of this talk was the patient's spontaneous insight that when she is disappointed about not getting what she wants, she believes *it is her fault and she has failed* to make something happen. She is a success if she gets what she wants, a failure if not. *She* failed when I denied her request to read the self-help book, and she felt ashamed of this failure.

Her shame reflects Winnicott's (1975) and Michael Lewis's (1992) view that shame is a consequence of having attained the developmental ability to feel self-conscious. When we discussed the enactment, she also could consider, perhaps for the first time in her life, that she is not omniscient, that another person plays a part in any rejection, that there are factors outside herself in any situation. Here I draw on Winnicott's (1975) conceptualization of the infant destroying the object (without the object actually being destroyed). In so doing, the infant realizes it is not omnipotent. The patient realized she was not omnipotent in her attempt to destroy me by shaming me – an important life lesson. Outcome (goal) was not all in her hands. The black and white of success or failure suddenly became much more complex, intertwined with the relationship with another (a process), and thus more interesting and alive.

## Perfectionism and being special

Cultural mandates for perfection and being special affect people's approaches to goals and process, success and failure. By perfectionism I mean obsessive, often dissociated and/or addictive pursuit of an ideal. This pursuit can be in almost any arena, e.g., work, love, status, money. Kohut (1984) described this compulsive need to reach or join the ideal. Others, particularly in self-psychology, have refined this idea (e.g., Lachmann, 2008). When expectations of perfection are thwarted or disappointed, narcissistic rage develops, often followed by grandiosity, then a terrible plummet in self-esteem. Shame accompanies every stage of this process. The sense of failure is often overwhelming and global.

Perfectionism is another way that goals trump process. One sometimes sees this in youngsters who practice gymnastics, ice skating, piano études, or study for Scholastic Aptitude Tests, not for the joy of mastering craft or gaining knowledge, but to win a competition or get into a top-level school. They lose track of all other values. They often suffer extreme distress if they do not succeed. These patterns follow many people into their careers as they seek perfection in business, arts, academia, or parenting. How do therapists break through such patterns and help patients reorient?

My patient, Elizabeth, in her late thirties, becomes obsessed about her marketing job because of her need to meet financial goals set by her boss. When she becomes overly focused on how much she has raised, on who says exactly what to the media, on writing just the right ads at just the right times, she loses perspective. She demoralizes her staff and herself with scathing criticism if aspects of work are not up to her standards. She works sixteen-hour days, neglecting family and health. Eventually she spirals into depression. We have many variations of the following conversation:

*JGB:* What happens when you get so wrapped up that you lose contact with everything else?

*E:* I just start to think I have to nail it, not miss a beat. Everything has to be perfect.

*JGB:* If you don't nail it, what will happen?

*E:* I grow intensely worried that the whole project will fail. If it fails, I fail.

*JGB:* Do you know how you can get some perspective on that global thought of failure when you are in the midst of it?

At this point in the discussion, Elizabeth often has become defensive because she feels she has to come up with the right answer. I tell her I want to take time out from talk about the job and shift focus to what is happening between us. Does she think I need or want her to be 'perfect'? She used to argue that I *did* want her to know 'the right answer,' to do therapy 'the right way.' She saw me as her critical father, demanding perfection. She would develop a biting tone in her voice that she recognized as the same one she can use at work with employers and employees. Now Elizabeth can usually quickly link to expectations placed on her as a child:

*E:* Oh, there it is again. I suddenly think I'm with my dad.

*JGB:* And when you are at work?

*E:* The same thing. I need to always remind myself when I get that feeling – the same one I just got with you – that it's about my dad threatening to have a fit if everything wasn't just right.

At those moments just prior to Elizabeth becoming perfectionistic, I think she is overcome by massive anxiety about possible failure that annihilates her ability to step back from the task, analyze, strategize, etc., including feeling her immediate emotions and analyzing her reactions. Instead, she shifts into a 'dissociated' state of mind in which it feels as if another person (another 'self-state,' in present-day psychoanalytic language) has suddenly taken over. This person is uncompromisingly perfectionistic. In those moments, she feels she must please the authority figure (including me) to be successful. Following any other, perhaps more measured, less rigid, agenda means failure.

By working through enactments such as the one just described, including linking present reality to historical past, Elizabeth has gradually come to recognize what happens when she becomes 'obsessed.' She often can work her way out of the dissociated state or, better yet, not fall into it in the first place, when triggers for perfection go off.

Another reason people are so easily seduced by goal achievement and perfectionism is extremely high cultural regard for 'the special' and extreme disregard for 'the ordinary.' Here, again, I draw on concepts of idealization and pursuit of the ideal (Kohut, 1984). I do not mean what I believe is a general characteristic of being human, i.e., that everyone is unique and needs to be recognized. Rather, I am referring to a distortion of this need that gets acted out in many ways, particularly overvaluing fame and status. We see it everywhere – in politics, sports, arts, academia.

In my practice, I frequently witness struggles about fame – for instance, a gifted writer who, despite other forms of recognition, cannot own the high quality of his work because it has not been published. When it is published, he will be successful. Until then, he has failed. He vacillates between feeling grandiose (with his talent, he *should* be published) and mediocre.

In romantic relationships, being special is measured differently. My patient, Ron, so valued his 'goodness' (he was a loving, kind person) he could not believe his lover broke up with him. When the breakup finally registered, Ron seesawed into deep depression, calling himself a 'retarded idiot' for having been so blind to his lover's and his own shortcomings.

In the workplace, being special is usually about being smart or working hard. People feel slighted by the superior or the institution that does not give the right promotion or raise. The patient I discussed earlier, Elizabeth, became depressed when she was not given the raise she thought she deserved. First, she could not believe her dedication and hard work were not recognized. Then she began to talk about having failed. If she had really done everything right, *then* she would have been rewarded.

In each example, the patient's notion of being special – as artist, lover, employee – was threatened. None of these patients could easily tolerate the possibility that what they had to offer might be just satisfactory, ordinary, or even inferior in the eyes of the other, and that a more neutral perception is OK. The therapeutic challenge is how to help these patients move off their rigid goal of specialness (perfection) to accepting the less glamorous, messier process of just being ordinary.

## How is psychoanalysis useful?

The specific issues discussed in this chapter – overvaluation of goals, lack of interest in process, perfectionism, the distorted need to be special – are hallmarks of ambition gone awry. Someone's wish for success has turned into failure. This feeling of failure usually leads to shame and loss of self-esteem. The person caught in this configuration is no longer good or even 'good-enough,' smart, worthy. Instead, they are bad, stupid, worthless. There is no in-between. Global hopelessness descends like a cloud of noxious gas, with depression and lifelessness moving quickly behind (Morrison, 1994). Some people go further and are ashamed that they are ashamed. No wonder people so often will do almost anything to avoid perceived failure!

A person in this demoralized state often makes choices based on faulty perceptions about what brings success and failure based on wishes of others or what is conventional or 'normal,' rather than what the person really thinks and feels. Often such people no longer believe they know, or trust, what they think and feel. Confusion joins hopelessness.

The particular skills of the psychoanalyst/psychotherapist often help someone in this predicament. Taking on the anxiety-provoking of task of working with the ambiguity and uncertainty of not knowing how one thinks and feels, including how to proceed when caught in failure, is relieving in itself. Clinicians also consider various theoretical points of view about how humans think, feel, and behave, thus widening the scope for patients about what is 'normal.' Listening to subtext and, between the lines, to the 'unconscious' and/or 'pre-conscious' is comforting. It also creates the possibility of finding patterns and making connections. Patients can sometimes explore idealized expectations, including their sense of omnipotence, as discussed earlier in this chapter, for the first time. The pain (and shame) of such exploration cannot be underestimated. Most human beings do not voluntarily go looking for these kinds of feelings. The therapeutic relationship offers a place for this kind of exploration, in addition to investigating the intimate relationship made possible in therapy, including transference/countertransference issues. This kind of intimacy is an experience many people may have never had and may sorely need when making important decisions that will affect their lives.

How one practices depends to some degree on one's theoretical stripe and, probably, temperament. Following in the analytic footsteps of Ferenczi, Independent British Object Relationalists such as Winnicott and Guntrip, and Kohut and other, more modern, self-psychologists, I usually do a lot of what practitioners call holding and mirroring at the beginning of a treatment, when people are often at their most vulnerable and also most defended. I try to understand the person's experience, making minimal intrusions, more reflecting back thoughts and feelings than interpreting. I try to remember that, for many people caught up with issues surrounding success and failure, the need for treatment is, in itself, often thought of as a failure (Ikonen et al., 1993).

The vignette with which I began this chapter exemplifies a more 'relational,' interpersonal, or intersubjective approach, in which the patient and I talk about what goes on between us, and I am more present with my own opinions. I usually do not find this approach possible at the beginning, and often not for a long time, especially with shame-prone patients struggling with issues raised in this chapter. A positive sense of self – OK me, good-enough me – has to be restored or perhaps created for the first time, before interpersonal matters can be looked at, or interpretations taken in. Through this restoration or development of sense of self, patients gradually access their own (not some other person's or the culture's) feelings and thoughts, and put them into play. Choices and judgments about success and failure begin to take on the nuance of a personal, felt life.

# References

Eisold, K. (2010). *What You Don't Know You Know*. New York: Other Press.

Frie, R. (ed.) (2008). *Psychological Agency: Theory Practice, and Culture*. Cambridge, MA: MIT Press.

Hayles, N.K. (1999). *How We Became Posthuman: Virtual Bodies in Cybernetics, Literature, and Informatics*. Chicago: University of Chicago Press.

Ikonen, P., Rechardt, P. & Rechardt, E. (1993). The origin of shame and its vicissitudes. *Scandinavian Psychoanalytic Review*. 16: 100–124.

Jacobs, L. (1996). Shame in the therapeutic dialogue. In R. Lee & G. Wheeler, (eds.), *The Voice of Shame: Silence and Connection in Psychotherapy*. Hillsdale, NJ: The Analytic Press, pp. 294–314.

Kohut, H. (1984). *How Does Analysis Cure?* ed. A. Goldberg. Chicago: University of Chicago Press.

Lachmann, F. (2008). *Transforming Narcissism; Reflections on Empathy, Humor, and Expectations*. New York: Analytic Press.

Lewis, M. (1992). *Shame: The Exposed Self*. New York: Free Press.

Lippmann, P. (2009). There ain't no cure for love: on the fate of dreams and psychoanalysis in post-human times. President's Address, September 2009, 2009–2010 White Society Colloquia Series, William Alanson White Institute.

Morrison, A. (1994). The breadth and boundaries of a self-psychological immersion in shame: a one-and-a-half-person perspective. *Psychoanalytic Dialogues*, 4: 19–35.

Orange, D. (2008). Whose shame is it anyway?: lifeworlds of humiliation and systems of restoration (or 'the analyst's shame'). *Contemporary Psychoanalysis*, 44: 83–100.

Winnicott, D. (1975). *Through Paediatrics to Psycho-Analysis*. New York: Basic Books.

# 4

# BLIND SPOT IN THE ANALYTIC LENS
## Our failure to address environmental uncertainty

*Elizabeth Allured*

We are now in uncharted environmental territory. While all landmasses and bodies of water have been discovered and explored, the frontier that lies ahead is the landscape of adaptation and extinction. This frontier contains dangers, opportunities, and losses. This paper is about our failure as an analytic community to address our uncertain future and its impact on the mental health of children.

In a prescient text about the psychological importance of the nonhuman environment written fifty years ago, Harold Searles (1960) stated:

> The thesis of this volume is that the nonhuman environment, far from being of little or no account to human personality development, constitutes one of the most basically important ingredients of human psychological existence. It is my conviction that there is within the human individual a sense, whether at a conscious or unconscious level, of *relatedness to his nonhuman environment*, that this relatedness is one of the transcendentally important facts of human living, that – as with other very important circumstances in human existence – it is a source of ambivalent feelings to him, and that, finally, if he tries to ignore its importance to himself, he does so at peril to his psychological well-being.
>
> (1960, pp. 5–6)

A conversation recently occurred in my office during a therapy session of two brothers, ages 11 and 12. David and Daniel were referring to a popular photo of the earth taken from space that hangs on my office wall.

David said, "Daniel, look at that picture. When do you think it was taken?"

"What picture?"

"That photograph of the earth on that wall. When do you think it's from?"

"I don't know."

"Daniel, look at the ice cap. Look how huge it is. That picture must be from the seventies. Or the sixties, even."

"Yeah, David, I guess you're right. The ice cap's not *nearly* that big now."
(Pause.)
(Me) "How do you feel about that?"
(Daniel) "Well, it doesn't really matter to me. I mean, there will be some big catastrophe and the earth will become uninhabitable to humans. Like, from global warming or species extinction or something like that. But it won't happen till I'm, like, 21 or something. And by then, I'll be able to drink and drive a car, and so it won't be so bad for me. I just want to be able to do those fun things, and I will. I don't want to live till I'm really old, anyway! Like, who would want to get wrinkles? I don't want to. The people I'm worried about are the kids being born today. *They* won't live longer than about my age, 10 or so. So they won't get to do any of the fun things that you get to do when you're a grown-up. I feel sorry for them."

(David) "I'm going to become an astronaut and escape in a spaceship and go to another planet. I'll just stay there. So it doesn't matter what happens on earth for me!"

"David, David, you can't *survive* on another planet for that long. There'll be no one left on earth to help you out when you have to come back *here*."

Two contemporary analysts have written about the connection of the child or adolescent analytic patient with the nonhuman world. Bodnar (2008) has begun to address the impact of pressing environmental changes upon the mental health and development of adolescents. She believes changes in the biosphere due to environmental degradation parallel self-destructive patterns of thought and behavior in adolescents and young adults, implying a close, but not fully understood relationship between the biosphere and mental health.

Santostefano (2004) wrote about child personality development within the non-human environment from infancy onwards as a dialectical, holistic process. He posits that human attachment relationships mitigate the use of the nonhuman environment, with healthier attachment leading to greater ability to make use of both human and nonhuman environments.

Freud spoke of the ego as a body ego. Many analytic writings developed this idea, elaborating the sensory, interactive dance of bodies between infant and caretaker from the first days after birth and onward. Rather than being a body-bound ego, the ego is now seen as existing also in the mindspace between individuals (Aron, 1996; Mitchell, 1988). We create and change emotional dialogue in our expectations and patterns of shared thought. The self is now a more fluid concept, with varied working definitions expressing continuity from self-in-isolation to self-as-cultural expression.

It is puzzling that our culturally rich psychoanalytic definitions of self are so little informed by the current environmental crisis. Psychoanalysts are slow to embrace relationships with the nonhuman world as important parts of culture and therefore of mental health and treatment, despite the fact discussed in current scientific literature that we are of and within the larger holding environment of the biosphere. Can we draw a boundary between our bodies, oxygen in our lungs and capillaries, and trees exuding oxygen? The line is arbitrary.

By the 1800s, when Freud came of age, the dominant anthropological evolutionary theory was unilinear cultural evolution. This involved belief that human development progresses from a primitive stage, which includes animism and magical thinking, through barbarism, which includes religiosity and superstition, including Judeo-Christian thought, on to the most advanced, rational, scientific reasoning involving increasing control and dominance over nature. To this Freud (1913) added atheism as a goal of human reasoning. This unexamined bias against those living close to the land, the "primitive," as Freud described them, reflected cultural biases. Since then, cultural anthropologists have informed us that our view of indigenous peoples as mentally inferior is misinformed ethnocentricity. Unilinear cultural evolution is now widely seen as a fallacy (Rohner, 1969). This theory which was at the root of Freud's view of mental functioning continues to underlie psychoanalytic thought, with little literature examining the role of the nonhuman environment in thought and culture. These unexamined roots continue to bias us against a more encompassing view of the connection of mental health to the nonhuman world of flora and fauna.

In the recent *New York Times* article, "Is there an ecological unconscious?" (Smith, 2010), the author discusses the growth of ecopsychology, which explores the link between mind and nature. Smith raises the question of whether we may be consciously or unconsciously experiencing "solastalgia," a phenomenon Albrecht defined as "the pain experienced when there is recognition that the place where one resides and that one loves is under immediate assault ... a form of homesickness one gets when one is still at 'home'" (Smith, 2010, p. 38).

A recent review article (Doherty & Clayton, 2011) differentiates between direct effects of environmental degradation and indirect effects related to anxiety about a changing global landscape far from one's own. "Acute and direct" impacts concern mental health symptoms related to extreme weather patterns, including increased natural disasters. Symptoms of this type are also related to adjustment to a degraded landscape and disrupted physical environment. Symptoms from direct, acute impacts include post-traumatic stress disorder, major depression, suicide, and increasing mortality.

"Indirect and vicarious impacts" concern observations of changing climatic conditions worldwide, and anxiety and other emotional symptoms reactive to these large-scale, fast-paced, unfolding events. Concerns about species loss and potential threats to human survival are in this category. Doherty and Clayton also describe a third category of psychosocial impacts, such as heat-related violence, migrations, and dislocations. This chapter, Blind spot in the analytic lens, is primarily concerned with indirect, vicarious impacts of climate change.

Some children attempt to process their reactions to environmental degradation in therapy. They know appropriate steps to take to mitigate their contribution. They use both sides of their drawing paper, insist on fluorescent lightbulbs in my office, and prefer not to use paper cups for water. They are more informed, but still anxious. Our school systems educate them in sustainable practices, but may make them more anxious in the process. Some children fear failure of the biospheric holding environment, leading to anxiety and defense. They no longer see the world as predictably sustaining, but rather as potentially toxic. How does this uncertainty affect personality development? How does it impact personal narratives? Do we need to begin contemplating the complexities of the attachment relationship to the nonhuman world, much as we have researched and defined attachment relationships to human caretakers?

In the journal *Ecopsychology*, Jordan (2009) develops the concept of an attachment relationship to the nonhuman world. He notes that attachment of infants to caretakers occurs within the context of the environmental landscape. Traditionally, this landscape contained animals, plants, sky, weather, and geological forms. Relationship with these elements was experienced by indigenous peoples as essential to survival, much as the maternal relationship is experienced by infants and, later, children. Jordan describes the psychological attachment styles developed by Ainsworth (secure and insecure attachment, and their expression as avoidant and ambivalent patterns of relating). He then discusses these same styles in relation to the nonhuman environment, introducing the idea that we may be in an avoidant relationship with nature. He asks whether we might be in a schizoid relationship with nature most or all of the time. Fear of dependency upon the biosphere could be seen as fueling defensive narcissistic, destructive behavioral styles that further disrupt an interdependent relation. As in human attachment, the way beyond the schizoid relationship involves acceptance of loss of grandiosity, sensitivity to the needs of the other, and appropriate feelings of guilt and reparation for one's aggression upon the other. Humans have tremendous destructive potential, but also great potential to love, empower, and heal that to which we are attached.

Returning to the two boys I described earlier, their dialogue concerning the melting polar ice cap can be analyzed. 11-year-old Daniel, who believed he would die at 21, used projection, seeing younger children as experiencing a sense of loss which he could not tolerate experiencing. He has a mild attention disorder, but is otherwise functioning well. 12-year-old David used an escapist fantasy (leaving via a spaceship) to deal with feared loss of life. Neither Daniel nor David could fully process their fears. A few months later, when I brought up this conversation with David, he said he had been "just joking." Several months later, he denied he had ever had the conversation. It is possible that initially he was joking, but something that looked like anxiety made him discuss the changing polar ice cap upon noticing the photo on my wall. David, who wanted to become an astronaut and escape troubles on earth, has a history of depression. His manic fantasy may relate to difficulties mourning losses, including those currently occurring due to ecological degradation. He has trouble discussing these difficulties, generally relying on grandiose hopes or avoidance. He has developed a generally positive self-image through treatment, but has variable ego strength.

Searles (1960) believed children experience themselves as more merged with the nonhuman environment than adults commonly do. He believed children experience a fully merged state with the nonhuman world at birth which gradually subsides, in Western societies, around age 12, Piaget's age for the onset of formal operational thought. At that time, young adolescents can experience themselves as separate from the environment. Younger children may feel the environmental crisis as occurring within themselves more than adults do, and may need more immediate defensive strategies to cope with this perception. Consider the following example.

In a recent session, I reminded Sasha, a 9-year-old girl with attentional problems, of something she had brought up the previous week that she had wanted to work on – focusing in class. "I'm better at that now!" she said. Sasha got up and walked over to the whiteboard. In colored letters she wrote: "Things that we can do for the earth." Below this she began a list: *Recycle; Take shorter showers; Plant a tree*. I asked her where she had heard of this idea of doing things for the earth.

"I saw a video about recycling at school. Any more ideas?" she turned to ask me, poised with her marker.

"How about planting a garden?" I offered.

"I already wrote 'Plant a tree'," she said with finality.

"How about riding your bike?"

She quickly wrote this down, then added, *Stop throwing garbage in the oceans*. "I know!" she said. "Reuse, reduce!" Her marker penned this out quickly. She paused thoughtfully, then added to her list, *Throw away less garbage*. "My teacher said we're producing so much garbage it will take the earth 3,000 years to repair itself."

"How do you feel about this?" I asked.

"Worried … She told us so much garbage is being made in New York City that it would fill up the entire Empire State Building every day."

"How did you feel about that?" I questioned.

"Even more worried."

"What are you worried about?" I probed.

"I'm afraid that the world will end in 2012."

"How would the world end then?" I asked with some concern.

"Global warming. And garbage, probably … I don't want to live to be so young. I want to grow up and be an author. And write books about how to take care of the earth. And maybe some fantasy books." Pause. Sasha went over and got her favorite stuffed animal, a small black-and-white dog that she had named Molly. She held Molly with concern.

"Is Molly worried about the world ending in 2012 ?" I asked sympathetically.

"Yes." Pause. Sasha began, "Let's make a salon for Molly. Maybe that will get her mind off of worrying about the end of the world." Sasha asked for a comb for the dog. Since I had none, I offered cardboard and scissors, with which she cut out a comb and began combing the silky, plush, animal fur. Sasha seemed to relax as she stroked the furry toy.

Sasha projected her fears into a stuffed animal that she initially tried unsuccessfully to comfort. Grooming the toy to decrease anxiety was used with some success. Sasha typically turned to objects, in preference to people, to comfort herself. She has coped with anxieties by creating a predictable, comforting, fantasy world. She can occupy herself with solitary play for hours. The first portion of treatment involved very little interpersonal interaction. Sasha set up all the toy figures and acted out dialogues with no input from me. As she began to venture into the interpersonal domain in treatment, she started to leave her solitary fantasy world behind for the more emotionally demanding social world of friends, cliques, and potential rejection. She has allowed herself to cry in therapy about feeling left out and different.

I am aware of my reluctance to reassure Sasha that the world will not end in 2012. As an environmentalist, a person who looks closely at my carbon footprint, I have experienced anxiety and a sense of loss concerning the future of the biosphere and the human race. Is my anxiety transmitted to patients? Are my activist leanings transmitted also? Would a lack of anxiety about this issue be a sign of mental health, or denial?

There is a growing literature concerning emotional reactions of adults to environmental degradation and climate change (Doherty & Clayton, 2011; Fritze et al., 2008; Randall, 2008; Stokols et al., 2009). This literature often refers to children's vulnerability and fatalistic tendencies about this issue. Should we reassure child patients, help them explore their anxieties, or both? Should we employ "grief work," as we would for a child with an ailing relative? Or should we use more traditional methods of storytelling and creative play to work through their feelings? We are swimming in uncharted mental health waters.

Children have never before been enlisted in a project as daunting as rescuing their very means of existence. Is this Children's Crusade to save the environment helping or harming their mental health? Children are confronted with images of tired, swimming polar bears with no ice floes to rest on; oil gushing from the ocean floor, fouling huge amounts of sea; and increasing numbers of devastating hurricanes and tsunamis as oceans warm. How does this affect children's expectations for their future? Why aren't we as analysts discussing this?

As with other failures, it seems important to accept our feelings of guilt, mourning, and anxiety as we help children deal with the changing landscape they will inherit from us. The possibility that our lifestyles may be contributing to our children having a foreshortened, or significantly degraded, future is perhaps too guilt-provoking for our minds to process consciously at this time.

Several recent popular films rated suitable for children and adolescents focus on environmental catastrophe: *WALL-E*, *Avatar*, and *2012*. These films contain graphic images of environmental destruction, toxic pollution, and terrified people trying unsuccessfully to escape. In *WALL-E*, the earth has been abandoned as unfit for life due to tremendous amounts of garbage. In the movie *2012*, billions of people are swallowed into a molten, unstable earth, while the relatively small number of survivors are carried off in metal, fortress-like mega ships. In *Avatar*, the sacred tree of life is bombed out of existence, to the horror of indigenous people.

Children have rarely before been confronted with images of mass annihilation and extinction related to scientific, ecological concerns. Many cultures share stories with children including mass exterminations (the Jews and Pharaoh, Christian martyrdom). These genocides were human atrocities, not upheavals of the very ground of existence, the ecosystem as a whole. In these cultural narratives, one can imagine oneself in the role of heroic survivor, like Moses, or those who escaped pogroms or plagues. The nuclear threat of the Cold War posed similar challenges for children. Unlike land war, the nuclear threat loomed as a possible end of life as we knew it. At that time, children and adults were told how to act in response, not how to prevent the catastrophe. The media promoted a belief in survivability that was reinforced by the U.S. educational system teaching "duck and cover."

A comprehensive review of the emotional impact of nuclear threat on children and adolescents was undertaken by Eisenbud et al. (1986). Their meta-analysis revealed that most children and adolescents did not believe in personal or family survivability of nuclear war (American, 84 percent; Swedish, 94 percent; Soviet, 97 percent). Many children believed nuclear war would happen within their lifetime (American, 38 percent; Swedish, 26 percent; Soviet, 12 percent).

Eisenbud et al. found in a study of Finnish children a positive correlation between frequent worry about nuclear war and other variables: high academic achievement; history of discussing nuclear concerns with others; and optimism about the preventability of nuclear war. The authors posit that anxiety and worry may be precursors to discussions with others leading to a search for solutions to the threat of nuclear war. These findings parallel those in a study of Californian adolescents, showing that students who were more worried about the possibility of a nuclear war had better self-esteem, adjustment, and were more hopeful (Goldenring & Doctor, 1984).

Researching how families with adolescents responded to nuclear threat, Zeitlin (1984) found many parents felt overwhelmed by the nuclear crisis. Many children appeared to protect their parents, reassuring them and not voicing worries, even though they were quite concerned. When parents voiced their feelings, adolescents responded in kind. Sharing nuclear concerns increased anxiety in parents more than children. When families appeared close emotionally, anxiety was typically higher.

While acknowledging parallels between the impact of nuclear threat in the Cold War era with the current impact of climate change threat on children, Fritze et al. (2008) noted an important difference. Unlike children in the Cold War, contemporary children have some influence on their fate and that of other ecosystem inhabitants. They note that children growing up in an era of climate change not of their own making may experience this reality quite differently than their parents.

There is a growing body of research about environmental education for children and its outcomes. A study of young children assessed environmental perceptions and "concerns for the future" (Barraza, 1999). This large project collected more than 700 drawings from 247 children, ages 7 to 9, attending five schools in

Mexico and three in England. This study asked for structured drawings in response to prompts (e.g., "You are approaching planet Earth in your spaceship. Draw it as if you were watching it from space. How do you see it?"). More than half (54 percent) believed the world would be in worse shape in fifty years. Children drew scenes including acid rain, loss of species, garbage, deforestation, pollution, earthquakes destroying the world, overpopulation, and nuclear holocaust destroying most of animate life. Nearly one-fourth (22 percent) of children expressed some hope for the future in their drawings, relying on technology, systems for cleaning air and water, and cessation of wars. The preponderance of pessimism over optimism occurred across all schools, except for one English school, where the dominant response was uncertainty.

From this preliminary research, it appears that discussing global catastrophe carries a burden of anxiety, of unknown degree, but often leads to learning preventive strategies and empowering children. Does the level of anxiety raised depend on the general levels of anxiety and depression in individual children? How can we as analysts tolerate our child and adult patients' anxieties while moving through a mourning process of our own? How can we help patients tolerate the inevitable mourning process on the way to reparation and mutative action? These questions concern the emotional impact of understanding one's own contribution to habitat destruction, and of understanding the small but real possibility of extinction of many species, possibly our own.

In my office recently, an 8-year-old girl discussed difficulties finding a group to play with at recess. She brought up possibilities: "Well, there's the monkey bar girls. And the hula hoop girls. And the peanut-free girls." In my hometown, each of the five elementary schools has a "peanut-free" lunch table for children who could have severe allergic reactions to peanuts and other environmental allergens. I recently worked with a boy who was so allergic to shellfish that having a terrarium with crayfish in the classroom was a major concern. Children currently are aware of peers so sensitive to environmental allergens that their lives depend upon avoidance. Few of us my age saw the environment as potentially toxic in this way. Poisonous chemicals such as those found in cleaning solvents could be easily avoided and did not limit our interactions with friends or the larger environment. Many of us grew up with a cultural philosophy that privileged "progress" and did not see monocultural farming, the destruction of habitats, or the virtual enslavement of indigenous peoples as leading to physical or mental health concerns. Rather, Western civilization was seen by the majority as a crowning achievement, a goal for all peoples.

Freud (1913) saw indigenous peoples' relationships with inanimate objects as containing projective processes, projecting their unconscious into trees, totems, or other objects. These objects, he believed, contained unknown aspects of self and could be related to without threat to the identity of the individual. According to Searles (1960), at times psychotic individuals use the inanimate world in a different, merged way. For instance, they may not have a separate self "doing," then moving on from the projection. A psychotic person may psychically merger with a nonhuman element, such as a tree, leading to a catatonic presentation.

Currently, it seems fitting to see each person as having a "real" relationship with the nonhuman world, as well as a transference relationship, much as patients have "real" and transference relationships with therapists. I have found that the nonhuman world can contain feelings and expectations related to the self as well as significant others in the patient's history. For instance, when I first brought the framed photo of the earth into my office, one patient spoke of the earth as "all alone … in a vacuum … so cold" (Allured, 2007). This related to her self-experience as well as her experience of her reportedly cold, distant mother. Exploring this transference phenomenon led to greater exploration of the patient's internal world and current functioning.

Perhaps it is significant that two of the children I quoted in this chapter have traits of Asperger's syndrome: social difficulties, often preferring to play alone, stilted speech, and less give-and-take conversational reciprocity. They have had speech therapy to address communication issues. In writing about her Asperger's, Temple Grandin (1995) noted that she felt greater affinity for the nonhuman world than for people. Those on the autistic spectrum may have greater sensitivity to changes in the nonhuman world than those we call "neurotypical."

This chapter raises many questions concerning helping children with their anxieties about environmental degradation. As analysts, we will hopefully at least begin to dialogue with ourselves and our children about our ambivalent feelings toward the nonhuman environment. We experience great longings for natural environments, while also fearing and aggressing upon them. As in the maternal relationship, we feel both blessed and damned by our dependency. Our love and aggression are expressed in countless ways as we interact with the biosphere on a daily basis, consuming and producing, creating, and destroying. As we dare become more conscious of this relationship of mutual influence, a secure attachment may develop to help us keep our "other mother" in mind. As an analytic community, we need to explore this crucial aspect of our patients' and our own psychic health.

## References

Allured, E. (2007). Welcoming the other mother into the analytic space: nature and the relational fourth. Paper presented at IARPP conference, Athens, Greece.

Aron, L. (1996). *A Meeting of Minds: Mutuality in Psychoanalysis*. Hillsdale, NJ: The Analytic Press.

Barraza, L. (1999). Children's drawings about the environment. *Environmental Education Research*, 5: 49–67.

Bodnar, S. (2008). Wasted and bombed: clinical reenactments of a changing relationship with the earth. *Psychoanalytic Dialogues*, 18: 484–512.

Doherty, T. & Clayton, S. (2011). The psychological impacts of global climate change. *American Psychologist*, 4: 265–276.

Eisenbud, M., Van Hoorn, J., & Gould, B. (1986). Children, adolescents, and the threat of nuclear war: an international perspective. *Advances in International Maternal and Child Health*, 6: 1–24.

Freud, S. (1913). *Totem and Taboo: Some Points of Agreement between the Mental Lives of Savages and Neurotics*. In *The Standard Edition of the Complete Psychological Works of Sigmund Freud*, vol. 13, pp. vii–162.

Fritze, J.G., Blashki, G.A., Burke, S. & Wiseman, J. (2008). Hope, despair and transformation: climate change and the promotion of mental health and wellbeing. *International Journal of Mental Health Systems*, 2(1): 13.

Goldenring, J. & Doctor, R. (1984). California adolescents' concern about the threat of nuclear war. In T. Solantaus, E. Chivian, M. Vartanan & S. Chivian, Impact of the threat of nuclear war on children and adolescents. *Proceedings of an International Research Symposium, Fourth IPPN Congress, Helsinki, Finland*. Boston, Massachusetts: IPPNW.

Grandin, T. (1995). *Thinking in Pictures*. New York: Vintage Books.

Jordan, M. (2009). Nature and self – an ambivalent attachment? *Ecopsychology*, 1(1): 26–31.

Mitchell, S.A. (1988). *Relational Concepts in Psychoanalysis: An Integration*. Cambridge, MA: Harvard University Press.

Randall, R. (2008). Loss and climate change: the cost of parallel narratives. *Ecopsychology*, 1(3): 118–129.

Rohner, R. (1969). *The Ethnography of Franz Boas*. Chicago: University of Chicago Press.

Santostefano, S. (2004). *Child Therapy in the Great Outdoors*. Hillsdale, NY: Psychoanalytic Press.

Searles, H. (1960). *The Nonhuman Environment*. New York: International Universities Press.

Smith, D. (2010). Is there an ecological unconscious? *New York Times Magazine*, January 31, pp. 36–41.

Stokols, D., Misra, S., Runnerstrom, M.G. & Hip, J.A. (2009). Psychology in an age of ecological crisis: from personal angst to collective action. *American Psychologist*, 64: 181–193.

Zeitlin, S. (1984). What do we tell mom and dad? *Family Therapy Networker*, 8(2): 31.

# 5

# FAILING BETTER

Working through chronic system/personal/
treatment failures in psychoanalysis

*Mark B. Borg, Jr*

In *Worstward Ho*, Samuel Beckett states, "Ever tried. Ever failed. No matter. Try again. Fail again. Fail better." In this chapter, I explore failing better through the dynamic intersection of the clinical-community border and how this was made manifest in one patient's analytic treatment. Through analysis of massive, chronic failures – personal, family, system, and even treatment – that pervaded this patient's history and contemporary life, I will show how years of widespread failure eventually became amenable to treatment as a consequence of a severe crisis – a psychotic episode that left the patient facing criminal charges – that finally allowed the patient to work through years of failure that were a central identity theme and see that he could go on and *fail better*. Through the analysis of transference-countertransference enactments between and among the patient, his analyst, and members of his Assertive Community Treatment (ACT) team, this patient's mental illness inherited, for the most part, from his family and community, revealed a complex history of conflict and failure.

## System failures

As a result of widespread system failures concerning adequate treatment for the mentally ill, the contemporary manifestation of the community mental health system's policy of deinstitutionalizing mentally ill individuals is Assisted Outpatient Treatment (AOT): mandated treatment for individuals who are violent, noncompliant, or otherwise unamenable – resistant – to voluntary mental health intervention (Borg, 2010b).

Treating mentally ill people without their consent is currently the most contested human rights issue in mental health law and policy (Ando, 2009; National Coalition for the Homeless, 2009a, 2009b; Wolff, 2010). Although 42 jurisdictions in the U.S. have statutes nominally authorizing outpatient commitment, until recently only a few states vigorously promoted and enforced such laws

(Korn, 2004; Baker, 2009; National Alliance to End Homelessness, 2010; National Coalition for the Homeless, 2009b; U.S. Department of Mayors, 2010). Interest in outpatient commitment soared with the passage of Kendra's Law.[1] Many states are now involved in a battle between advocates of "assisted treatment" (the term preferred by proponents of outpatient commitment) and critics of these "leash laws."

What if *community* itself could be conceived of as a system-level defense against the overwhelming anxiety of society itself? Might we then be able to suggest that the community mental health system has been mandated to provide a kind of policing tactic geared toward keeping society safe from its most marginalized population while simultaneously attempting to treat mental illness generated by what Erich Fromm (1956) facetiously referred to as the "sane society"? With these questions in mind, I will present the case of Mr. G, whose treatment brought us into the epicenter of the intersection – the collision – of the community in the clinical and vice versa.

## Blue lightning strikes

Two years into Mr. G's psychoanalytic treatment, I, his therapist, was subpoenaed regarding an incident for which he had been incarcerated and was being held, without bail, pending my evaluation. The verdict of this court proceeding would lead into the heart of the dynamic processes associated with AOT.

Mr. G's presenting problem(s) revolved around the fact that he had recently been granted custody of his 11-year-old daughter whose mother, from whom he had been estranged for years, had died of cirrhosis (related to long-term alcohol and heroin abuse). Mr. G is an attractive Puerto Rican in his early forties. For the first year of his three-times-a-week analysis, he severely minimized his history of mental illness. At the time of intake, he had recently experienced major upheaval (custody of his daughter), so he seemed eager to get to work. I referred him to a psychiatrist who is part of the community consultation group with which I am affiliated. He and I set up monthly consultations to assess Mr. G's progress.

During initial consultation, Mr. G mentioned he had been psychiatrically hospitalized in his early twenties, diagnosed with Bipolar I Disorder (recurrent, severe, with psychotic features). Complying with treatment, he experienced no further episodes (delusions, hallucinations) since then. This was not true. Slowly but surely, he revealed a history of severe mental illness going back to his early teens. Hallucinations and delusions were religious. He believed he had "special powers," communicating directly with some higher being (or beings, ancestors). When necessary, he could shoot blue lightning from his fingertips. This power could heal and/or destroy. He was destined to be a great "Shaman" for his community, a powerful expectation that influenced much of his thinking, feeling, and behavior. Though his family members were concerned about his psychotic symptomatology, they had been convinced by local religious leaders that Mr. G was a powerful spiritual being whose powers should be controlled and enhanced locally.[2] He began revealing a history where the best efforts of family and community to contain his powers were not able to keep him out of the emergency room. He had been psychiatrically hospitalized numerous times.

Developing a safe therapeutic alliance during his first year of treatment, Mr. G revealed salient aspects of his history. He undertook the role his community bequeathed upon him – as a *healer*. He took this role most seriously with his daughter's mother. She had been in and out of detox, rehab, and psychiatric hospitals. When they had a daughter, they both "cleaned up [their] acts." They "kicked" (i.e., got sober), joined twelve-step programs, attended individual and family therapy, and began recovering. When his partner relapsed, Mr. G's powers failed. He could do nothing for her. She grew emotionally distant, moved back with her (collusive) parents, and proceeded toward her own death.

About twenty-one months into his treatment, Mr. G revealed he had been meeting hostility on the streets ("again"). He was a street vendor. Experiencing paranoia, he believed others could "tune into" his power, perceiving him as a "threat" they wished to challenge and destroy. He began feeling electricity building up in his body, resulting in his ability to shoot blue lightning from his fingertips. Significantly, his daughter, at the time, had been acting out in school. She was detained by police for possession of a small amount of marijuana. Evidently, he was failing her as a healer, just as he had failed her mother (or so he felt). Blue lightning loomed on the horizon.

Mr. G was devastated and humiliated by any suggestion that his "powers" suggested mental illness. His community's perspective on his powers served to protest (deny) the dreaded diagnosis that lurked behind his "healing" role. Mr. G, the "Shaman," was a stand-in for Mr. G, the mentally disturbed. Treatment compliance over the first year was contingent upon a kind of *don't ask, don't tell* approach. He attended regularly and minimized his psychiatric history. As he described his current psychotic experiences, it was as if his whole history of psychosis that had been effectively dissociated, even in treatment revelations, returned to him. This return of the repressed had but one clear message to him: *You have failed.*

This was not *mandated* treatment, so when it became apparent that another psychiatric hospitalization was imminent, Mr. G, enshrouded in a gloomy message of failure and despair, disappeared. The psychiatrist and I attempted numerous calls to Mr. G. The line was dead.

Three months later, I was sitting in a courtroom in Lower Manhattan looking at Mr. G standing with his lawyer in front of a judge. Evidently, during his psychotic episode, he created a delusional system wherein he and his daughter were under attack. Beams of radiation were being fired into their apartment. The world had been destroyed. His blue lightning failed him, failed to protect his daughter. He felt terrified and alone. In bewildered terror, he tried to protect his daughter by lying on top of her (to absorb the radiation blasting into their apartment). He told her they were the last two people on Earth. It would be their responsibility to propagate the human species. Police intervention, incarceration, and Child Protective Services were the next steps that led to the courtroom.

According to his lawyer, the best-case scenario for Mr. G would be mandated AOT in lieu of incarceration in the overcrowded, overtaxed, criminal justice system. His lawyer suggested the treatment team include his current therapist and psychiatrist. So began a year of AOT.

## Assisted Outpatient Treatment

Some mental health consumers have difficulty engaging in rehabilitation and present high risk to themselves or the community. AOT strives to enable these individuals to live safely in the community, avoid repeated hospitalizations, and have access to comprehensive outpatient services. Through court-ordered treatment, consumers have the opportunity to better engage in treatment, then graduate to less restrictive mental health rehabilitation services.[3]

There we were, in front of a judge, just a few blocks from where Mr. G had spent his life on the Lower East Side – me with a folder of case notes and treatment plans, Mr. G with a psychiatric history that had caught up with him and was unfolding before us. The blue lightning had turned against him. He was being sentenced to do what we had been doing over the last two years, though now under intense scrutiny. During the AOT sentence, Mr. G's physician could determine whether he needed involuntary admission to hospital, and could recommend he be retained for up to 72 hours to determine if inpatient treatment was necessary. Refusal to take prescribed medication, or failure of a test to determine medication compliance, alcohol or drug use, would be considered in reaching the determination regarding involuntary admission. Any decision to retain him beyond the initial 72 hours must be in accordance with the procedures for involuntary admission set forth in Mental Hygiene Law.[4]

Mr. G had been through similar procedures, numerous times. Through AOT, he was assigned an ACT team.[5] His psychiatrist and I would collaborate as core members. The team that would deliver the majority of treatment, rehabilitation, and support services required by Mr. G also included a court appointed social worker, child protective services, program coordinator, and the county mental health director.

## Community character analysis

Communities, like individuals, develop unique characters with unique psychological defense systems (Borg, 2002). *Community character* describes group-level self-protective mechanisms, styles of interaction reflecting unconscious, unwritten, unstated, but ever-present laws that decrease group anxiety by governing and limiting the ways people interact (Borg, 2004, p. 155). These laws grow out of historical events, circumstances, and experiences to which the community has adjusted. There are direct connections between community and individual character. Individuals are formed in part by the character of their communities. Experiences and behaviors inconsistent with community character must be dissociated and *enacted*.[6]

In the case of AOT, the *character* of the community mental health system contains dissociated elements of how our society handles our mentally ill. AOT represents an enactment of this handling. The larger society dissociates this anxiety into the community mental health system that has containment procedures to control the mentally ill (after the family's attempts to implement the rules of the community character have failed). Although AOT recipients frequently benefit from the treatment (and containment) offered, AOT often becomes a means of decreasing anxiety and increasing security in specific communities at the expense of those who are being contained and treated. The community (mental health system) was incarnate in the ACT team, becoming a screen and receptacle for the historical and contemporary fears and hopes that Mr. G experienced in his complicated relationship with his community.

Character formation based on acclimation to a pathological society can produce psychopathology (Cohen, 2009; Fromm, 1941, 1956; Volkan, 2009). This is true for community character as well. Community character is organized into patterns of social interaction, relations, and connections – the sum total of conscious actions and unconscious enactments of a particular community's stakeholders (Borg, 2004, 2010a). Through repetition, these enactments lead to the establishment of rules, regulations, taboos, and stereotypes. Community character sets up and regulates community expectations. The expectation implicit – and explicit – in the community character of the community mental health system as manifested in AOT is relatively clear: *Comply*. Compliance includes the collaboration of the individual who is being treated. It is imperative to assess this collaboration during the mandated AOT period.

## Assessing the dynamics of AOT in community-clinical intervention

It is a complex task to get back to the starting point of the long series of behaviors that ultimately result in a person like Mr. G winding up in AOT. In his AOT year, it was revealed that he had previously experienced a complicated series of failed attempts at treatment (psychiatric hospitalization, criminal justice intervention, incarceration, homeless shelters, substance abuse treatment). The infamous FTC (Failure To Comply) label had haunted him as he attempted to deny and dissociate his mental illness throughout his adult life.[7] Community character *qua* anti-anxiety/security system is an unconscious, system level prediction, plan and assessment – an *a priori* expectation for how behavior should/must be conducted, and a retroactive assessment of whether its members are in compliance with these rules and regulations. Non-compliance is failure (FTC).

Many failures – system and other – along the way to AOT were part and parcel of Mr. G's sense of self. How many of these belong to him specifically? He felt like the very incarnation of failure, yet his symptomatology also represented large-scale failures in the community mental health system. He was a living indictment of the system. He was a scapegoat for system failures, a receptacle for society's most dreaded projections (fears, insecurities) about being, ourselves, potential victims of system failures (Borg, 2007, 2010a; Borg, Garrod, Dalla & McCarroll, 2009; Borg & Porter, 2010). This complex social defense against anxiety sets up a multidetermined, bidirectional (between individuals and representatives of the system) process where a whole series of failures – personal, interpersonal, community, society – are experienced as belonging solely to the individual.

Midway through AOT, Mr. G missed four sessions in a row, and an appointment with his psychiatrist. He would not return phone calls. Protocol stated that FTC was to be met by emergency measures. The team discussed how to handle this non-compliance. Based on the data each team member presented, we suggested to the director that one of us reach out to Mr. G to indicate to him that our primary task was to support and serve him (and not the reverse): "Would you please consider returning to *your* treatment?" The ACT team had become, countertransferentially, the living representative unit of the *System*. I was chosen to be *its* spokesperson. True to the nature of transference-countertransference enactment (Levenson, 1991, 2009, 2010), Mr. G responded to me as such.

Clearly agitated when he returned, he said he was "giving up," he "deserved to go to jail," and society had "no place" for him. He felt he was under constant surveillance by me (i.e., the ACT team, i.e., the *System*). He was. He believed the consequence for missing his sessions would be (re)incarceration. He was awaiting my betrayal (from the initiation of his therapy, not just his mandated treatment) and was ready to preempt that by turning himself in.

At this point, Mr. G's bitter struggle to comply confronted him with his own ambivalence about "getting well." In the enactment, I became the *System*. I was threatening – through the treatment itself – to take away his place in the symbolic order (his inherited place in his community/society, the place carved out just for him, without which he would, in an intersubjective sense, cease to exist).[8] The wager of returning to treatment was between the obliteration of the core of his being versus the possibility of going forward into unknown and uncharted territories, unmoored from the familiar coordinates of his previous sense of who/what he had been, and surviving in that profoundly alienated state.

At the end of that session, Mr. G said, "When I was gone I was lost. I shed all inhibition. I was walking toward my death. It was the only option to this [treatment], and so I came back."

"I had been told, and came to believe," said Mr. G through heaving tears, "that my hallucinations, my paranoia, were demonic attacks on my Holiness" (manifest in blue lightning). We uncovered/discovered that there were severe, delusional expectations – secret pacts between Mr. G and various family members and community leaders – that rode beneath the wings of his blue lightning powers. For instance, his mother held Mr. G responsible for the congenital birth defect of his younger brother. Mr. G was expected to heal him. He was responsible for curing his father's alcoholism and repressed – but well-known – homosexuality. Community leaders, in hushed voices and coded messages (according to Mr. G), telepathically communicated that through blue lightning he would halt the tide of gentrification rushing in from the East Village, and cease the rampant drug use and gang violence in his community.

This mandate ran surreptitiously throughout the course of his illness, forging the trajectory of his life. It was a major component of his sense of self, shored up by mirroring responses from his community. The degree to which this sense of self was context-dependent became evident when he took custody of his daughter. Mr. G's original plan for caring for her included a series of commitments that had been made to him by relatives from her mother's family, his family, neighbors, the school system, etc. Soon after he gained custody, community support diminished, then disappeared. As he mourned the loss of his partner (and experienced a deep sense of failure and guilt regarding his inability to save/heal her), his daughter acted out in familiar, destructive ways.

Mr. G felt betrayed by the systems of support he relied on to help him raise his daughter and manage his emotions and behaviors, which, in turn, led to denial and dissociation of his needs. He attempted to overcompensate by working more hours, diminishing social contacts, and exiting therapy. His sense of betrayal infected the transference and allowed us to explore Mr. G's history of family and community betrayals – the first of which was the denial of his condition.

Since community character runs on the dynamics of repetition, change at the system level is influenced by repetitive, highly resistant to change, processes. Since dissociation and denial were in the mix, Mr. G was unable to experience how he was being impacted by the dramatic changes in his social/community system. His response to feeling betrayed and abandoned caused reactions within him that resulted in behaviors that did not comply with the rules of the community character (of the community mental health/family/society system) that exerted *sub rosa* profound control over him. When this system breakdown became personalized (and enacted in treatment), a flood of previously dissociated trauma rushed into the treatment. The long and arduous process of working through his history of personal-community conflict became our primary task.

## Unleashing blue lightning

Toward the end of his AOT sentence, Mr. G came to perceive and believe that the blue lightning that held the power to both heal and destroy was (and always had been) not solely in(habiting) him. It also was charged by the community system(s) of which he was a part. The process of disembedding himself from identification with the mirror image that this system projected into/onto him was often harrowing. This dynamic manifested in the transference-countertransference enactment between us, and also in interactions he had with ACT team members. He began working through powerful transferential currents related to the community mental health system which the ACT team represented, upon which he had projected his deepest fears (that he was "mad and incurable"), as well as his most profound hopes (that he could be "cured" and still maintain his specialness).

In the transference-countertransference enactment, Mr. G became the personification of the failures in the community mental health system, while I represented the oppressive elements of the same system. In this process, dissociated elements of his historical engagement with this system revealed his deep ambivalence and conflict regarding the intricate web of social networks he had been entangled in since childhood. To comply with treatment, work through his psychopathology, and take medications meant relinquishing his special powers. We trudged through the war zone of these deep-seated conflicts with the numerous systems that had wounded him, yet had given a profound sense of meaning and purpose to his life.

After a year of AOT, it seemed the system had effectively mitigated the danger potential of/in Mr. G, but not without a back-loaded, high price. He had been ingested by, absorbed, and metabolized into the (community mental health) System – setting up a bidirectional, mechanistic assemblage that was as much a part of him as he was It (*das Ding*). As we attended the final court date and he was released from AOT, it was clear that mourning would take central stage for his post-AOT analysis.

In this exploration, Mr. G often felt as if he were struggling for his life (vs. the sense of himself as a product spit out at the end of a production line), for his dignity (vs. the adhesive psychopathological labels that would haunt him for the rest of his life), and for his rights as a human being. Can one person's psychotherapeutic treatment enact the dynamics of the fight for civil rights of oppressed individuals and communities? The fight for civil rights is an ongoing struggle on the part of any group oppressed by institutions and ideologies that ignore unique histories, cultural formations, individual and family identities, and the needs of those groups to be adequately represented within a daily societal context. Middle-class values legitimate and regulate cultural hierarchies that demean marginalized groups and reinforce racial, economic, cultural, and ableistic – that is, who is considered ill vs. who is healthy (i.e., disability oppression) – inequalities that are often reflected in legislation that targets their struggles (Borg & Porter, 2010). Such inequalities are reinforced by legislation that purports to remedy them (Illich, 1976). In the struggle for equality, institutional forms of domination that affect the lives of the disabled cannot be separated from cultural ones (Berger & Neuhaus, 1977; Foucault, 1975). It should come as no surprise to anyone familiar with the history of the civil rights movement that the same dynamics that historically oppressed groups enact continue to play out within policies and interventions aimed at individuals with mental disabilities and, as we have seen, were dramatically – and painfully – brought to light (life) in Mr. G's one-year sojourn through the AOT program.

In that year, Mr. G articulated his chronic sense that his psychosis had, for years, been a wild X factor that existed both within and outside him, like an undead entity possessing a life of its own. Working through transference-countertransference enactments, we came to understand (and experience) this spectral presence as his inheritance, bequeathed upon him by his family, community, and society. This entity would be transmogrified in the crosshairs of the AOT process.

The System had been, and would be, inscribed into his psyche ad infinitum. Mr. G and I sensed that treatment, itself, had taken on a life of its own, an obscure remainder of the AOT treatment and the now, more or less, phantasmagorical residue of community character specific to Mr. G's history, establishing a new, co-created territory at the clinical-community boundary.

We would walk on together … to FAIL better.

## Notes

1  In January 1999, a 30-year-old man with schizophrenia, Andrew Goldstein, pushed 32-year-old Kendra Webdale in front of a Manhattan subway train. Goldstein was convicted of second-degree murder. New York State enacted legislation providing for involuntary outpatient commitment to community-based mental health services ("Kendra's Law").

2  Based on collateral interviews with family members, work I have been involved in with other patients, and consultations and work with other practitioners in the Lower East Side of Manhattan, I have every reason to believe that the religious leaders in Mr. G's community did believe his illness constituted a high degree of "specialness," i.e., was not simply delusion.

3  A person may be ordered to receive AOT if a court finds s/he: 1) is unlikely to survive in the community without supervision, and 2) is at least 18 years of age, suffering from mental illness, and 3) has a history of non-compliance with treatment which has led to two hospitalizations in the preceding three years or at least one violent act toward self or others, or threats of serious physical harm to self or others, within the preceding four years (time period may be extended in the event of current or recent hospitalizations), and 4) is unlikely to voluntarily participate in outpatient treatment, and, 5) based on treatment history and current behavior, is in need of outpatient treatment to prevent a relapse or deterioration likely to result in serious harm to self or others, and 6) will likely benefit from AOT (Drake, Goldman, & Leff, 2001; Institute of Medicine, 2001; National Coalition for the Homeless, 2009a; Wolff, 2010; World Health Organization, 2008).

4  Data from the New York State Office of Mental Health (2005) on the first five years of implementation of Kendra's Law indicate that of those participating, 77 percent fewer experienced hospitalization. A tragic consequence for many individuals with untreated mental illnesses is homelessness. Compared to three years prior to participation in the program, 74 percent fewer AOT recipients experienced homelessness (NYC Department of Homeless, 2009; National Coalition for the Homeless, 2009b). Arrests were reduced by 83 percent, plummeting from 30 percent prior to the onset of a court order to only 5 percent after participating in the program. Kendra's Law resulted in dramatic reductions in the incidence of harmful behaviors for AOT recipients at six months in AOT, compared to a similar period prior to court order: 55 percent fewer recipients engaged in suicide attempts or physical harm to self; 47 percent fewer physically harmed others; 46 percent fewer damaged or destroyed property; 43 percent fewer threatened physical harm to others. The average decrease in harmful behaviors was 44 percent. The number of individuals exhibiting good service engagement increased by 51 percent. The number of individuals exhibiting good adherence to medication increased by 103 percent. Individuals who received a court order under Kendra's Law were 58 percent more likely to have a co-occurring substance abuse problem, compared with a similar population of mental health service recipients. At six months in AOT, 49 percent fewer abused alcohol and 48 percent fewer abused drugs (Coalition for the Mentally Ill, 2009).

5 Assertive Community Treatment (ACT) provides comprehensive, local treatment to people with serious, persistent mental illness. Unlike other community-based programs, ACT is not a linkage or brokerage case management program connecting individuals to mental health, housing, or rehabilitation agencies or services. Rather, it provides highly individualized services directly to consumers. ACT recipients receive multidisciplinary, round-the-clock, 365 days-a-year staffing of a psychiatric unit, but within the comfort of their own home and community. To have the competencies to meet a client's multiple treatment, rehabilitation, and support needs, ACT team members are trained in psychiatry, social work, nursing, substance abuse, and vocational rehabilitation.

6 Transference-countertransference *enactments* are what happens "when the analyst unwittingly actualizes the patient's transference and, together with the patient, lives out [the] intrapsychic configurations ... [Enactment] is viewed as the patient's unconscious effort to persuade or force the analyst into a reciprocal action: a two-party playing out of the patient's most fundamental internalized configurations" (Hirsch, 1998, p. 78). System change is created through a practitioner's "ability to be trapped, immersed, and participating in the system and then work his [or her] way out" (Levenson, 1972, p. 174). I use the term *enactment* to include system-level dynamics or interaction patterns (familial, community, societal) as they are played out – unconsciously – among and between individuals or groups.

7 Mr. G brought in medical records from psychiatric hospitalizations where he had been given such diagnoses as Schizoaffective Disorder, Bipolar I Disorder, and Polysubstance Dependence.

8 See Lacan (1973) and Žižek's (2008, 2010) use of this concept in their analyses of failed political and ideological systems.

# References

Ando, N. (2009). *Introduction to Community Psychology: Foundations, Developments, and Practices*. Tokyo: Shinyo-sha.

Baker, D.L. (2009). Bridging the deficiency divide: expressions of non-deficiency models of disability in healthcare. *Disability Studies Quarterly*, 29, 136–145.

Beckett, S. (1983). *Worstward Ho*. New York: Grove Press.

Berger, P.L. & Neuhaus, R.J. (1977). *To Empower People: From State to Civil Society*. Washington, DC: American Enterprise Institute.

Borg, M.B., Jr. (2002). The Avalon Gardens Men's Association: a community health psychology case study. *Journal of Health Psychology*, 7, 345–357.

Borg, M.B., Jr. (2004). Venturing beyond the consulting room: psychoanalysis in community crisis intervention. *Contemporary Psychoanalysis*, 40, 147–174.

Borg, M.B., Jr. (2007). Just some everyday examples of psychic serial killing: psychoanalysis, necessary ruthlessness, and disenfranchisement. In B. Willock, R. Curtis, & L. Bohm (eds.), *On Deaths and Endings: Psychoanalyst's Reflections on Finality, Transformations and New Beginnings*. London: Routledge, pp. 180–195.

Borg, M.B., Jr. (2010a). Community psychoanalysis: developing a model of psychoanalytically-informed community crisis intervention. In N. Lange & M. Wagner (eds.), *Community Psychology: New Directions*. New York: Nova Science Publishers, pp. 1–66.

Borg, M.B., Jr. (2010b). Disability, social policy and the burden of disease: creating an "assertive" community mental health system in New York. *Psychology*, 1(2): 134–142. Retrieved September 7, 2010 from http://www.scirp.org/journal/psych/

Borg, M.B., Jr., Garrod, E., Dalla, M.R., & McCarroll, J. (2009). Can psychoanalysis exist outside the consulting room? In B. Willock, R. Curtis, & L. Bohm (eds.), *Taboo or Not*

*Taboo: Forbidden Thoughts, Forbidden Acts in Psychoanalysis and Psychotherapy.* London: Karnac, pp. 180–195.

Borg, M.B., Jr., & Porter, L. (2010). Following the life-course of an expectation: examining the exchange of expectations in a homeless shelter in New York City. In P. León & N. Tamez (eds.), *The Psychology of Expectations.* New York: Nova Science Publishers, pp. 1–47.

Coalition for the Mentally Ill (2009). Outpatient commitment. Retrieved March 2, 2009 from http://www.homelessmentallyill.org/homeb.html

Cohen, A.C. (2009). Many forms of culture. *American Psychologist*, 64, 194–204.

Drake, R.E., Goldman, H.H., & Leff, H.S. (2001). Implementing evidence-based practices in routine mental health settings. *Psychiatric Services*, 52, 179–182.

Foucault, M. (1975). *Discipline and Punish: The Birth of the Prison.* New York: Vintage.

Fromm, E. (1941). *Escape from Freedom.* New York: Holt, Rinehart & Winston.

Fromm, E. (1956). *The Sane Society.* New York: Rinehart.

Hirsch, I. (1998). The concept of enactment and theoretical convergence. *Psychoanalytic Quarterly*, 67, 78–101.

Illich, I. (1976). *Medical Nemesis: The Expropriation of Health.* New York: Pantheon.

Institute of Medicine (2001). *Envisioning the National Health Care Quality Report.* Washington, DC: National Academies Press.

Korn, M.L. (2004). Approaches to assertive community treatment. *Medscape.* Retrieved August 4, 2010 from http://www.medscape.com/viewarticle457029

Lacan, J. (1973). *The Four Fundamental Concepts of Psychoanalysis.* New York: Norton.

Levenson, E. (1972). *The Fallacy of Understanding.* New York: Basic Books.

Levenson, E. (1991). *The Purloined Self.* New York: Contemporary Psychoanalysis Books.

Levenson, E. (2009). The enigma of transference. *Contemporary Psychoanalysis*, 45, 163–178.

Levenson, E. (2010). The schism between "drive" and "relational" analysis. *Contemporary Psychoanalysis*, 46(1): 7–9.

National Alliance to End Homelessness (2010). Snapshot of homelessness. Retrieved November 3, 2010 from www.endhomelessness.org/section/about_homelessness/snapshot_of_homelessness

National Coalition for the Homeless (2009a). Why are people homeless? *NCH Factsheet #1.* Retrieved August 3, 2010 from http://www.nationalhomeless.org/factsheets/why.html

National Coalition for the Homeless (2009b). How many people experience homelessness? *NCH Factsheet #2.* Retrieved July 6, 2010 from http://www.nationalhomeless.org/factsheets/How_Many.html

NYC Department of Homelessness (2009). Mayor Bloomberg and Homeless Services Commissioner Hess announce decline in street homelessness for the third consecutive year. Retrieved April 22, 2009 from http://www.nyc.gov/html/dhs/html/press/pr030408.shtml

NY State Office of Mental Health (2005). *Kendra's Law: Final Report on the Status of Assisted Outpatient Treatment.* New York: Office of Mental Health.

U.S. Department of Mayors (2010). HUD issues proposed regulation on definition of homelessness. Retrieved November 4, 2010 from www.usmayors.org/usmayornewspaper/documents/05_03_10/pg11_HUD.asp

Volkan, V.D. (2009). Large-group identity: "us vs. them" polarizations in the international arena. *Psychoanalysis, Culture & Society*, 14, 4–15.

Wolff, T. (2010). *The Power of Collaborative Solutions: Six Principles and Effective Tools for Building Healthy Communities*. San Francisco: Jossey-Bass.

World Health Organization (2008). *Primary Health Care: Now More Than Ever*. Geneva, Switzerland: World Health Organization.

Žižek, S. (2008). *In Defense of Lost Causes*. London: Verso.

Žižek, S. (2010). *Living in the End Times*. London: Verso.

# Part III

# FAILURE IN THE FAMILY

# 6

# WHOSE REPORT CARD IS IT ANYWAY?

## Helping parents move from empathic failure to empathic attunement

*Stephen Hyman*

Many children are brought into therapy by their parents as a result of academic difficulties. In an effort to be helpful, parents often get involved in their child's homework and school projects. It can be supportive for parents to be interested and available to work with their children on school assignments. When the "help" continues after it becomes evident that it is counterproductive, contributing to arguments, tantrums and heightened tension in family life, it is important to understand what propels parents to perpetuate this behavior.

As emphasized by Winnicott (1965), facilitation of a child's maturational growth occurs when parents are able to reasonably contain their needs and focus on the unique needs of their child. When parental self-preoccupation is not adequately contained, their capacity for empathic attunement to their child is compromised. This chapter focuses on psychotherapeutic work with parents whose sense of emotional wellbeing and feelings of success as parents were dependent upon their child's academic achievement.

Complexities inevitably arise when parents need their children to be a certain way in order for the parents to defend against feelings of disappointment, anxiety and personal failure that they are not able to contain. This dynamic, a symptom of a lack of selfhood in the parents, results in misattunement to the child's individuality. It contributes to a variety of developmental problems, especially in attachment, separation/individuation, self-regulation, and in the child's experience of having a mind of his/her own.

Thoughts and interventions mentioned in this paper have been influenced by the work of Fonagy and Target (1998) and Slade et al. (2005). They stress the importance of treatment interventions that enable parents and children to develop mentalization or reflective functioning skills. The goal is for parents to be attuned to their child, to see the world through their child's eyes, and thus to keep the child's separate mind in their own mind when relating to the child. This kind of attunement is not so easily developed by many parents.

Parenthood as a developmental phase has been discussed by several writers, including Winnicott (1965), Mahler, Pine, and Bergman (1975), Fraiberg (1980), Novick and Novick (1999), Green (2000), and Rustin (2000). The birth of a child "provides a powerful motive for positive changes in parents ... A child's birth can be experienced as a psychological rebirth for parents" (Fraiberg, 1980, pp. 53–54).

Many parents seek therapy for themselves because they realize they are doing hurtful things to their children. They often express regret that they are, or were not able to be, better parents. I usually remind them that our kids have a way of hanging around for a long time, giving us lots of opportunities to make corrections. The same is true of our patients. Whether they say it or not, often they are waiting for us to "get it right," hoping we keep their minds in our mind, understand their struggles, and have the knowledge, patience, and skill to help them move beyond their parental introjects so they can learn to see their children as dependent, yet separate individuals.

Philosophically we may prize individuality, but we generally give approval most readily for alikeness. Comments made by family members ogling newborns bear this out. After marveling and feeling relief that the child has five fingers and five toes, the next most frequent observations are: "He/she looks just like his/her father/mother/grandparent, etc." From hair to nose to size to strength of cry, there is often immediate focus on alikeness to link the child to the family. When alikeness is all that can be seen and/or when uniqueness cannot be enjoyed or even accepted, the risk for problems in the child's identity formation is heightened.

## Case example

Daily life for the L family was organized around their teenage son, Jonathan's, homework and, ultimately, his school achievement. Comments from both parents indicated that their sense of worth required that Jonathan be a diligent, successful student. When questioned about their constant involvement in his school life, they commented: "Good parents make sure their children don't fail ... We wouldn't be responsible parents if we didn't push him to get his homework done and get good marks." When the possibility of letting Jon be responsible for his grades was raised, Mr. and Mrs. L had a ready response: "When teachers call and tell us he's not doing his homework, what are we supposed to do – just forget about it? What would people think of us if we just let him do whatever he wanted?"

Completion of homework frequently was a condition for including Jon in family activities. On one occasion, Jon was told he could go on a family outing only if he finished his homework. When he had not done this at the time his parents were ready to leave, he protested. Blocking the door, he refused to move unless they would allow him to go with them. After much yelling, crying, and threatening on all sides, Jon unblocked the door and the parents parted with frayed nerves all around. The content varied, but the emotional theme of this family scene was repeated frequently.

The parents' comments indicated they needed Jon to be successful in school to ward off their ever-looming feelings of being seen as failures as parents. They also depended on his high achievement to contain other anxieties. "If he doesn't do extremely well in school," Jon's father commented, "he won't be eligible for scholarship money and will not be able to go to a more expensive college because I don't have the money to pay for his tuition." He also said: "If Jon doesn't succeed in school and get a good job, he won't be able to take care of us if we need that ... If he's depressed and lonely it will be clear that I have passed my depression genes on to him." Mrs. L often commented about being embarrassed and nervous when she received phone calls from Jon's teachers. She felt judged by what others would think of her son's actions, especially in school.

Jon internalized his parents' expectations about the importance of schoolwork. He also internalized their values in ways they had not intended. They expected him to be what they needed him to be to maintain their own sense of worth and to contain their anxieties. He expected them to be what he needed them to be to maintain his sense of worth and stability. Thus he had many symbiotically based, anxiety-reducing expectations of others that were "reasonable" to him. He agreed he should finish his homework, study, and do well on tests but, in order to accomplish these goals: "I need my mother to pay attention to me when I'm doing homework. They know I have trouble concentrating ... They [especially mother] should want to help me by staying in my room with me so I can focus my attention. If they really cared, they'd stay with me." Following his parents' model, Jon expected them to eliminate frustration and anxiety from his life. When Jon's expectations for merger were not fulfilled by his parents, he relentlessly bullied them verbally to agree with him. This pattern occurred at home and in public.

Jon's insistent hounding of his parents and his frequent tantrum-like reactions called to mind Coates' (1998) description of the failure in self-regulation or containment that often characterizes children who have experienced limited parental attunement. They "develop symptoms that are repetitive enactments with primary caretakers who are experienced as unmetabolizable introjects or alien presences (Britton, 1992) (i.e., others who do not mirror the child's self)" (p. 125). Many of these children "show object hunger ... and are anxious, moody, irritable and explosive to the point that they compel responses from the environment" (p. 125). This last comment describes Jon's desperately trying to compel responses from his detached, withdrawn father and stress-avoidant, emotionally constricted mother.

I first saw Jon for psychotherapy when he was entering kindergarten. Delayed toilet training was a concern. He was described by teachers as bright and capable, but provocative to classmates and immature in social relatedness. Impulsivity, limited frustration tolerance, and social awkwardness contributed to difficulties with peers and disruptive behavior in class and at home. Parent counseling and consistent reinforcement helped accomplish consistent bowel control. Treatment continued through first grade.

I next heard from the parents when their son was entering high school. They were pleased Jon had been accepted into the school of his choice, but they had little confidence in his ability to meet the academic demands. In addition to much family tension about schoolwork, they reported serious arguments that pitted one or both of them against their son. If he did not get his way, he hounded them, following them around until there was either a violent outburst, usually by father, or until they begrudgingly did what he wanted.

During initial sessions with Jon, he only vaguely remembered the content of arguments with his parents. He asked to have them come so they could give more information. Since they seemed more distressed than him, family sessions were scheduled to work on improving their relationships with one another.

At times family sessions felt like a battle zone. Non-empathic relating on everyone's part resulted in heated arguments and fruitless debate. Whenever Jon wanted to watch movies on television and wanted his father to join him, power struggles ensued. Father, on various medications to control depression, stated: "I need my space. Why can't he just leave me alone? If I watch television with him whenever he wants me to, it feels as if I have no power. He can't just boss me around like that. I'm the father. In addition, if he's watching television, he's not doing his homework and then he'll get all upset and expect us to do the homework with him late at night."

When Jon would angrily respond that he knew his father would like the program and that he felt rejected by his father's refusal, dad would retaliate with the following: "Well, I just don't believe you. You're just trying to be manipulative. You can't take no for an answer. You always want your way. Well that just can't be!" This was a frequent theme. For Jon, his parents saying "no" felt like intolerable rejection. For father, a request from his son felt like coercion. Mother could not believe Jon honestly felt his parents were not attentive enough. The fact that he calmed down when given what he wanted left her with the impression that his protests were only a way of bossing his parents around. Nonetheless, the threat of either Jon or her husband getting angry caused her severe anxiety. Her impulse was to appease Jon and not make waves.

I felt several countertransferential issues in working with this highly defensive, emotionally avoidant family. I needed to be alert to hold onto an analytic stance and not join the family members in their focus on details of schoolwork and their constant attempts to project blame for their uncontainable feelings onto each other. Suggestions I made about handling homework and study issues were inevitably rejected as unworkable or otherwise disregarded. Sessions often left me feeling frustrated, useless, alone, and a failure. I realized I was experiencing a range of feelings that family members were trying to avoid, especially their disowned, intolerable feelings of inadequacy or failure. I realized I was joining the family system in also becoming rigid and pessimistic. I was aware of feeling angry and critical of the parents and I wondered if I was being fooled by Jon.

Coates (1998) refers to a personal communication with Fonagy in which he discussed therapeutic processes that foster reflective functioning skills. He stressed the importance of the therapist's openness to having the patient *colonize* his/her mind, and recovering so as "to be able to offer the patient a fresh perspective upon their own mental functioning" (p. 127). I took some comfort in knowing I was successful in being colonized. The task remained to contain my reactions and offer family members a fresh perspective on their mental functioning in order to enable them to contain, rather than act upon, their unpleasant feelings.

My self-doubts helped me recognize the extent to which each family member was struggling to maintain a fragile sense of selfhood. Independent, non-merger preferences and decisions were interpreted as being based on malevolent motives. When expectations of alikeness were not fulfilled, the result was intense conflict. The idea that family members could each be separate individuals and that each of their minds could be valid, although different, was emotionally foreign. Comments by each parent indicated they struggled, and continued to struggle, with separation/individuation issues in their relationships with their parents.

The importance of helping parents recognize when and how their own parental introjects are being enacted in their relationship with their children is the focus of works by Frick (2000) and by Novick and Novick (1999). In a comprehensive article on the topic, Herman (2005) stresses the importance of meeting with parents of children in treatment to work on:

> exploring, understanding, clarifying, and interpreting the nature of the parents' interrelationships with their child as expressions of unconscious attempts to repeat in order to redo or undo, master, and repair introjective identifications formed in their relationship with their parents, which are projectively identified into their child.
>
> (2005, p. 450)

When parents become rigidly frozen in enacting their own introjects, it is not possible for them to be attuned to their own individuality, nor to the separate identities of their children.

Mother, father, and Jon acknowledged they each had separation-related issues. I suggested we change the format of sessions to foster greater separateness for all by scheduling separate sessions for Jon and for his parents. They agreed to try this approach. Therapy evolved to include sessions with Jon, separate sessions with his parents, and full family meetings as needed. In this more flexible format I focused on following my own curiosity, my own mentalization about what was motivating the actions and reactions of each family member. This emphasis set a model that was meant to foster family members' use of reflective functioning and to be attuned more empathically to each other's needs. I believe these skills are gradually being internalized by them.

Understanding the misattuned parenting each parent had experienced was helpful to them and to me. It became evident that mother and father were bringing significant aspects of their parental introjects into their relationship with their son. Although they were each bright and articulate and were trying to be more self-reflective and more understanding of their son, alternative ways of responding did not emerge spontaneously from awareness alone. The void in selfhood in the parents had seriously limited their interpersonal flexibility. I therefore introduced the family to problem-solving processes, heavily influenced by mentalization-enhancing activities, meant to expand relational possibilities.

The topic of one recent session is an example. The session centered on father's annoyance with Jon poking him in the stomach. This occurred especially when father and son were in the elevator, leaving their apartment. Attempting to help everyone, including myself, understand the motive for this behavior and to further the process of reflective functioning, I asked Jon to explain what the poking meant to him. Was he trying to annoy or hurt his father? Was he angry at him? Was he trying to make contact? Was it a tic-like, obsessive action? Jon replied: "Does everything have to have a reason?" I answered, "Of course, especially when your father has told you over and over again that the poking is annoying to him." Jon responded that he did not think he was angry at his father, but he did like the tactile feel of poking his father in the stomach. That gelatinous sensation was an important element in the action. The parents laughed quizzically, but the father repeated that it was unpleasant for him and he wanted Jon to stop it.

To learn more about Jon's father's mind, I asked him to elaborate on what the poking felt like to him. He repeated something he had said in the past – he does not like physical contact. Poking felt like assault. Jon's persistence in doing it left him feeling he was being disregarded.

At this point I noted that they faced a dilemma. I framed their conflict in the context of their differences in neurosensory sensitivity. Jon needed deep muscle stimulation, while Mr. L needed very light, or even no, physical touching. I asked them to stand and demonstrate the poking procedure, cautioning Jon to be very careful not to hurt his father. They did so. I then asked if they had any ideas about an alternative way of meeting their differing sensory contact needs. Father suggested he could put his arm around his son. When they tried that, it felt awkward to each. As they stood next to each other simulating their position in the elevator, their hands were side by side, almost touching. I asked if they would feel OK making contact with the back of their hands. Each agreed that felt OK. Jon agreed to use this form of touching instead of poking. His father also accepted this form of contact. So far, the poking has pretty much stopped.

Was the gelatinous feeling Jon described his metaphor for mocking his father for being a soft weakling? Was it his way of trying to experience a softer, more pliable father? Was it a combination of the two? I suspect the substitute behavior has become a concrete form of being in contact that respects each of their needs. I also believe the process of building attunement to each other's needs has enabled them to lower the power struggle and be more flexible in their responses to each other.

About a month after this incident, Mr. L called in distress to discuss a significant blowup that seemed to have been set off by Jon seeking physical contact with his father in a way that repelled the father. As we discussed the event and made some possible connections to poking, Mr. L, an aspiring playwright, said with surprised self-realization that he had just been working on a short play on the theme of people "touching" in both literal and emotional ways. Early in the play, the female protagonist smacks a guy in the face because he had touched her face in a semi-romantic way. Gradually she comes to like the man. At the end of the play, she pushes her inhibitions aside and, in the playwright's words, "throws herself at the guy."

We both reacted to the similarity between the theme of the play and father's ambivalence about making contact with his son. Mr. L added that, in earlier versions, the main character never did release her emotions, but the work did not play well until the rewrite. I noted that perhaps he was in the midst of trying to rewrite his relationship with his son. He agreed, noting that the theme of making contact is evolving in his writing and hopefully in himself.

There is still much work to be done with this family. The marital relationship and the impact of mother's identification with her son have not been discussed in this chapter. Jon's schoolwork is no longer in the forefront. A focus upon being more self-reflective and empathically attuned to each other's needs has been set.

I conclude with two examples that reflect Jon's movement toward appreciating his own mind as well as the minds of others. First is a poem he wrote a while ago and brought into a recent session. "I want to write a symphony / I want it to be good / But more than bringing fame to me / I want it to be understood." What a powerful message this teenager was conveying about what is meaningful for his developing self-worth.

A final example reflects Jon's growing empathic ability. In one of the last sessions of the year, Jon was talking about a final exam: "Dr. Hyman, it was really interesting. The essay was on the theme of separation. But it wasn't the way I was thinking about separation. It was about the way parents feel when their children go to college. I never thought about it, but the example story given was about a father who was having anxiety about his daughter going away to college. I'm involved with anxiety about my separation from my parents. I never thought about it the other way around."

I thought to myself: *By our children we'll be taught … if only we can be open to hearing them.*

## References

Britton, R. (1992). Keeping things in mind. In R. Anderson (ed.) *Clinical Lectures on Klein and Bion*. London: Tavistock/Routledge, pp. 99–110.

Coates, S.W. (1998). Having a mind of one's own and holding the other in mind: commentary on paper by Peter Fonagy and Mary Target. *Psychoanalytic Dialogues*, 8(1): 115–148.

Fonagy, P. & Target, M. (1998). Mentalization and the changing aims of child psychoanalysis. *Psychoanalytic Dialogues*, 8(1): 87–114.

Fraiberg, S. (1980). *Clinical Studies in Infant Mental Health: The First Year of Life*. New York: Basic Books.

Frick, E.F. (2000). Parental therapy – in theory and practice. In J. Tsiantos (ed.), *Work with Parents: Psychoanalytic Psychotherapy with Children and Adolescents*. London: Karnac Books, pp. 65–92.

Green, V. (2000). Therapeutic space for re-creating the child in the mind of the parents. In J. Tsiantis (ed.), *Work with Parents: Psychoanalytic Psychotherapy with Children and Adolescents*. London: Karnac Books, pp. 25–45.

Herman, J. (2005). Psychoanalytic insight-oriented parent counseling based on concepts of projective identification and reparative repetition: an object relations perspective. *Journal of Infant, Child and Adolescent Psychotherapy*, 4(4): 442–456.

Mahler, M.S., Pine, F. & Bergman, A. (1975). *The Psychological Birth of the Human Infant*. New York: Basic Books.

Novick, J. & Novick, K.K. (1999). Parent work in analysis: children, adolescents and adults. Part one: The evaluation phase. Paper presented at a joint meeting of the Philadelphia Association of Psychoanalysis and the Philadelphia Psychoanalytic Society, January.

Rustin, M. (2000). Dialogues with parents. In J. Tsiantos (ed.), *Work with Parents: Psychoanalytic Psychotherapy with Children and Adolescents*. London: Karnac Books, pp. 1–23.

Slade, A., Sadler, L., De Dios-Kenn, C., Webb, D., Currier-Ezepchick, J. & Mayes, L. (2005). Minding the baby: a reflective parenting program. *Psychoanalytic Study of the Child*, 60: 74–100.

Winnicott, D.W. (1965). From dependence towards independence in the development of the individual. In *The Maturational Processes and the Facilitating Environment*. Madison, CT: International Universities Press, pp. 83–92.

# 7

# FAILURE IN COUPLE RELATIONSHIPS – AND IN COUPLE PSYCHOTHERAPY

*Molly Ludlam*

## Introduction

When a couple's relationship breaks down, they may turn to couple psychotherapy as a means of managing the difficulty. In this chapter, I explore a key concern that motivates them to seek such a resource and that the psychotherapist must hold in mind if the therapy is to have any useful outcome. This key concern is the fear of failure. Couples may be troubled by a maelstrom of feelings, including anger, hatred, contempt, confusion, guilt, grief, disappointment, distrust and disillusionment, but generally, underlying all of these, is fear. This fear concerns not only loss and abandonment, but also fear of failure, or of being thought to have failed in maintaining the relationship. Moreover, fear of failure weighs the more heavily because of its close relationship to primal feelings of shame and humiliation. My aim is to reflect on the impact of these feelings, both during relationship breakdown and in couple psychotherapy.

With the help of two case vignettes, details of which have been disguised to protect confidentiality, I also identify three particular pitfalls which experience has taught me await the unwary therapist: (1) the assumption that couples seeking psychotherapy want to be helped, (2) the assumption that our role is to repair relationships because break ups signify failure – the couples' and our own and (3) the failure to offer a containing relationship to the couple, through opting, instead, to defend against their and our own powerlessness with active interventions and intellectualisation.

As the third of these pitfalls indicates, I shall make particular reference to the contribution of W.R. Bion (1970) in assisting the couple psychotherapist to understand that offering a container–contained experience is vital to the effectiveness of therapy.

## Failure of the couple relationship

Couple psychotherapy is predicated on failure. Although one could say that most psychotherapeutic encounters are made to avert an impending breakdown or to address one that has already happened, in the case of therapy with couples it is almost always the only reason for seeking help. If the couple's aim is to avert a breakdown, then clearly there is much at stake for them, and arguably more than for the individual patient. If the therapeutic endeavour were to fail, there is so much to lose. As well as loss of relationship with a partner, there may also be loss of relationships with children, probably with the partner's family, and possibly loss of home. Nothing will be the same again. A couple relationship breakdown is a root-and-branch crisis.

Records in the UK show the rate of divorce to be declining, but this is because fewer couples are getting married. Reluctance to commit to marriage may serve as, and express, a defence against anticipated failure of the relationship. At the very least, it may be an attempt to mitigate the loss should breakdown occur.

Of those who marry, couples in their twenties have the highest rate of divorce. We might draw from this finding that divorce after shorter periods of marriage is most common. Figures for the incidence of relationship breakdown in non-married couples were not available at the time of writing, but it seems likely that statistics on the longevity of marriage reflect but a small part of a much larger picture.

Among couples, the threshold for seeking help in a crisis is high. Only a relatively small proportion seeks couple counselling or psychotherapy, and often only after their difficulties have become entrenched and intractable. What deters couples from seeking help? It might be supposed that they are inhibited about exploring publicly an intimate relationship which, by general consensus, is considered to be rather private. That an aspect of that privacy involves protecting the couple's sexuality and their sexual relationship is, of course, significant. To expose their intimacy, or lack of it, to an outsider's intrusive gaze risks vulnerability and shame. Some couples experience profound hurts and grievances, perhaps following sexual and/or emotional infidelity. The wounded party may choose to avoid any potentially mediating resource in order to punish the offending partner by precluding any opportunity for reparation or forgiveness. Others may harbour a belief, born from early experience, that, once broken, relationships cannot be mended. It is preferable to burn one's boats.

If only a relatively small proportion of couples seek our help, are we to assume that these couples are hopeful? They may express hopes and expectations of being helped, but one of the first errors a couple psychotherapist can make is to assume that a request for help constitutes a desire to be helped. On the contrary, a couple may be seeking the confirmation that, in spite of trying everything, nothing can be done. Asking for professional help is a way of telling themselves that they have done as much as might be expected of them, and are thus permitted to let the relationship go.

In such circumstances, however, the couple may also be seeking awareness on the part of the psychotherapist that each partner has a significant internal relationship with failure, and that this internal relationship with failure has become an intrinsic part of the couple's shared belief about their relationship. It is this belief, and their joint and several relationships with failure, which must be contained and detoxified. Couple therapy can then provide the chance for these relationships with failure to be thought about and worked through. In order to be able to offer this kind of container–contained experience, the psychotherapist must come to terms with her/his own relationship with failure so that it does not contaminate the therapeutic process. In accordance with Bion's (1967) maxim, we must be ready to suspend our own desire for any particular outcome.

The second erroneous assumption the psychotherapist can make is that it is primarily up to her/him to repair the couple's relationship because of a belief that if the couple breaks up it is always a sign of failure. The couple's success may be to achieve separation, which then allows room for both partners' respective emotional growth. Failure, after all, is often a prerequisite for further development. In order to be creative, we may need to be destructive. We deconstruct, so we can start again (Bollas, 1999). Seen from this perspective, the definition of 'failure' lies in the eye of the beholder. Writing about the goals of Object Relations Couple Therapy, Savege Scharff and Bagnini (2003) stress that they:

> do not privilege marriage over divorce. Our role is to help the couple appraise their marriage, explore what can be done to bring satisfaction to each partner and arrive at a commitment to marriage or divorce. Divorce is not necessarily a failure of couple therapy … Only if the therapists can face the possibility of failure of the marriage, can they deal with the anxieties that compromise the couple's relationship.
>
> (2003, p. 304)

## Case vignette A

At a consultation for couple therapy, John and Jane state that for the sake of their three children they want to find a civilised way to end their fifteen-year relationship. Preoccupation with the children – two of whom have congenital heart conditions – has detrimentally limited Jane's sexual and emotional availability to John. As a result, he has frequently turned to other women for mothering and sex. Recently he declared he had found an alternative 'love of his life' and wants to leave the family home.

In a dynamic where communication has been reduced to projection and projective identification, we might formulate that, for John, these affairs have constituted angry protests about being abandoned by Jane. The betrayal involved in the affairs has elevated them into angry spoilers, which prevent any resolution because of the humiliating challenges they pose for Jane. To forgive them would require Jane to acknowledge her failure to command John's love and loyalty. Through the affairs, especially the latest, John has turned the tables on Jane by now rejecting her. Jane is torn between love for John and loss of her dignity and has reluctantly agreed to separate.

Their request to me is for a *brief* series of meetings to discuss how to arrange separation amicably and to think about how best to respond to their children's distress. They present as thoughtful and tearful, but find it hard to be in the same room. There is much to be angry about, much to be mourned.

In terms of countertransference, I am aware of the urgency of their needs, but I also feel set up. It will be impossible to achieve their aim of making amicable arrangements or to think about their children's distress without openly addressing their feelings of outrage, rejection, humiliation, loss and betrayal. To be creative requires tolerating the experience of feeling destructive. They have a need to mourn and maybe even to explore an unconscious phantasy that there was something ill matched and fundamentally shameful in their union which damaged their children's health. A brief series of meetings will not allow me to contain their hurts sufficiently for them to come close enough to disentangle their knots. Paradoxically, without re-engaging, they will not be able to separate.

The impossibility of my task with them may reflect their sense of having been expected as a parental couple to undertake the impossible. Do I in turn represent for them the parent who expects too much, and whom they must disappoint? How can we, as a threesome, manage between us the feeling of powerlessness, without relating to it as if powerlessness constitutes personal failure?

Whilst this couple has asked for help, we might wonder whether help is truly expected. As well as being a couple, a collective 'they', John and Jane are typical in being two warring people whose conflict is expressed in having differing hopes for outcome of the therapy and for their relationship. It is very common when couples present that one partner is more ambivalent than the other about attending therapy, and one partner is more hopeless about the future of the relationship.

## How might each partner view the break-up?

I return here to the role of internal relationships with failure and to suggest that each partner may perceive relationship breakdown in a number of ways:

1   Relationship breakdown is the ultimate consequence of a series of successive failures to resolve tensions in the relationship. In its finality it may echo previous experiences of lost loves.
2   Break-up may be felt to constitute failure, at a very deep level, perhaps reflecting the infant's sense of powerlessness to engage and hold mother or father's love, and thus represent a reopening of a deep narcissistic wound.
3   Alternatively, break-up may be considered as a catastrophic inevitability, evoking a sense of nameless dread. (This conviction mirrors a sense of paralysis in response to hopelessness.)
4   The break-up may be experienced as an unfortunate, but necessary, defence against intimacy and loss, because commitment to the relationship would lead to greater loss of the self. (For some, this defence is repeatedly adopted in serial attachments, enactments of a defence against growth.)
5   For committed parents, break-up may represent a devastating blow to hopes for the family's future because of a feeling of having let down the children.

6    More positively, break-up may be viewed as a somewhat bittersweet experience which enables developmental growth, sometimes leading to a renewal of the broken relationship or, alternatively, to developing another that is more lasting.

## How might a couple relationship breakdown be perceived psychoanalytically?

When two people form a couple, they may be conceived as seeking a new container within which to manage past and present experience (Colman, 1993). This container can operate either as a defence against change and growth or as a means of fostering it. Relationship breakdown signifies that the container is not functioning to meet the partners' respective needs.

Commonly, couples report disappointment arising from the mismatch between their expectations and experience of dependency. The impending loss of this relationship resonates with earlier losses sufficiently to confirm a conviction that another's love cannot be sustained. Moreover, the hope and/or expectation that the chosen other would be able to compensate for and correct previously unresolved relationship conflicts have proven illusory (Pincus, 1962).

At separation, partners may find themselves re-enacting the unresolved conflicts and developmental tasks of separation that they first experienced when leaving their respective parental homes and that have remained unresolved in the couple relationship.

## How might the psychotherapist play a part in the failure?

The couple psychotherapist is on the receiving end of conflicting demands and powerful transferences from two people in distress. This makes us vulnerable to the third and most serious failing. In the face of witnessing painful breakdown in relationships and our patients' perceived sense of failure, we easily move mentally to what we can grasp most assuredly. Intellectualisation proves a profound defence against pain and we may find ourselves acting it out with interpretations designed to inform and instruct, and even to tell ourselves that we know what this is all about. Acting on and out of this defence, we move away from urgent and very present feelings of failure, helplessness, hopelessness, and especially of shame – our own, as well as those of our patients. It is then that we as clinicians fail, because we fail to contain patients' pain and confusion. This failure is the greater because it carries the risk of repeating the adult partners' experience as infants – that of losing a containing other.

## Case vignette B

The most challenging experience for couple therapists is not necessarily when couples seek to end their relationship. More testing still is to respond to couples who are stuck. They cannot happily live together and yet they cannot separate. With such couples, the therapist, too, can become stuck.

In the case of Sam and Grace, I felt seduced by their desperate request for a competent therapist because, apparently, previous attempts by couple therapists had failed. At the initial consultation, I asked what they each were hoping for from our meeting. Grace deferred to her husband, saying, 'He asked for this meeting …' When I turned to Sam, he said he was hoping for a 'miracle'!

My heart sank and I felt, *Then you are sure to be disappointed.* My counter-transference read a desperate desire for rescue, but not until afterwards did I register their contempt. I said: 'You are saying that you expect to be disappointed because you are certain that nothing can be done to change the status quo.' This conviction turned out to be the most positive belief the couple shared.

Now in their late thirties, they had been sweethearts in secondary school. On the eve of going to university, Grace became pregnant. They both felt ambivalent about having a baby but, fearful of their parents' shame, they married. Grace miscarried. Although they subsequently had three other children, they never together mourned the first loss. They held on separately to their disappointment in their lost futures. They displaced this disappointment on to other grievances, which became their creation, in lieu of their first child. After a few sessions, our meetings ended abruptly when they decided to separate.

What was my part in it all? Emotionally I felt I had failed them, in spite of intellectually knowing that neither believed in the marriage sufficiently to take the necessary risks for it to survive. I wondered subsequently whether I had responded to their distress by trying too hard to be a maternal figure that could make it right for them. I recollect being relatively active in our meetings, as if I were trying to keep something alive.

After their sessions ended, I was able to think more clearly. I realised that they did not believe that the other could bear to contain their grief at the losses they had sustained at that early crucial transition point in their lives. Not only had they lost the baby, but the promise of further education and the possibility of making other relationships. They had felt trapped into marrying, complying with parents to keep their approval, but doomed to a sense of frustrated disappointment. Now that they no longer needed to hold the relationship together, they perhaps needed to thwart whatever hopes for a successful resolution – a 'miracle' – they had projected on to me as a parental psychotherapist.

## Conclusion

I have described three pitfalls: (1) the assumption that couples seeking psychotherapy want to be helped, (2) the assumption that our role is to repair relationships because break-ups are a sign of failure and (3) the failure to contain the couple by defending against powerlessness through active interventions and intellectualisation.

The first two are common fallacies and are reparable. We can learn from experience, even in the course of relatively non-intensive therapy work with a couple. The psychotherapist can helpfully model the efficacy of learning from experience and that it is not irremediably shameful to 'get it wrong'. Freud's maxim that 'one must try to learn something from every experience' (1908, p. 121) suggests that the experience of failure can allow something creative to happen.

The third pitfall may prove much more difficult to override. In failing to contain their pain, we risk conveying to the couple, in a re-traumatising way, that we too cannot bear the shame of their failure. Sadly, the complexities and constraints of the couple psychotherapeutic process may not allow us time to repair the damage.

## References

Bion, W.R. (1967). Notes on memory and desire. *Psychoanalytic Forum*, 2(3): 271–280.

Bion, W.R. (1970). *Attention and Interpretation*. London: Tavistock.

Bollas, C. (1999). *The Mystery of Things*. London: Routledge.

Colman, W. (1993). Marriage as a psychological container. In S. Ruszczynski (ed.), *Psychotherapy with Couples*. London: Karnac, pp. 70–99.

Freud, S. (1908). Letter from Sigmund Freud to C.G. Jung, February 17, 1908. In W. McGuire (ed.), *The Freud/Jung Letters: The Correspondence Between Sigmund Freud and C.G. Jung*. Princeton: Princeton University Press, pp. 119–121.

Savege Scharff, J. & Bagnini, C. (2003). Narcissistic disorder. In D.K. Snyder & M.A. Whisman (eds), *Treating Difficult Couples*. New York: Guilford Press, pp. 285–307.

Pincus, L. (1962). *The Marital Relationship as a Focus for Casework*. London: Tavistock.

# 8

# CLUTCHING DEFEAT FROM THE JAWS OF VICTORY

## Failure, self-destruction, and the Icarus myth

*Robert Mendelsohn\**

## Introduction

Psychoanalysts have long noted how certain people self-destruct just when they have achieved a significant success. Freud (1924) saw such people as *moral masochists*, distinguishing them from those whose masochistic perversions involve sexual stimulation via physical pain. I have treated several males who have clutched failure from the jaws of victory. They seemed to have an almost uncanny ability to self-destruct in their professional and/or family lives just when they might have been able to enjoy their greatest professional and personal successes. I have also treated men whose history involves a parent who failed dramatically and who now live their own lives in a marginalized, restrictive way, as if *one false move* would send them into self-destruction.

I will present two patients who avoided success, one in each of these ways. Though they took different approaches to hampering success, they had an interesting commonality: lifelong fascination with the Greek myth of Icarus. I will discuss the idea of personal myth and psychological connotations of the Icarus myth and their role in these patients' psychologies.

## Myths and the personal myth

Myths are fantasies that attempt to provide a solution to basic psychological dilemmas shared by large groups of people. These cultural stories are passed down through generations, orally or in written form. Myths, fantasies, and day-dreams are compromise-formations expressing wish-fulfillments and defenses. In a broad sense, myths are fantasies. We call a fantasy a *myth* when certain criteria are fulfilled: the fantasy deals with heroes and heroic actions … in an elaborated, coherent and structured narrative … that expresses a broad spectrum of the myth reader's representational world.

When asked for an earliest memory, many people will present a myth or fairy tale *as if this production had actually been part of their own history* (Freud, 1913). The myth has become a part of the person's life narrative.

Green (1991) shows that identification with a myth may occur not only on a cultural, but also on a personal level. The personal myth is a narrative that includes what Green calls a heroization (creation of a heroic figure who goes on quests, battles enemies, and vanquishes forces of nature). From a psychoanalytic view-point, heroic deeds such as these have long been understood as a displacement of a fight against the father. According to Green, the myth is also about liberation from the mother. The hero liberates himself both from the part of the mother who wishes to freeze the individual's development, to keep the child in a dependent position, and from the part of the child who wishes to comply and remain in the dependent, infantile position. The unsettling realization by children that they do not own their mothers exclusively, that their mothers are also attracted to others, constitutes a powerful motive for the creation of heroes and personal myths.

Green believes that the core function of myth is to provide answers to funda-mental psychological conditions related to human biology. One condition is the child's prolonged dependency on the mother. To obtain psychological separation, children must go through a long, complex developmental process. In this chang-ing context, the myth is a rich psychological phenomenon, serving multiple func-tions. It gives freedom, while simultaneously preserving privileged access to mother. The myth thus provides a solution to the insoluble! It brings comfort in the dramatic, but inescapable reality of separation and individuation.

## Psychological facets of the Icarus–Daedalus myth

There are many different myths about heroic feats that can offer freedom from, and disavowal of, needy feelings. People are drawn to and fascinated by specific myths and characters that narrativize their unconscious conflicts. Biographers, particularly psychobiographers, of important, troubled historical figures often struggle to find the key *narrative/myth* that would help explain irrational, self-destructive actions. Examples would be those who have written about two recent United States presidents, each of whom self-destructed at what seemed like their moment of greatest success: Richard Nixon (Volkan & Dod, 1997) and Bill Clinton (Maraniss, 1986).

The Icarus myth has several themes and symbols that people respond to uncon-sciously. Daedalus and his son, Icarus, are exiled on the island of Crete. Daedalus, a talented craftsman, fashions wings of wax and feathers so they can escape. Before flying, he warns Icarus not to fly too close to the sun, or too near the sea. Overcome by the giddiness of flying, Icarus soars close to the sun, which melts the wax. He keeps flapping his wings, but soon realizes he has no feathers left and is only flapping his bare arms. He plummets into the sea. The location where he fell now bears his name – the Icarian Sea near Icaria, an island southwest of Samos,

Greece. Different psychoanalysts have offered slightly different perspectives on the myth.

The Icarus myth, Mitchell (1986) argues, underscores the powerful relationship between child and parental illusions:

> We have all been born of imperfect parents, with favorite illusions about themselves and their progeny buoying their self-esteem, cherished across a continuum ending with addiction to illusion. We have all come to know ourselves through participation in parental illusions which have become our own. Like Icarus we have all donned Dedalus' wings. It is the subtleties of parents, gone lazy with these illusions which greatly influence the nature of the flight provided by those wings – whether one can fly high enough to enjoy them and truly soar ... or never leave the ground.
>
> (1986, p. 199)

Weinberger and Muller (1974) suggest the meaning in the Icarus myth is that of the phallically fixated young man, whose male identification with his father is incomplete, who falls while ascending higher than his father. Unless the incomplete identification is worked through analytically, the young man is bound to endlessly repeat the pattern of soaring and falling.

Kohut (1966) suggests infantile grandiosity must undergo a lengthy developmental alteration and integration into the total personality organization if "the reasoning ego is to perform at the (request) of the grandiose self in a realistic way" (p. 257). This pathway to building up psychic structures necessary for solid achievements and real success may also lead through the flying fantasy. Persisting archaic claims of the perfect self lead to painful psychological repetitions of the Icarus experience – the self-annihilating feeling of falling from the heights of unmodified grandiosity. This proposition regarding the role of grandiosity in the "success of the individual or ... his downfall" (Kohut, 1966, p. 253) is analogous to the basic psychoanalytic proposition regarding the Oedipus complex – namely, that the developmental tasks posed by this constellation can lead to balance and differentiation of the personality or to psychopathology.

## Two examples of the Icarus myth as personal myth

Two patients had been fascinated by the Icarus myth for most of their lives. For them, it was a powerful personal myth. One case illustrates psychological progression from Icarus' fall from the heights. The other shows identification with Daedalus' desire to be careful and safe. The Daedalus myth contrasts disastrous flight driven by archaic grandiosity with a more tamed, modulated form of original grandiosity that infuses reality-oriented goals and ambitions and is channeled into acquiring personality attributes and skills through which these "upward strivings" can be realized.

## *Case One*

Andrew is a 51-year-old married father of a 19-year-old son and 17- and 12-year-old daughters. This CEO of a publicly traded company presented for psychotherapy after a tumultuous affair with the wife of the Chairman of his company's Board of Directors nearly cost him his job and marriage.

Andrew met his girlfriend at a company dinner. They were immediately smitten. Both were married. Their affair lasted several months. When caught, it was in a public, shaming way. Andrew debated leaving his wife. For several months, he obsessed about what he should do. During his deliberation, the husband of Andrew's girlfriend pressured Andrew to quit the company, then attempted to restrict Andrew's access to Board officers, and finally pushed to have Andrew fired. When these maneuvers failed, the husband left the Board, taking on a consultative position in the organization. While Andrew currently has no contact with either his former girlfriend or her husband, he occasionally worries this former boss will extract revenge. Andrew acknowledges the affair was a lapse in judgment, very harmful for his reputation. He understands he chose an affair with a woman similar in many ways to his unstable, seductive, ultimately destructive mother.

## *History*

Andrew is the youngest in a large family (three sons, three daughters). His father was a moderately successful attorney and businessman, his mother a housewife. To Andrew's knowledge, mother was never formally diagnosed, but he believes she had substantial mental health problems. Sometimes manic, she was often rageful towards both of Andrew's brothers. At other times, she was too depressed to get out of bed. At age 12, Andrew began interceding on behalf of his oldest brother in their fights with mother. "I should have become a lawyer like my dad … I would represent my brother, plead his case and sometimes even put myself between my brother and father who had been ordered to hit my brother by my mother."

## *Andrew and the Icarus myth*

Andrew had a lifelong fascination with Icarus. He first read about him in a cartoon book about Greek myths when he was 7 or 8 years old. Icarus was a major part of his fantasy life: "Perhaps every day for much of my childhood … I would think about how Icarus could fly. I would never make the same mistakes [falling into the sea]." Andrew had numerous flying dreams and fantasies, including those in which he could "fly like superman" and, later, wished to become a "fighter pilot."

A bright, precocious youngster, Andrew was always tall. By early adolescence, he was over 6 ft (185 cm). This growth impacted all aspects of his life: "Everything changed ... I became popular, President of my sophomore and junior classes, got very athletic, and got into an Ivy League college."

Andrew had unusually early success in his corporate career, rising through the ranks of a major company, from junior management to CEO in just over a decade. Since having his affair exposed, he sometimes fears for his job, but believes he will most likely hold it. He sees himself as well liked and thought of as extremely competent. On self-reflective occasions, Andrew allows himself to be baffled and bewildered by what he now realizes as an act of self-destruction.

Like Icarus, Andrew is attracted to the sky. During therapy, he returned to an old passion, skiing. While always a talented skier, he has developed those skills, and expanded to skiing several seasons per year. He travels around the world to ski in spring and summer. He has taken his young adult son with him on several excursions where their group reaches slopes by helicopter. Andrew loves instructing his son in these advanced settings. He has been delighted by my interpreting connections with Icarus and Daedalus. Skiing with his son has helped Andrew in several ways. He developed a loving, patient manner with his son that he never experienced in his own childhood. Meanwhile, Andrew continues in couples therapy and reports success in repairing the damage his affair did to the marriage.

This case suggests the wide spectrum of unconscious meanings associated with the Icarus myth that symbolizes multiply determined phallic, Oedipal, and pre-Oedipal conflicts.

## Case Two

It will soon become apparent that Andrew and the patient to be presented below had several commonalities in their histories: self-absorbed narcissistic fathers who *failed* in some way; mothers who were cold, undermining, and often seductive during their boyhoods.

Jerry, a 50-year-old attorney, is father of a 12-year-old son and 9- and 7-year-old daughters. He came to therapy at the urging of his wife, who felt Jerry is depressed, drifting through life "with no joy or pleasure." Jerry reported a life pattern of "taking no chances," always making the least risky choice in his career and other arenas. A partner in a small firm, he earns a "respectable living." Most of his colleagues who attended Jerry's Ivy League law school have enjoyed much more success and prosperity. A few obtained senior partnerships in major firms.

### History

Jerry's careful, constricted life is the polar opposite of how Jerry's father and uncle led their lives as reckless risk takers who *crashed and burned*. They were disbarred after being involved in schemes and shady dealings. Jerry's father faced possible imprisonment when Jerry was 11 years old. His father's brother experienced similar problems when Jerry was younger. While Jerry did not learn the full circumstances of his uncle's legal and financial difficulties until he was a grown man, Jerry remembers his mother telling him his uncle had died of a "broken heart," a similar phrase to the one she would later use to describe her husband's death, when he suffered a massive heart attack, dying "a broken man" when Jerry was in law school.

Jerry describes his early years as a nightmare. Enuretic until age 7, he was teased mercilessly by his mother. She was joyless, constantly angry, usually at Jerry's father, who "was always busy working, never home ... and when he was home he would only want to tell me stories about his great business deals." Jerry learned later that these *deals* were fantasies, schemes that never came to fruition. At age 12, he complained about his mother to his father. His father criticized him bitterly for this, while praising Jerry's mother. Jerry remembers being confused by his father's response, particularly the praising. He decided that day to never complain to his parents or look to them for comfort.

Jerry strove to avoid his family's "craziness" by retreating into fantasy. He was an unhappy, isolated, withdrawn child and adolescent. He did well academically, enrolling at a prestigious, out-of-town college. Becoming depressed, with suicidal ideation, he was unable to complete his first year. Ultimately, he completed college and law school and slowly became independent from his family.

Jerry married the first woman he dated in law school. They have three children. While Jerry claims he and his wife take great pride in all their children, he is particularly proud of his son: "He's everything I never was ... handsome, athletic, popular ... and happy."

### Jerry and the Icarus myth

Jerry was introduced to Icarus during latency, when he spied a book of myths at a friend's house. Whenever he visited that home, he read the story over and over. He fantasized about Icarus every day for much of his latency and had recurrent flying dreams. One in early adolescence featured Jerry flying pleasurably over his community until he discovered he had no wings or other apparatus to carry him. At that point, he would "wait for the fall ... I knew it was inevitable but I didn't know when. This part was terrifying but it was like I was paralyzed ... suspended." Thus, many nights, Jerry experienced his personal version of the Icarus story.

## Andrew and Jerry: flying fantasies

Andrew and Jerry, different in many aspects of their histories, shared a childhood fascination with the Icarus myth and fantasies of flying. While Andrew's focus was on the thrill of flight, Jerry's was on dangers inherent in flying too high. The myth served as an organizing personal narrative for each – perhaps predictive of future life choices.

Freud (1900) attributed the origins of typical flying dreams to toddlers' "flying" sensations in supporting arms of playful adults. Pre-psychological roots of the fantasy probably arise in connection with sensations of being lifted, then carried around by mother at a time when her lifting and supporting arms are not yet consciously perceived and simply belong to the earliest body–mind experiences of the undifferentiated phase. More active sensations and experiences, and their ideational elaboration in fantasies of power and prowess later in development (such as Freud described in connection with toddlers' excitement at their new abilities to interact physically with their new environments), add new components to the passive, effortless lift sensations of the symbiotic merger. These later experiences add psychological content and new layers of psychological meaning to the flying fantasy.

The Freudian (1900) explanation of flying dreams that receives most attention in the literature is "the remarkable phenomenon of erection which involves an apparent suspension of the laws of gravity" (p. 394). It seems to me and other authors (Green, 1991; Kohut, 1966) that, whatever these later meanings, at its core the flying fantasy repeats the primal pleasure experience of the infant in arms, and this experience invariably enters into the formation of the grandiose self.

Later "derivatives" of the baby-flying-in-the-air feeling can be found in a broad range of psychological phenomena, ranging from severely pathological to healthy. As Kohut (1966) suggests, in the severe part of this spectrum are psychotic states of grandiose soaring. In the more borderline range are narcissists with rigid, grandiose fantasies. In the normal/neurotic range, we see high self-esteem, humor, creative states and experiences, and normal psychological buoyancy. These healthy states are "triumphs" of infantile narcissism (Freud, 1927).

Andrew and Jerry struggled with feelings of infantile flight, feelings that are exhilarating in large part because of the feelings of individuation they stimulate in the infant. While Andrew and Jerry experienced somewhat different fathers – one a moderate success, the other a success followed by dramatic failure – both were self-absorbed, narcissistic fathers who did not make it easy to *fly away from maternal symbiosis*. When we add to this mix that each of these patients had mothers who were somewhat undermining and discouraging of their son's autonomy, one can see the difficulty each man had achieving non-ambivalent individuation.

### Andrew and Jerry: Icarus in treatment

Both Andrew and Jerry were initially resistant to accepting the importance of analysis and the analyst. Newirth (1987) points out two characteristics of this type of man in treatment. Men with these conflicts refuse to recognize the analyst for anything more than functional qualities and they resist change in their internalized selfobject. Both these qualities have analogs in the Icarus myth. First, though Icarus acknowledges his father's advice about not flying too close to the sun, he does not fully internalize this directive. He is only superficially attached to his father, having not internalized his wisdom, knowledge, and goals. In this same way, Andrew and Jerry, for a long time, could not internalize my presence or analytic stance. The second form of resistance, what Newirth (1987) calls "the refusal to modify the internal selfobject, to modify the existing grandiose structures," seems to me to reflect fear the patient will *crash and burn* if he succeeds and begin to act on the basis of internalized hopes and goals. As I understand Newirth, I believe both Andrew and Jerry have internalized the father's infanticidal wishes for his son, while each is reacting in different ways.

Finding himself too close to the sun, Andrew crashed to earth. For Jerry, failure internalizing father's ideals, strength, and hope led, instead, to a *fear of* flying too close to the sun and crashing. This failure is seen in his burdensome, plodding, joyless experience of life reflecting absence of development of the idealized selfobject.

Treatment for Andrew and Jerry has been to help them understand and work through their personal Icarus myths. To do this, we explored all the Oedipal and pre-Oedipal implications the myth contained. Having a son has helped each man make the transition from Icarus to Daedalus. Each has been able to stop the repetitive cycle of using one's child as a narcissistic extension. In the process, each has experienced the joy of true generativity. Parenting their sons, both men have been able, to some degree, to re-father themselves.

## Conclusion

I have discussed the psychological implications of personal myths, particularly the Icarus myth. I presented two patients who had a childhood fascination with Icarus. I have shown similarities in their family histories, including narcissistic, self-absorbed fathers and mothers who undermined their son's attempts to separate and individuate. I attempted to show how both men repeated aspects of their childhood narrative in their adult lives: Andrew, by having a dramatic personal failure; Jerry, by living his life in an inhibited, marginal way, as if not being extremely cautious and constricted would place him in the same situation that Icarus confronted when he discovered, to his horror, that his wings no longer adhered to his body. I suggested the Icarus myth became each of these men's *personal myth*, influencing each in profound, conscious, and unconscious ways. Finally, I discussed implications for treatment in recognizing the dynamic issues related to the use of *myth* as a *personal narrative*.

## Note

* The author wishes to thank Margaret Klein for help preparing this chapter.

## References

Freud, S. (1900). The interpretation of dreams. In J. Strachey (ed. and trans.), *The Standard Edition of the Complete Psychological Works of Sigmund Freud* (vol. 4). (Original published work in 1900.)

Freud, S. (1913). The occurrence in dreams of material from fairy tales. In J. Strachey (ed. and trans.) *The Standard Edition of the Complete Psychological Works of Sigmund Freud* (vol. 12, pp. 279–287). (Original published work in 1913.)

Freud, S. (1921). Group psychology and the analysis of the ego. In J. Strachey (ed. and trans.) *The Standard Edition of the Complete Psychological Works of Sigmund Freud* (vol., 18, pp. 65–144). (Original published work in 1921.)

Freud, S. (1924). The economic problem of masochism. In J. Strachey (ed. and trans.) *The Standard Edition of the Complete Psychological Works of Sigmund Freud* (vol. 19, pp. 159–170). (Original work published 1924.)

Green, A. (1991). On the constituents of the personal myth. In *The Personal Myth in Psychoanalytic Theory* P. Hartocollis. & I. D. Graham. Madison, CT: International Universities Press, pp. 63–84.

Kohut, H. (1966). Forms and transformations of narcissism. In C. Strozier (ed.), *Self Psychology and the Humanities*. New York: Norton (1985), pp. 97–123.

Maraniss, D. (1986). *First in his Class: A Biography of William Jefferson Clinton*. New York: Touchstone.

Mitchell, S. (1986). The wings of Icarus – illusion and the problem of narcissism. *Contemporary Psychoanalysis*, 22: 107–132.

Newirth, J.W. (1987). Idealization and interpretation. *Contemporary Psychoanalysis*, 23: 239–243.

Tolpin, M. (1974). The Daedalus experience: a developmental vicissitude of the grandiose fantasy. *Annual of Psychoanalysis*, 2: 213–228.

Volkan, V. & Dod, A. (1997). *Richard Nixon: A Psychobiography*. New York: Columbia University Press.

Weinberger, J.L. & Muller, J.L. (1974). The American Icarus revisited: phallic narcissism and boredom. *International Journal of Psychoanalysis*, 55: 581–586.

# 9

# YOU CAN'T GO HOME AGAIN

## Henry M. Seiden

This chapter is a meditation on an inevitable failure, one that takes a variety of forms but is endemic in the human situation. As is the usual case with our deepest ambitions (the Oedipus struggle, the wish for eternal life, the wish for merger with a loved one), the wish to go home again cannot be fulfilled. The only successful adaptation is accommodation to failure.

My childhood home was a five-room apartment in a "prewar," six-story building on the once elegant Grand Concourse in New York City's West Bronx, just a block or two up the hill and across Franz Sigel park from Yankee Stadium. That location, the apartment, the building, the broad, tree-lined avenue that I looked out on from my fourth-floor bedroom window, still figures prominently in my dreams – although I have no (daytime) thought of going back. I live in another borough now, across the bridge in Queens, and have for most of my adult life.

The last time I saw that building, also called the "Franz Sigel" (for the so-honored Bronx resident and German general in the American Civil War) – saw it in the light of day, that is – I was on my way to a Yankee game with friends. We parked on my old block, where I found myself playing a new part in an old, familiar scene. When I was a kid in the 1940s people heading for the Yankee game on summer afternoons would walk by us as we played our own variations on the big game on the sidewalks and in the side streets off the Concourse – our "stickball," "punch ball," "baby baseball." Later, they walked by again, the other way, carrying their scorecards. "Hey, mister!" we'd call, pausing a moment in our own game. "What was the score?"

As for the building itself, now in the first decade of the twenty-first century, there was just a hint of its former elegance: a poured-concrete faux balustrade enclosing the oval entrance courtyard where once there had been a formal garden, now a shred or two of windblown plastic caught in the stalky hedges. The geometric tiled flooring was still there in the lobby that by this time was long empty of the heavy armchairs and the low tables that had been there in my childhood. Such a small shabby place it seemed to me now. What had been the center of my universe was just one more place in the universe – and a small and forgotten corner of it at that. Nothing there to go back to – except in my dreams.

In a recent paper (Seiden, 2009), I argued for the importance of recognizing the longing for home as a motive worthy of serious psychoanalytic consideration – this, despite the fact that, although universal and recurring in our cultural and personal narratives, it is largely ignored, reinterpreted, or reduced in the psychoanalytic literature.

The awareness of a home of origin, the sense of coming from somewhere, and the inevitable (if sometimes conscious and sometimes submerged) longing for return that attends it can be seen to orient our most important life choices and to give definition to a sense of self. The place we continue in one way or another to look back to, like the West Bronx for me or the island of Taiwan in the extended vignette below, influences the way we live our lives – and does so long after we're not there, and, indeed, choose not to be there any more. What one might call a shadow longing for an idealized version of one's home can be seen in myriad expressions of self – in small and inconsequential things, like the foods we want to eat, and in large, important ones, like the way we engage our husbands and wives and raise our children.

It is, however, a longing that can never be fulfilled. As Thomas Wolfe (1934) put it famously in his novel of that title, "You can't go home again." In the variety of efforts at return (be they literal or symbolic), success can only be limited, fleeting, or approximate; *failure* is inevitable. I'm going to use the story of a friend of mine, along with personal reflections and literary examples to examine the psychological consequences of a kind of dialectic: the longing for home as against the impossibility of going home again.

Important to say, there are any number of things that can make going home impossible. For one, by the time we get around – as adults – to experiencing a longing for return to a particular place and time *we* will have changed. The home we have left could not accommodate us anymore in any case. And then, the home we long for may *never* have been what we wanted it to be. It may have failed us to begin with – and sent us out looking, the rest of our lives, for a home that corresponds more nearly to the one we idealize, and with a longing disguised even to ourselves.

Still, there are ways of reconciling the wish for return and the impossibility of its fulfillment. In what follows I will consider some of these.

## Andrew

My young colleague and friend Andrew tells me he has a recurrent dream. It's this: his house has burned down – or half of it is missing, or something has gone badly wrong with the renovations or is about to go wrong.

His house is one on a block of frame houses in the borough of Queens, just east of New York City's largest Chinatown in Flushing. Andrew, who is a boyish-looking man in his early thirties, has lived in this house since he was 15. He arrived here from Taiwan when he was 12. He lived at first with a woman he calls his "godmother," his mother's cousin, and her four children in the house next door. Then his mother bought this place – for him.

Remarkably, from age 15 until 19, when his younger sister joined him, he lived in his house by himself. His mother, who, he says, worked hard to make the monthly mortgage payments so that her children could live and go to school in America, was in Shanghai where she had been living since her divorce from his father. His father was in Taiwan and lives there still. Andrew did have his godmother's family next door. And he had tenants, mostly graduate students, to help pay the mortgage. But in the early years he lived essentially on his own, making his way in the American world in which he found himself. He says this with a smile and a shrug. He went to high school – got himself up in the morning and went. It's not clear who signed his report card. Andrew just smiles at the question and shrugs again. In some ways it was better, he says: "No parents around at parties!" He hung out with other Taiwanese kids. He went to college locally, then to graduate school in Manhattan and the Bronx. He ate his meals in restaurants in Flushing. His parents "visited," his mother once or twice a year, his father every year or two. It's not hard to understand why he might to this day have anxious dreams about the house that sheltered him and (presumably) about his capacity to maintain it.

Remarkably, Andrew did well in school despite obstacles presented to a speaker of English as a second language. He got a PhD in Psychology. He is a college teacher on a tenure track. He does research and lectures on health psychology and on mindfulness meditation (he is a practicing Buddhist). For someone so young, he has an impressive number of published papers on his resume. He works as a psychotherapist at a local clinic and is beginning private practice. (We met when he was in graduate school; I was one of his psychotherapy supervisors.)

These days Andrew and his wife live in that house – the house he has bad dreams about. She, too, is from Taiwan. They met through the Buddhist service organization to which they both belong. She has a busy professional life in another field. They don't plan to have children, he tells me – with the same kind of small, perhaps sad, smile. "It's just us," he says. And it's all here: "There's the house and nothing for us in Taiwan, although it's nice to visit there."

Over the years Andrew and I have made it a point of meeting for lunch in Flushing – Chinese food being an interest we have in common. At a recent meal at a quiet table in a new, upscale restaurant off Main Street, Andrew tells me that much of his childhood was spent in a rural village at the edge of the sea in Taiwan. (One of his earliest memories involves a water buffalo outside his door.) He lived with his grandmother and aunt in what was his uncle's house. In Chinese (Andrew speaks Mandarin as well as Taiwanese) there's an expression for "living under someone else's roof." The expression in full, as he translates it, is, "When you live under another's roof, you have to keep your head down." Being dependent on a (sometimes grudging) hospitality that could be withdrawn, he explains, means a suppression of self-assertion and a chronic sense of transiency. It involves always being reminded that one is not at home.

Andrew has had much of living under another's roof, both then and now. Flushing – with its large Taiwanese population, its shops and restaurants and signs in Chinese (and Japanese and Korean) characters, and its crowded streets – feels like an Asian city. That helped and has continued to help ameliorate the strangeness. Although he became a U.S. citizen while in graduate school, he always feels like an outsider here. This is especially so when he ventures out of Flushing. He says, when I ask him directly, "No, I don't see this country as my country."

When I visit his home at his invitation, Andrew shows me the recent renovations proudly. The house is sparse and serene, reflecting sophisticated, modern Asian taste: white walls, dark floors, tatami mats, minimal low furniture. His computer is on a low table. The only other furniture in the room is a bookshelf holding his professional books. He works at his computer sitting cross-legged on a low cushion. He and his wife meditate daily; their "meditation hall" is in a corner of the glassed-in front porch.

Although his home for more than half his life has been in America, Andrew thinks of himself as Taiwanese. The modern capital city, Taipei, and the rural village his family came from constitute the world of his origin and anchor his identity (not unlike the way the West Bronx and the Grand Concourse do for me). But (also like me) his home of origin is a place he can return to only as a visitor. I think it's fair to say that Andrew is ever under another's roof. His recurring dream is revealing. His anxiety – long in the building, and building no doubt on the anxieties of his adolescence – is that the house which has been his home away from home won't stand, that the roof will fall in.

When Andrew says of Taiwan that there's "nothing there" for him. I'm reminded of Philip Larkin's (2003) poem "Home Is So Sad." " [Home] stays as it was left," he says, "a joyous shot at how things ought to be, long fallen wide."

Andrew's history, of course, reflects still another iteration of the failure of that joyous shot. Taiwan, it could be said, was already failing him when he lived there. This was what his mother recognized early when she arranged to send him away – no doubt with a great sense of personal loss, her sacrifice only one variation on a universal immigrant story.

As for falling wide, it's certainly too late now for Andrew to expect Taiwan to "comfort" him, because by now *he* has changed. The culture, even of contemporary Taiwan, could not support his new identity, his new way of being in the world: psychologist and American college teacher. He is American despite his uneasy acceptance of that identity. The Taiwanese equivalents of Larkin's pictures, cutlery, and vase, which is to say the Taipei he grew up in and perhaps the water buffalo and the village by the sea, are matters of nostalgia. His original home is a place to visit.

## Anna

And then there are other inevitabilities: losses wrought not by change in place but by time itself. Here's another New York story, this of a woman who never moved. A patient of mine, whom I'll call Anna, is a 73-year-old woman who lives with her husband in the house she was born in. First as a child, then as a young married woman in the upstairs apartment, then when her parents died in the apartment downstairs – she lives in what was once a solidly Italian-American enclave in south Brooklyn. Her parents were immigrants who spoke little English. Cousins and people from the same town in Italy lived on the block. They worked hard at maintaining their neighborhood and community even as other Brooklyn neighborhoods were changing around them. People stayed, resisting the late twentieth-century temptation to move to sunnier suburbs or more upscale locations. Anna never had children – having had enough housekeeping and caretaking as the only sister in a family of six children to last her a lifetime. By now her brothers – all but one – have passed away.

I had seen her over the years for anxiety attacks that we could trace to her childhood experiences with an authoritarian father. These are largely under control. She returned to treatment recently because she was "feeling her age" (although she is in good health), but more: everything is unsettled, "stressful." When I ask her to tell me more, she begins to talk about her neighborhood. The familiar faces are disappearing, the old folks dying, the young ones moving out. Her new next-door neighbors (in the attached house in which they share a common wall) are black Jamaicans. They play their strange music on the back porch on summer evenings; their kids ride their bicycles on the street – where she as a child rode hers. Their patois fills the air. A West Indian market has replaced the Italian deli on the corner.

"Your home doesn't feel like your home anymore, I think," I say.

"Yes," she says sadly. "We know we have to sell."

The impossibility of return is not simply a reflection of the fact that things (the place, the times) have changed. The idealized home of origin – and therefore even the fantasy of return – is subject to other, more internal, destructions. In Thomas Wolfe's *You Can't Go Home Again* (1934), for example, the alter ego protagonist is a young writer living in New York, who writes a semi-autobiographical novel based on events and characters he knew in his hometown in the South. The more closely he looks at where he comes from, the worse things look. Now he can't go back: for one thing, the townspeople are enraged with the picture of them painted in his bestselling book. He has damaged their idealization of their town, their South. More important, his deconstruction of where he comes from has damaged that idealization for *him*.

Taiwan or Brooklyn or Ashville: there are lots of ways the joyous shot goes wide.

The world is such that moving is inevitable, be it in space, or in time, or in sensibility, or in what we come to value. Often the distance is very great. A chronic sense of dislocation is a milder, but I think inevitable, consequence of the experience; often we feel like exiles, whether it be from our country of origin, or childhood home, or from the home we thought (or wish) we had. I think of all the first-generation immigrants like Anna's parents, who never adequately learned, and never wanted to and never will, the language of their new homeland, who cling to the language of the old. I think of Andrew's struggle, even as he lectures in his college classroom – a struggle he's all but given up on – with the elusive mystery of English verb tenses. And I think of all those who have acquired comfort with only some of the most necessary customs of their new home, always strangers, never home here and can't go back there, for whom a chronic sense of exile is inevitable and painful. (In some sense we're all psychic immigrants, having left some of our self behind along with the childhood context that supported it. But this is the subject for another chapter.)

## Adaptation

Important to say, though: not every adaptation to exile is unhappy. The sense of dislocation can become part of the texture of a new life, giving one's new home a coloration and enriching it.

Some years ago my wife and I were vacationing in Greece, where I was collecting a little background for the first paper in this series which began with a consideration of Odysseus's *nostos*, his longing for home (Seiden, 2009). We spent a few days on the island of Samos in the southeastern corner of the Aegean. One day, up in the hills, we stopped in a little village hidden away from the sea, a village named Mitylene (named, it is significant to add, for the island of Mitylene, from which centuries earlier the founding population had been forced to flee). There was a small museum, a modern building of two floors around a sun-baked courtyard, just outside the village. The museum had been donated to the village by a local man who had gone off to Australia and gotten rich. It was largely devoted to local history, traditional crafts, farm implements, old photographs, and the like. But, in one room, something else: artifacts of Australia, prominent among them a stuffed kangaroo! The native son's stuffed kangaroo. He couldn't or wouldn't come home again, but he built a museum and he sent his kangaroo. A way of saying, "I'm both here and there." One imagines that living in Australia, he made quite a point of being Greek.

Like that prideful and happy Greek in Australia (I assume he's happy, but can't prove it – maybe it's the love of Samos, maybe it's the kangaroo), we do make our adaptations. We, all of us, build our own museums, it might be said, honoring the old, honoring the new. And we can build a new home that partakes of many worlds; that embraces the new even as it borrows elements of the original and reflects what we valued (and long for) in the original. Having spouses and children helps in this accommodation. (Perhaps it hasn't escaped your notice that neither Andrew nor Anna has children.) Good work, and a good workplace to do it in, serve the accommodation. Community – everything from professional organizations to religious fellowship to the local PTA – can perform this function.

My friend Andrew lives in a little new Taiwan surrounded by the signs, shops, language, food, and street smells of the old. He lives in a modern Asian home. His Buddhist practice and service provide community. He tells me that the banner that hangs above the hall in their retreat center says, "Hui Jia Le," which he translates as "Returning home!"

## Absence as presence

Psychoanalysis tells us that absence can be a kind of presence. The lost object Freud (1917) says of "melancholia" (that is, depression) is internalized, becomes part of the self. As part of the self it is subjected to – that is, the self is subjected to – all the ambivalent feelings, the loving and raging, that pertained to the lost object. Again, in *The Ego and the Id* (1923) Freud writes, "The character of the ego is a precipitate of abandoned object cathexes and ... it contains a history of those object choices" (p. 29). Not only object choices (i.e., people), I would say, but worlds. Our lost worlds, for better and for worse, are part of us.

One's home of origin is inevitably for adults, an absence: a thing lost. But "the shadow" of that home, to borrow Freud's felicitous phrase, falls upon us. This would seem to be a characteristic of mind. Absences are shadow presences – lost loves, lost childhoods, lost gods, lost homes. We spend our lives in chronic longing for and chronic celebration (which is a form of longing) of what has been taken away from us, what we will never have again, or have dreamed of but now know we'll never have at all, or will know was never there to begin with. That longing and those absences and those celebrations become part of us.

Can the meaning of Brooklyn for Anna, or of Taiwan for Andrew (or the Bronx for me), be separated from the sense of having lost it? The longing, the sense of value, the sense of safety, identity and belonging, but also the feelings of abandonment, the sense of dislocation or exile, the sense of irredeemable loss, are all turned inward.

This is not all bad news. There's a sweet, if sad, sense of being anchored in knowing where you come from, a reconciliation of the longing for and the impossibility of return. The reconciliation becomes apparent in a perspective on the world: a "What would my mother, father, uncle, grandma (in my own case, especially my grandma) say about this?"; a "What would they call this where I come from? What would the neighbors say?" which provides a psychic bottom line. While we can't go home again, the home we've lost is in us and stays a part of us. The lost Bronx (not just the Bronx, the *lost* Bronx) is in me, his lost Taiwan is in Andrew – and I dare say whatever lost place you come from that's in you.

## References

Freud, S. (1917). Mourning and Melancholia. In J. Strachey (ed. and trans.) *The Standard Edition of the Complete Psychological Works of Sigmund Freud*, vol. 14, pp. 237–258. (Original work published 1917.)

Freud, S. (1923). The Ego and the Id. In J. Strachey (ed. and trans.) *The Standard Edition of the Complete Psychological Works of Sigmund Freud* (vol. 14, pp. 1–66). (Original work published 1924.)

Larkin, P. (2003). *Collected Poems*. New York: Faber and Faber.

Seiden, H.M. (2009). On the longing for home. *Psychoanalytic Psychology*, 26: 191–205; also in B. Willock, L.C. Bohm & R. Coleman Curtis (eds) (2012), *Loneliness and Longing: Conscious and Unconscious Aspects*. London: Routledge, pp. 267–279.

Wolfe, T. (1934). *You Can't Go Home Again*. New York: Harper Collins.

# Part IV

# THERAPEUTIC FAILURE

# 10

# DORA AND THE BATHWATER

## A relational perspective on shame and psychoanalytic failure

*Amira Simha-Alpern**

A little over a year into Alyssa's analysis, I had a dream in which I invited her into a warm, cozy bed, covered with a down comforter and fluffy pillows, in the middle of an open prairie, blanketed with thick snow. Alyssa stood with a group scattered in the distance, wearing heavy winter coats, shivering. She turned down my invitation. Dressed in flannel pajamas and wrapped in a comforter, I felt warm and cozy, but confused and disheartened by Alyssa's rejection.

A few weeks later, Alyssa had a dream in which she was on her way to session but found herself going to Canada instead (the opposite direction to the treatment facility). Realizing she would never make the session on time, she called to cancel. A short time after reporting her dream, Alyssa decided to quit analysis, saying she could not tolerate being "vulnerable" three times a week.

The distance between Alyssa and me was palpable. It is apparent from both dreams that we equally felt the gap. While I seemed to be the one unsuccessfully attempting to close the gap, Alyssa was moving further away. She declined my suggestion for wrap-up sessions, saying they were not necessary. She knew I had done my best. She had told me "some," but was unable to tell me everything.

When I think of Alyssa, I think of Freud's (1905/1989) Dora, his famous case that inspired development of classical theory and technique. That case actually described a treatment failure. Dora, a young woman with histrionic symptoms, left analysis after only eleven weeks, by no means "cured." Her departure (one may say flight) was neither planned nor recommended. Freud acknowledged that one of his errors was his failure to recognize her erotic transference. Because of the many gaps in his understanding of Dora and her flight from therapy, some contemporary psychoanalysts are ready to throw away what can be learned from this failure. Many contemporary writers, especially feminists, attribute Freud's failure to his lack of consideration of the power differential between males and females in Viennese society at that time and his lack of empathy for Dora's struggle as a woman in patriarchal culture. A relational perspective on this striking failure argues that Freud "went too fast" in interpreting Dora's unconscious sexual desires. While his interpretations may have been legitimate, he expected her to hold in her mind shameful parts of herself that she was desperately trying to disown (cf. Bromberg, 2003).

I have always wondered whether intolerance to shame is what thwarted Dora's ability to benefit from the "brilliant" but overly exposing interpretations Freud offered. Freud's own shame may have prevented him from recognizing where he went wrong. I maintain that "therapeutic failures," which frequently result in premature terminations or therapeutic impasses, are often associated with attempts to avoid insufferable shame. Failure to establish a deep emotional connection between patient and analyst is often a manifestation of the patient and/or the analyst maneuvering to avoid experiencing shameful self-states. Important questions informing this chapter are: What are the roots of this shame? Of what are we ashamed? How do we attempt to avoid feeling shameful?

In the psychoanalytic literature, shame is understood as a reaction to "the absence of approving reciprocity" (Ikonen & Rechardt, 2010, p. 112), particularly when one's love is not accepted (Karen, 1998). "When the infant notices that he does not meet the mother's gaze ... he is ashamed of his false expectation" (Ikonen & Rechardt, 2010, p. 112). In other words, the infant is overwhelmed with shame for having false expectations when she realizes that her belief that she is the mother's center of attention is incorrect. Winnicott (1971) suggested a similar perspective when he quoted one of his patients as saying: "Wouldn't it be awful if the child looked into the mirror and saw nothing!" (p. 133).

Fairbairn (1941/1952a) argued that all psychopathology results from a failure to obtain a mutually loving relationship with a real object. He suggested that frustration in being loved or having one's love accepted "is the greatest trauma that a child can experience" (p. 40), and that shame is rooted in the infant's experience of intense humiliation when she recognizes that mother is unloving and rejecting of her love (Ogden, 2010, p. 104). "The experience is one of shame of the display of needs which are disregarded and belittled" (Fairbairn, 1944/1952b, p. 113).

Similarly, attachment theorists attribute overwhelming shame, or rigid defenses against it, to insecure attachment resulting from an early relationship with a rejecting, or oblivious, significant caretaker. This caretaker ignores or criticizes the child's pleas for affection or other expressions of need states, leaving the child with a profound experience of inefficacy and a sense that his feelings, thoughts, and needs are inadequate. Moreover, the child grows to believe parts of him or her are ugly and, if shown, will chase the other away (Karen, 1998). Research (Cassidy, 1990) has shown that, with insecure attachment (avoidant, ambivalent), individuals develop low self-esteem and reduced tolerance to shame. In contrast, securely attached individuals enjoy strong feelings of self-worth and are able to acknowledge their imperfections. They are neither tormented by shame nor deny feeling shameful.

Alyssa was a bright, competent, hard-working, energetic, promising woman in her early twenties. Pursuing a graduate degree, she was the departmental protégée.

She sought psychotherapy to handle persistent, confusing panic attacks. Her first attack occurred on her way to visit her ex-boyfriend's parents, who disapproved of their relationship. In their minds, their son was destined for greatness and a better bride. While she and her ex-boyfriend were driving to his family event, she wanted both of them to believe everything would be fine. She managed to keep her spirits up most of the way until finally she found herself unable to breathe. He had to stop worriedly on the side of the road. Alyssa had "no clue" as to what precipitated the panic, as is often the case with panic attacks. Only later were we able to understand that collapsed mentalization and paralysis vis-à-vis her feelings at that time reflected her need to purge from her mind the experience of shame. Alyssa could not tolerate her boyfriend's parents' humiliating rejection and the shame associated with her sense of worthlessness.

Alyssa experienced several more attacks after the initial one. By the time she began once-a-week psychotherapy, she was negotiating a painful breakup with this boyfriend. He had moved out of town and she was developing a romantic relationship with another student. After a year of therapy, she was referred to me for analysis because her therapist assessed her as insightful, open, and ready for more depth. As I worked with her, I realized that what looked like perceptive insight was actually a cover-up for a profound sense of abandonment. Alyssa's superior intellectual and verbal abilities gave her apparent access to mentalization and insight but actually covered profound emptiness and aloneness (Benjamin, 2009, p. 446). She used sophisticated psychological reflection, valued self-observation, shared a rich fantasy life, and seemed to pursue insight. Her involvement with others seemed complex and multilayered, with great sensitivity and perceptiveness to nuances. As we worked together I gradually recognized her psychological understandings were prematurely applied to offset overwhelming, unarticulated experiences and "ward off knowledge of primitive conflicts and islands of unintegration" (Fogel, 1995, p. 793). Her talent for reflection, eloquent articulation, and "responsiveness to others were, in effect, exploited at the expense of full psychological growth" (p. 793). Her psychological-mindedness was actually a defense against confusion and vulnerability.

Alyssa's early experience with a passive, dependent mother implied that without an external, competent, holding object to assist her in organizing her experiences meaningfully, Alyssa used her own mind as a holding, nurturing, organizing object. As a precocious child, she used immature psychological perceptions to formulate and understand experience, temporarily relieving chaos, ambiguity, and disorganization but, in the long run, leaving her mind with lacunae of uncontained, unrepresented, unintegrated experiences and sense of self. As an adult, she avoided situations that challenged her tenuous integration and subjective sense that everything is fine. On occasions where primitive self-states were activated, Alyssa found herself feeling disoriented and overwhelmed (Fogel, 1995).

For our early morning sessions, Alyssa often was dressed in pajamas after a sleepless night. Unlike Dora, Alyssa was a sexually liberal woman. Although she preferred committed relationships and easily maintained exclusivity, she was quite comfortable with "one-night stands" and playful "hooking up." Far from being sexually inhibited, she felt superior and powerful with her open sexuality. I believe this attitude reflects our new era where sexuality and desire are not the main sources of shame and inhibition.

Alyssa's real struggles were with dependency and yearning to be loved. She was overwhelmed with shame and felt profoundly inadequate when these needs were exposed through her dreams or enactments. Her new boyfriend communicated to her in many ways that he was not interested in, or was unable to maintain, a committed relationship. Although he was open about his liaisons with other women, Alyssa had a hard time letting go. She drove by his house obsessively to see if his car was parked there overnight or whether there was an unfamiliar automobile in the driveway. She incessantly texted him and needed to know his whereabouts. Yet she felt shamed when she was seen as needing him too much.

When Alyssa reported on her pursuits, she tended to flip the story. Rather than portraying herself as a desperate woman begging for affection and acceptance, she depicted herself as a heroine who ran to her ex-boyfriend's rescue whenever he got into trouble (which he often did). Like a Greek character facing danger and adversity, or acting from a position of weakness as the desperate, rejected woman, Alyssa turned herself into the "savior," displaying courage through self-sacrifice and care. She stood by her ex-boyfriend when he did not get the job he wanted, was forced to admit that his academic record was tarnished and was unable to graduate, and was arrested by the police for drunk driving. By maintaining the higher moral ground and not retaliating against his rejection of her, Alyssa protected herself from shame associated with recognizing her dependency and unreciprocated desperation to be loved.

In working with Alyssa, I gradually concluded that shame and defenses against it played major roles in her personality formation. Initially informed by a classical formulation, I believed Alyssa was inhibited by guilt over Oedipal rivalry triggered by the realization that she had surpassed her dependent mother and gained the respect of her father. Alyssa recalled blatant childhood fantasies and concrete communications with her father about replacing her mother. Her choice of emotionally unavailable men with whom she could never develop mature, reciprocal love could be perceived as her way of negating Oedipal victory. Her obsessive attachments to men who pursued other women easily lend themselves to this formulation. Later, however, I realized that her de-identification with her weak, dependent mother and her identification with father were part of a shame-based drama (Osherson & Krugman, 1990). Alyssa expressed contempt towards her childlike, dependent mother who was "only" a kindergarten teacher, incapable of handling anything more challenging. When Alyssa faced parts of herself that evoked her devalued mother, she became overwhelmed with a sense of shameful worthlessness.

I developed the suspicion that Alyssa had more tolerance for experiencing guilt than for feeling dishonored by shame, and that her guilt may have been a defense against humiliating shame. Guilt was about something she *did*, while shame was about who she *was* (Ikonen & Rechardt, 2010; Morrison, 2008). Alyssa reported on her visit to a local bar she often enjoyed with friends. Her ex-boyfriend joined her after having rejected her invitations multiple times in the past, insisting that they were no longer together. During that evening, Alyssa left with another male and found herself "going down on him" in the hallway. She was confused about her behavior: "How could I do it when he [ex-boyfriend] was there?" "Is it possible that you did it *because* he was there?" I replied. Alyssa paused, perplexed. My question seemed jarring. She returned to my comment many times in following sessions with apparent distress. She thought I meant she intentionally attempted to make her ex-boyfriend jealous in retaliation against his rejection of her love. She felt awful, mean, remorseful. It was now my turn to be perplexed. This was not on my mind when I made that comment. I was referring to her tendency to lose clarity and become disorganized in the presence of a rejecting object, as well as her counterphobic exhibitionism when she felt her love was not reciprocated. It occurred to me that she may be better able to tolerate guilt for being aggressive than shame of being needy and hurt.

Alyssa's difficulty was not only that she was unable to establish and maintain a loving tie with an object capable of giving and receiving love. She was also incapable of extricating herself from futile efforts to wring love from external objects who were experienced as unloving (Fairbairn, 1944/1952b; Ogden, 2010). She was often caught in a web of tantalizing-rejecting object ties, perpetually attempting to transform unloving/unaccepting objects into loving, accepting ones. Powerful, uncontrollable attachment to the alluring aspect of her ex-boyfriend's short-lived moments of acceptance kept her hopelessly attached to his rejecting aspects. I believe hope of changing the object from unloving and unaccepting into a loving, accepting one (Ogden, 2010) detoxified her shameful sense of unlovability and kept her "addictively" attached to the rejecting object.

The main struggle for me was not my difficulty accepting Alyssa with all her parts. At least consciously, I had great compassion for her struggle and great admiration for her fights against internal demons. I wished she would give herself permission to need, rather than camouflage and dissociate need states. It seemed, however, that Alyssa had difficulties accepting my acceptance of her. What I hoped would be empathic reflections were experienced by her as a penetrating, exposing surgeon's scalpel. She felt more intruded upon than understood. Encouraging her to speculate on why she behaved in a certain manner, or what parts of her dreams meant, only exacerbated her need to escape.

The challenge was that the disapproving objects of Alyssa were internal parts of herself.[1] Her internal "judge," or internal saboteur, as Fairbairn (1944/1952b) phrased it, constantly attacked her libidinal ego.[2] The following dialogue (Ogden, 2010) may have played in her mind:

> The internal saboteur, filled with self-hatred for its own "dependence dictated by … [infantile] need" (Fairbairn, 1944, p. 114), turns on the libidinal ego … The internal saboteur disdainfully, contemptuously

attacks the libidinal ego as a pathetic wretch, a sap, a sucker for the way it continually humiliates itself in begging for the love of the exciting object: "You [the libidinal object] never learn your lesson. You get kicked in the face [by the exciting object] and drag yourself to your feet as if nothing has happened only to get kicked and knocked down again. How can you be so stupid as not to see what is plain as day? ... [He] [exciting object] toys with you. Leads you on, and then dumps you every time. And yet you keep going back for more. You disgust me."

(2101, p. 111)

The internal saboteur demeans and shames the libidinal ego for its infantile longings and attacks the exciting object for its endless appetite for tantalizing, seducing, deceiving, and humiliating. The fury and contempt that the internal saboteur heaps upon the libidinal ego and the exciting object stem from a glimmer of recognition of the shame and humiliation it feels about its own absolute dependence on, and loyalty to, the rejecting (internal) object (Ogden, 2010, p. 112). When Alyssa left analysis saying she could not tolerate being "vulnerable," she probably meant vulnerability to attacks by her internal saboteur and the overwhelming shame it elicited in her.

The psychotherapeutic process itself was shameful for Alyssa, just as it had been for Dora. There was no insight without shame. Throughout our work, I sensed the following intricate paradox: I am doomed if I am compassionate to her needy part, legitimizing her desire to be loved. I am equally doomed if I empathize with the part of her that endorses her right to be accepted by a better partner who is capable of reciprocating her love. If I am too empathic with her need for love and affirmation, then I am pathetic, worthy of scorn. If I ally with her competent, high-functioning parts, then I am critical and shaming. If I recognize her functioning, presentable, good self, I am oblivious to her disgraced parts. If I recognize her dissociated, desperate, shameful self, I push her into the abyss. Holding in mind both her strength and her psychic pain was not possible yet. I could not be with both parts as they could not be together (Benjamin, 2009). Instead, feeling excluded from her internal drama, I became the useless, helpless, bystander mother. I believed there was nothing I could do to soothe her, to make her feel recognized and known to me. Powerless, I retreated into observing her rather than engaging with her.

The challenge at the heart of therapeutic work is inviting patients to experience, own, and articulate shameful, disowned self-states, finding the optimal balance of experiencing shame without becoming overpowered by it. Growth and transformation are the *sine qua non* for expanding this ability to simultaneously experience multiple self-states. Benjamin (2009) refers to this process as developing an analytic third: "An important sign of re-opening thirdness is being restored to the capacity to hear multiple voices – I can hear both your voice and mine as can you without one canceling the other out; I can hear more than one part of yourself, you can hear more than one part of yourself" (p. 442).

Holding this therapeutic goal in mind, I could not avoid feeling like a fundamentally ineffective therapist – I was not the right analyst for Alyssa, someone else would do a better job. When she decided to leave, I offered to refer her to someone else (a referral she declined). Her terror of being exposed as inadequate resonated with own fear. I was a beginning analyst. Alyssa was my first analytic case. My taped sessions were closely scrutinized in weekly supervision with someone whom I respect greatly. I was serious and thoughtful, attempting to say the right thing and, like Alyssa, afraid to be exposed as worthless.

It was only after Alyssa's premature termination that I dared bring my dream to supervision. I was embarrassed by what I was afraid would be identified as my need for Alyssa, my unreciprocated longing for her affirmation of my sensitivity and competence and what could be interpreted as my homosexual desire for her. I was inhibited by shame about Alyssa's rejection of my offering warmth to her. In the dream, I was publicly humiliated by being left "hanging there," my inviting hands outstretched. For a few moments, I was her (dressed in pajamas like her) and she was the rejecting object.

Ogden (2010) poses a question I often grappled with while struggling with my inability to connect with Alyssa. He asks whether it is the mother's failure to convince the child of her true love, or the child's failure/inability to be convinced/accept love? Was I unable to convey to Alyssa my true appreciation and affection towards her, or was she unable to recognize and accept it?

I am not sure what could have been done differently and whether the analysis could have been "saved" had I taken a different approach. I wonder if a more playful approach, with a healthy sense of humor and freedom of expression, would have helped us bond better, softening Alyssa's internal parts that harshly judged and demeaned her other parts. Benevolently laughing at our shortcomings and failures could have expanded the collapsed transitional space and, like an analytic third (Aron, 2006; Benjamin, 2009), could have facilitated a more benign perspective towards – and acceptance of – disdained self-states. It is possible in my serious attention to her narration, Alyssa "looked into the mirror and saw nothing." She may have needed a more active, enthusiastic engagement from me, more delighted reaction to her sexual conquests, professional triumphs, and benevolent rivalries. I saw those parts of her as "false self" or "manic defenses" against a more despondent "true self." I had the goal of helping her recover her "true self," reclaim uncharted parts of herself, and wanted no part in colluding with her defenses. Perhaps I left her to play alone in the sandbox.

## Notes

* The author wishes to thank Ms. Shulamit Falik for her valuable editorial comments on this chapter.
1 Fairbairn suggested that, in an effort to control the unsatisfactory object, the object is internalized and divided into two parts: the tantalizing and the rejecting object and self-representations. Furthermore, these parts are split off from the main ego and become "not me" states.

2 The libidinal ego (LE) contains the exciting object(s) and the internal saboteur (IS) contains the rejecting object(s). Both the LE and the IS are unconscious (Ellman, 2010, p. 348).

# References

Aron, L. (2006). Analytic impasse and the third: clinical implications of intersubjectivity theory. *International Journal of Psychoanalysis*, 87: 349–368.

Benjamin, J. (2009). A relational psychoanalysis perspective on the necessity of acknowledging failure in order to restore the facilitating and containing features of the intersubjective relationship (the shared third). *International Journal of Psychoanalysis*, 90: 441–450.

Bromberg, P.M. (2003). Something wicked this way comes. Trauma, dissociation, and conflict: the space where psychoanalysis, cognitive science, and neuroscience overlap. *Psychoanalytic Psychology*, 20: 558–574.

Cassidy, (1990). Theoretical and methodological considerations in the study of attachment and the self in young children. In M. Greenberg, D. Cicchetti, & E.M. Cummings (eds.), *Attachment in the Preschool Years: Theory, Research, and Intervention*. Chicago: University of Chicago Press, pp. 87–119.

Ellman, S.J. (2010). *When Theories Touch: A Historical and Theoretical Integration of Psychoanalytic Thought*. London: Karnac Books.

Fairbairn, W.R.D. (1952a). A revised psychopathology of the psychoses and psychoneuroses. In *Psychoanalytic Study of the Personality*. London: Routledge & Kegan Paul, pp. 28–58. (Original work published 1941.)

Fairbairn, W.R.D. (1952b). Endopsychic structure considered in term of object relationships. In *Psychoanalytic Study of the Personality*. London: Routledge & Kegan Paul, pp. 82–132. (Original work published 1944.)

Fogel, G.I. (1995). Psychological-mindedness as a defense. *Journal of the American Psychoanalytic Association*, 43(3): 793–822.

Freud, S. (1989). Fragments of an analysis of a case of hysteria ("Dora"). In P. Gay (ed.), *The Freud Reader*. New York: W.W. Norton & Company Inc, pp. 172–239. (Original work published 1905.)

Ikonen, P. & Rechardt, E. (2010). *Thanatos, Shame, and Other Essays: On the Psychology of Destructiveness*. London: Karnac.

Karen, R. (1998). *Becoming Attached: First Relationships and How They Shape Our Capacity to Love*. New York: Oxford University Press.

Morrison, A.P. (2008). The analyst's shame. *Contemporary Psychoanalysis*, 44: 65–82.

Ogden, T.H. (2010). Why read Fairbairn? *International Journal of Psycho-Analysis*, 91: 101–118.

Osherson, S. & Krugman, S. (1990). Men, shame, and psychotherapy. *Psychotherapy*, 27(3): 327–339.

Winnicott, D.W. (1971). *Playing and Reality*. New York: Routledge.

# 11

# THINKING THROUGH THERAPEUTIC FAILURE CONCERNING A SUICIDAL PATIENT

*Marsha Aileen Hewitt**

The Truth is past all commiseration.
Maxim Gorky (in Laing, 1965, p. 178)

One year after leaving analysis, Mr. M returned to his country of origin. Two years later, he died. He might have succumbed to his serious physical ailments, or he might have committed suicide, which I believe is more likely. Although such outcomes are not often written about in the psychoanalytic literature, our field is better served if "hard" cases, failures, the ones where we wonder what might we have done differently, are discussed so we can learn and serve patients more effectively.

Although there could be endless debate about this clinical material, such cases inevitably confront us with the question of the limits of analytic theory and practice (with certain patients, or generally) as we engage the ultimate mystery that lies within each human being. In every treatment, we encounter a unique inner universe, with its own specific narrative, both conscious and unconscious. As formidable and encouraging as our theorizing may be in helping patients live fuller, more satisfying lives, there are countless moments in treatment, even in a single session, when theory cannot bridge the gulf between analyst and analysand. Occasionally a patient remains lost to us despite our best efforts. Sometimes, even as that knowledge becomes painfully conscious, we carry on, shifting between the affective polarities of hope and despair. This experience may become especially acute in work with suicidal patients.

Some questions informing this chapter are: How does the sustained threat of suicide shape the analytic work? What elements of the analytic process become dissociated or unconsciously enacted between analyst and analysand when the Damoclean sword of suicide perpetually hangs over them? How can the analyst navigate the oscillating, fragmented dialectics of fear, shame, love, hopefulness, and hatred that are often present in work with deeply depressed, sometimes hostile, suicidal patients?

A therapist who sought treatment while in deep personal crisis resulting from the suicides of two patients earlier in his career explained that he was depressed for months afterwards, thinking perhaps it was his fault: "I am a highly trained therapist. I should have known this was coming, I should have done something differently, but for the life of me I could never figure out what, and that did me in. I felt ... *if I had been a better therapist, they'd be alive today.*" Similarly, I wonder, if Mr. M did commit suicide, could it have been prevented in the way I worked with him?

With such patients, death is omnipresent – not only the risk of their death, but also the "death" of the analyst's sense of professional skill and public reputation. Analyst and analysand may have dissociated fears of being "killed" by the other. Multiple subtle, and not subtle, power dynamics (domination, submission) may play out, diminishing the analyst's capacity to think. The analyst may become emotionally paralyzed, fearing her patient may kill himself. The patient may become terrorized by the feared loss of the analyst that he believes will be his fault. If these anxieties remain dissociated, the treatment is threatened. Suicide may well result.

To explore these and other issues, I will present a detailed clinical picture that will hopefully evoke the intense immediacy of the analytic experience. Given that there are many competing psychoanalytic perspectives from which to organize and understand any case, I will consider several that open a deeper understanding of Mr. M and what played out between us. I engage those analytic discourses that feel most appropriate to this case rather than *excluding* discourses that may have valuable insights as well.

I met Mr. M very early in my analytic career while he was a psychiatric inpatient being treated for depression accompanied by compelling suicidal thoughts. He had been hospitalized several times in the previous twenty years for suicide attempts. The last two were especially serious. Although most were preceded by some failure in his life, two followed significant successes. Both failure and success could pull the psychic supports out from under him. What linked these attempts were feelings of shame, despair, and dissociated rage related to his abiding sense of powerlessness. Suicide, representing control over his life, was preferable to feeling helpless.

Mr. M's inner world was a dark reservoir of cumulative, unresolved trauma occasioned by horrific, unexpected losses originating in and extending across his childhood. He had no one to help him understand and integrate the sudden disappearance of his parents. Left to his own emotional devices, this abandoned, terrified little boy had no way of working through or regulating the jumble of contradictory, tumultuous feelings accompanying his losses. As far as his caregivers were concerned, his problems were his own fault. Mr. M knew he was unloved and, tragically, concluded he was unworthy of love. Shamefully dependent upon his extended family for financial support, this fact gave his relatives license to dictate his life.

Mr. M had little capacity for negotiating relationships (Pizer, 1998) because he had no real experience of the mutual recognition and reciprocity of healthy intersubjectivity. For him, disagreement and benign difference *were* rejection and persecution, and he retaliated accordingly. His relationships were characterized by repetitive, exhausting struggles for control which he exercised in ways verging on emotional extortion. He had no hesitation reminding anyone who disappointed him that he was a fragile, depressed person who might kill himself if things did not go his way. Suicide was often the only way he could imagine taking charge of his life, controlling others' power over him.

## The first crisis

During our first holiday break, Mr. M wrote me emails describing how depressed he was while wishing me a peaceful holiday. One letter, sent Christmas Day, concluded with a harrowing description of the most effective way of slashing one's wrists with an X-Acto knife, which he had beside him as he wrote. In this letter, he urged me to intervene with someone who had rejected one of his projects. I was to point out that Mr. M's emotional state and physical survival depended upon that person reversing his position. Acknowledging that my time is limited, Mr. M drafted the letter I was to sign. Given his history, I took his suicidal threat seriously. I had to find a way of helping him through the crisis without gratifying his demand that I get tough with his adversary. This was the first of many "life and death" conflicts with which he and I would struggle, where either I had to be destroyed in my analytic identity in order to "help" Mr. M, or he would kill himself. Whatever I chose, it seemed one of us was doomed.

Observing that some patients are a "heavy emotional burden," Winnicott (1975, p. 194) argues that analysts must be conscious of "hate" toward patients.[1] Thinking about his list of "reasons" why mothers hate their babies, and Gabbard's (2000, pp. 418–419) reformulation of them with respect to the analytic relationship, it became apparent to me that with this letter (and others), Mr. M was accusing me of having abandoned him and driven him to the brink of suicide in asserting my needs over his in taking a holiday. My vacation underlined his helplessness, evoking feelings of vulnerability and shame associated with parental loss in childhood. He had no control over my "leaving." I was no different from his parents who selfishly abandoned him when he was a vulnerable child needing their support and protection. If I *really* cared, I could repair this injury by using my professional power to force his colleague to comply with Mr. M's wishes, atoning for the humiliation and abandonment I inflicted.

From Mr. M's point of view, I failed him and I knew it. This awareness aroused in me a sense of shame that I had not only failed him in taking a vacation, but that I would fail him again as I had no intention of signing that letter. Feeling boxed in and helpless, my only recourse was a feeble attempt at "responsive understanding" (Pizer, 1998, p. 32) in which I acknowledged the conundrum we shared and wondered if there might be more effective ways of addressing the problem. This response satisfied him momentarily.

## Disgust and shame: irresolvable dilemmas

There were times when being with Mr. M was almost unbearable. He exuded a beastly body odor that lingered for hours, giving me headaches. Sometimes his smell aroused such visceral disgust that it impeded my ability to focus analytically or maintain empathic attunement. I delayed confronting this issue given my worry about shaming him, thus possibly precipitating another suicide attempt. My feeling of having to put up with his intense odor indicated the powerful transference/countertransference field that sometimes felt like an inescapable prison. I felt like an emotional hostage, "forced" to relinquish my needs in submitting to the tyranny of his suicidal threats.

Mr. M maintained precarious, illusory grandiosity in delicate balance with profound self-loathing and shame. These almost separate selves existed in a state of dissociation vital to his stability and self-preservation. The idea of "dying of shame" metaphorically infused most of his experience, occasionally resulting in suicide attempts. Intense shame provoked him to shame others, providing an illusory refuge where he felt relieved and revitalized.

Given the early stage of the analysis, my interventions were few, conservative, and largely mirroring. I often felt I was stumbling along in a darkened landscape full of hidden dangers.

Once Mr. M raised the issue of his smell, reporting somewhat angrily that his physician pointed it out. Excited that we might be able finally to open a new line of communication, I thought it might be safe to address his odor. With all the neutrality of tone I could muster, I responded: "I wonder what it was like for you, him telling you that." Mr. M retaliated with familiar harshness: "I like his manner. He is East European, like me. Refreshing. Not like overbearing, repressed Anglo-Saxons." Mr. M paused, then continued in a withering tone that was, at the same time, strangely light: "He isn't like *you*. *You* are an Anglo-Saxon." I was so stunned by this aggression that suddenly broke through that I barely registered that he was shaming *me* for shaming *him* in pursuing the matter of body odor. Before I could think of how to respond, he continued, "It's so obvious with YOUR name! Anglo-Saxons are so repressed and intimidating!"

Not willing to lose the moment of tackling his odor, I wondered whether he knew how difficult it was for others and if he planned to correct it. He gave me one of his scornful looks and informed me that he sustained his smell not so much by foregoing bathing, but by going days, maybe weeks, before changing underwear. "BO is symptomatic of depression. That is how depressed people are." His tone was patient, pedagogic, and arrogant as he explained the inevitable link between body odor and depression, making it clear he was not about to change.

This interchange reminds me of Pizer's (1998, p. 33) patient, Donald, who used his body odor as a means of asking people to accept him for who he was. With Mr. M, it was more aggressive, a way of forcing people to accept him as a depressed person. His smell was emblematic of his depression. To lose his depression would be to lose his identity, his way of experiencing himself and being in the world. As long as he maintained this dramatic symptom, he maintained some sense of internal stability. His symptom also served to keep others at bay, especially me. If I had a problem with his odor, that was because of my "repressed, Anglo-Saxon" nature, not because of him. There was no opportunity to pursue this matter further before analysis ended.

## Re-traumatizing dangers of therapeutic change

Despite these challenges, there were promising signs that our work was having positive effects. At times Mr. M idealized me, though rarely without caveat. He "couldn't believe his good luck" in being in analysis, telling me, "You seem reasonably sure of what you are doing. You are a nice person. Best of all, you are conveniently located to my home."

Mr. M began experiencing affects he was not used to, such as feeling "warm and safe" in sessions, but often "freaking out" when he left. Since he was "always very nervous when things are good," and since being in analysis he was feeling better, that also scared him. Having been depressed for so long, it had become "habit-forming, like cigarettes … Depression feels more real to me than feeling good."

Most scary of all, to "give up" his depression would be to "move away" from "the family." They were obliged to support him because he was "sick." He was the family's spot of infection, their designated madman. This role allowed them to maintain a sense of stability, sanity, and cohesion by disavowing their familial and individual pathologies (Laing, 1969a, 1969b). Problematic though these family dynamics were, Mr. M had a defined role and sense of belonging. They had no choice but to accept him, however grudgingly.

Mr. M had been dependent on his extended family since age 6. He recalled being happy (though he could not remember concrete examples), until one day his mother "disappeared." No one mentioned her again. They refused to discuss what happened. His father disappeared a year later, having lost custody of his son to one of Mr. M's distant relatives, who promptly moved him into another relative's crowded house, where Mr. M slept mostly on the floor. When he was 7, Mr. M's guardian took him for a ride. They stopped at a graveyard. Mr. M was shown a headstone with his mother's name on it. He was told she died from "a gas leak." Mr. M eventually figured that she committed suicide. Years later, he discovered his father had moved to the US, where he started a new family. When Mr. M was in his mid-twenties, his father contacted him in an effort to resume a relationship, which Mr. M spurned. There was no further contact.

Mr. M became the victim of repeated abuse and neglect after his mother's death. At age 11, he was caught stealing pennies from a bed-ridden, elderly aunt's purse, which he spent on toys. He did not think of himself as stealing or doing something to hurt his aunt, although he knew it was wrong. The toys comforted him, providing momentary happiness, perhaps permitting him to experience some of the wellbeing he knew prior to traumatic parental loss. Winnicott's (1990) description of the "anti-social" gesture is relevant to Mr. M's need to "get back behind the deprivation to the state of affairs that obtained when all was well" (p. 204). Stealing pennies may be understood as unconsciously restoring a relationship where he was loved as a little boy who played with toys.

His relatives saw his action as another sign that he was his immoral father's son. His thievery deserved harsh punishment. They beat him, dragged him out of the house, and banished him to a housekeeper's care for several months. His attempted self-soothing traumatically exacerbated his despair. When allowed back home, no one spoke to him for two months. This period in his life was "terrifying, really horrible, the worst experience."

Given this traumatic attachment history, it was not surprising that Mr. M experienced me at times as both loving *and* dangerous. "Feeling good here is like swimming with sharks ... Warm, nice, safe, not thinking about dangers ... but it isn't safe at all. Not when I go out of this room."

Mr. M often spoke of fear immediately accompanying any happiness he felt. Change was dangerously destabilizing. His dilemma was how to maintain his sense of identity while changing. In the meantime, he presented dissociated feeling states utterly disconnected from each other.

I was dangerous in my efforts to interpret his experience so we could understand it. He resisted me with increasing force in the sense described by Bromberg (1995):

> "Resistance"... is an enacted communication that an analyst's effort to interpret meaning is being experienced at that moment as requiring the patient to trade off some domain of his own self-experience for something he is being offered that is "not me" ... "This is not who I am!" is part of the dialectic between loyalty to old patterns of self-meaning and the consensual construction of new meaning and increased ability to state "This is who I am!"
>
> (1995, p. 176)

Happiness and success were intolerable because they had no connection with Mr. M's self-experience as a depressed failure. Some of his suicide attempts occurred immediately after achieving a major success. As we discussed this, Mr. M recalled occasions where his caregivers thwarted his efforts to seek happiness, such as interfering in his first romance, with the result that his girlfriend ended their relationship. That loss provoked his first suicide attempt. For Mr. M, positive experiences always come to grief.

As he began to experience inchoate attachment feelings toward me, I became another dangerous persecutor who threatened his core identity as a depressed individual. He began "feeling pressure" to relinquish familiar, grounding despair in favor of disorienting, unfathomable hope that generated terrifying dread and pain (see Pizer, 1998, ch. 5).

As we explored his feelings of isolation, rage, and helplessness, I focused on details of his interactions with others past and present. Once I pointed out that he seemed to feel contempt for a woman who upset him. His initial reaction was angry denial. In the following session, he said my remark seemed to "loosen" something in him, like a "tight knot." He felt better as he realized the "truth of the word." Deeply ashamed of feeling contempt, he recalled how his caregivers expressed contempt for "lower classes." It was "devastating" and "ugly" to think he, too, might have contempt for others. He had not yet been able to bring to awareness the full force of his caregivers' contempt for *him*.

Mr. M longed for and hated women. They humiliated and rejected him. Like "dogs," women sense need and fear. "They smell my need and don't want to be with me." I believe he was also expressing dissociated awareness that I didn't want to be with him, telling me what it was like to endure my (unarticulated) disgust at his smell, and his fear I would leave, as his mother did, as women always did.

The momentary shame Mr. M felt toward that woman was displaced and subsumed by contempt and rage at women generally (and, unconsciously, me) for "smelling" him. He could not imagine I might choose to remain with him, despite his odor. Neither of us was capable of addressing what was unfolding. He seemed to have instantly "forgotten" his shame and, I think, remorse for feeling contempt, in order to protect himself from the dangerous insight that his caregivers and I had rejecting feelings toward him. Without that forgetful protection, he would see himself in their minds (and mine) as a contemptible, stinking creature, which he unconsciously experienced himself to be.

Pizer's distinction (1998) between distributed and dissociated multiplicity of self-states pertains to Mr. M's defensive maneuvers in such moments. Over the course of his childhood and adolescence, traumatic overload led to "dissociative damage control," leaving him no alternative but to oscillate between separate "islands of relational experience" (p. 73). Internal "meaning-and-affect centers" developed in communicative isolation. He was capable only of selective focusing, unable to tolerate or bridge "a range of paradox." For example, he could only fleetingly experience shame about his contempt for women he longed for and needed. The fragile links of consciousness between these contradictory feelings collapsed almost as soon as they were established. Longings for intimacy were sequestered in another part of his mind to which he allowed himself no access.

Women rejected him because of their doglike nature, not because there was something about him that inhibited them from entering into loving relationships with him. Since women were not subjects in their own right, Mr. M could not consider their point of view. He was barely a subject himself.

Behind his contempt for women lay deep, unresolved mourning for his mother, coupled with shame and rage at having been abandoned by her. If he had been able to mourn her loss, and the loss of his childhood, the frozen, dissociative structures of his mind that were shaped and defined by both distinct and cumulative traumas (Khan, 1963) might have begun to develop into a more conscious, integrated self.

I now have a clearer understanding of what it might have been like for Mr. M to be with me as I increasingly disliked being with him. (My thanks to Stuart Pizer for bringing this, and parallels in his own work with "Everett," whom he disliked, to my attention.) Although I did my best to stay with Mr. M in an empathic manner, there were times when I could barely stand him. He could be savagely humiliating toward me and others. He stank up my consulting room and (in my mind) embarrassed me with other patients, although I carefully sprayed the room and opened windows after each session.

With growing awareness of my aversion toward him, I felt guilty, frustrated, and ashamed for harboring such feelings toward a patient, particularly one so damaged and traumatized. Nearly all his relationships were permeated by rejection, despair, shame, and rage. As those feelings were aroused in our distorted relational field, they became increasingly unspeakable. I imagine he must have experienced me as abandoning him. My moments of failed empathy likely reinforced his belief that *he* was to blame for his mother and father leaving him, and for all failed, broken relationships in his life.

I felt sad imagining Mr. M as a scared little boy whose mother vanished, leaving him to endure a life devoid of love, acceptance, and support. I felt angry at this mother for abandoning her child, and at his caregivers for treating him with emotional and physical brutality. They made him who he became, I reasoned. At the same time, he was responsible, like all of us, "for what we make of what we are made of" (Laing, 1968, p. 25). The aim of therapy is that patients "own up to" wishes, conflicts, and defenses generated within themselves (Loewald, 2000, p. 93).

I struggled to speak to Mr. M from a place of compassion where I connected with the lonely, frightened, abused, neglected man-child he was. It nevertheless remained difficult to address other parts of him that were repulsive and infuriating. When I felt angry at his humiliating, nasty remarks, I remained silent, battling temptation to retaliate. I wonder if that was one way I may have failed him, meeting his authenticity with inauthenticity, motivated by fear of retraumatizing him, thereby tilting him toward suicide.

Nine months into analysis, Mr. M came dangerously close to suicide. Repeating an all-too-familiar pattern, he fought with a colleague he respected, admired, and needed for help with his career. When this person very understandably broke off all contact, saying, "I have reached an impasse that I have no energy to struggle with further," Mr. M was crushed. There ensued a flurry of pleading, accusatory, threatening emails, all copied to me. It was painful reading. I was often at a loss as to how to help him understand what happened between him and the other.

Any possibility of helping Mr. M see his (considerable) role in these events was foreclosed by his inability to see himself in the mind of another, distinguishing between his internal fantasies and motivations, and their intentions, thoughts, and feelings. The closer he got to others, the more they became clusters of projections reflecting his working models of self and (persecutory) other.

Given his chaotic attachment history, Mr. M had a serious inability to "mentalize" self/other relations (Fonagy et al., 2002). Reflective function was severely compromised by his sustained experience of trauma, which included absence of a mentalizing, mirroring other. Relating in ways that were projective and repetitive of his earliest pathological attachment experiences resulted in relationships infused with defensive actions designed to protect him from drowning in overwhelming feelings. He was always the victim, the other persecutor. Always he was right, the other wrong.

Encountering others who suffered depression, Mr. M was initially excited, but they existed more as twinned, projective aspects of himself than as separate subjects. Seeing them as unconditionally accepting playmates whom he could dominate, he seemed to feel these kindred spirits would understand him effortlessly, accept him no matter what he did, agree to whatever he proposed. With them, he possessed an instant, imagined community that would save him from his isolated existence. When he invariably discovered this was not the case, that no matter how depressed they might be they were different and distinct subjects, he felt betrayed and duped and savagely retaliated against them, citing vituperative catalogs of their failures and inadequacies.

Enduring Mr. M's angry, dismissive assaults toward me as well, which intensified as time went on, challenged my analytic identity. Immersed in his internal world, I began to experience powerfully what it must be like to be him: held in contempt, despised, and helpless to do much about it. My acknowledgment of any responsibility for hurting him on occasion was not for him the result of mutual negotiation of a relational experience, but a sign of his victory over an opponent. Trying to maintain balance between who he needed me to be and who I was (Fonagy et al., 2002, p. 370), I occasionally lost my ability to focus on the analytic work. The analysis was in danger of drowning in prolonged enactment.

Mr. M could not tolerate the slightest difference of perspective between us. Sorting out miscommunications was painstaking. When I tried to explore his anger and hurt with me and others, he became enraged by my attempts to unravel these tangled webs of miscommunication. Things happened as *he* said. He took my silences as assent to his irrefutable logic. Satisfying himself that there was only one correct point of view, he would move on to discuss something else. In such moments, I often felt backed into a corner from which there was no escape. Increasingly, I remained silent during his rages, mostly because I could not think of anything else to do. My silences had a soothing effect on him. He became more relaxed and friendly. It felt like the less there was of me, the better for him.

## Dreams and shit

One area that became a "battlefield" between us was dreams. In the first year, Mr. M reported a number of them. In his first, he sought breakfast food, but could only find dry dog biscuits. As with most dreams, he felt "nothing, rather flat, actually." He was, however, astonished that he appeared in this dream. This had never happened before. Usually he "watches" his dreams from outside, a removed spectator. He was curious about this glimmer of emerging subjectivity. While he insisted he had nothing further to say, we were able to return to the dog biscuits.

They became a metaphor for the lack of emotional nourishment and the psychologically dry atmosphere he experienced growing up.

In other dreams, Mr. M did experience feelings. He felt happy in one where he stabbed a "bad relative" to death for refusing to give him money. He dreamed of a playful, sexual scene with a former girlfriend: "It was a really nice feeling. Happy, like kids."

For a while, we could investigate dreams and associations. My remarks were conservative and few, mostly confined to exploring feelings. I did not want to impinge upon him with interpretations. He was amazed in the change he experienced with dreams, such as having feelings in and about them. Then, quite suddenly, he informed me that my interest in his dreams bothered him. It made me "shrinky" and "predictable," two qualities he found "deeply disappointing." Dreams were of no importance, except to women. "Dreams are excreta, bowel movements of the brain." He feared analysis was about compliance. He was being pressured to "manufacture" dreams to fit "your agenda, although I don't really feel like you have much of one. But this is analysis, after all, and I might be forced to come up with stuff that is relevant, and if I do, if I do it to be nice, well, that is really scary. I worry about planting evidence. I am not used to dreaming. I am not used to feeling dreams are important. I resist them."

I told Mr. M I could understand his fear of compliance. With his caregivers, compliance was the price of survival. Since they supported him, he was forced to walk a fine line between physical survival and existential death. Compliance meant he had no room to develop his self his own way. I wondered if another part of his fear had to do with revealing himself to me, thereby expressing a need for connection. Mr. M shot back, "That's the *positive* interpretation. What I am worried about is being a good boy and *that* is a waste of time!"

## Triumph of the fates

As the analysis moved into its second year, Mr. M seemed increasingly desperate, contemptuous, impatient. He accused me of "s/mothering" him when I urged him to see his physician about serious physical symptoms he was self-medicating. My caring unnerved him. In those moments, I "lowered" the discourse and was "profoundly unprofessional."

Mr. M was agitated and dismissive when I said anything that did not precisely match his perspective, and then when I said anything at all. It felt like he was on a ruthless campaign to undo me as an analyst, to destroy me with savage verbal attacks and ridiculing insults. Sometimes it seemed he brought dreams to pique my interest (they invariably did), only to dismiss my efforts to explore them.

Underlying his views about dreams as brain shit was, I think, a feeling of himself as shit: shitty, smelly underwear; shitty feelings; shitty dreams. Though deeply mistrusting that I might care about his shitty self, he once remarked, "You are a saint to put up with my dismal crap." I can't say I didn't privately agree with him.

To regain control of what he experienced as a threatening relationship, Mr. M fought my efforts to work with him. I felt the analysis was failing, thus I was failing my patient. Grimly determined to stick with him, I hoped we would get through this bad patch. I tried to think of myself as a Winnicottian mother who comforts and regulates her baby with her determination and capacity to survive his assaults.

There were reasons to believe there was light beyond the darkness. Often Mr. M marveled at himself and "new thoughts" he was having. Though he usually found vacations "boring," he excitedly contemplated visiting a cousin in South America, getting to know her children. In vitalizing moments, we shared his enthusiasm about his changes. For stretches of time, he did not feel depressed. He felt himself "reorganizing." Although this new awareness often left him agitated and frightened, he also marveled: "I don't know how analysis works. It is really strange, like a kind of poetic vagueness. It's hard to say, but I think it's working."

Despite these hopeful feelings, Mr. M felt he could not "escape fate, that I really am nuts." He might never escape his past, was not even sure he wanted to. Poignantly he said, "The past defeats free choice. There is an old saying in my native language: your fate is carved on your forehead."

Although a tentative, fragile part of him could experience progress and hope in his emerging attachment to me, Mr. M worried that fate would win. He had to fight against being "vulnerable." Overwhelmed by emotions when younger, he trained himself not to feel. He had been dehumanized and compelled to dehumanize himself. Having so little sense of his humanness, he could only relate to me by increasingly "dehumanizing the analytic relationship" (Bromberg, 1995, p. 177).

Mr. M complained I took his focus off work. He needed work "not to feel." Believing I was "inviting him to expand" his ways of thinking about himself, he became agitated, accusing me of "blind-siding" him. In these moments, I mostly listened, because if I said anything, he became upset, looking at his watch, out the window, drumming his fingers on his knee, and interrupting me.

Always vigilant, Mr. M scanned my tone and facial expressions for signs of danger. He could be disrupted by a simple greeting, demanding to know, "Why are you smiling at me like that? What's wrong?" My friendliness confused him, since, in his experience, all caregiving was dangerous seduction, offering false hope. He would be rejected in the end. His defensive attacks became more frequent and relentless.

Toward the end of our second year, a month before summer break, Mr. M announced that *he* would be taking a break from *me*. In a tone that struck me as far too upbeat, he told me he felt like taking control, since I control everything – times, fees, breaks. Now it was his turn. Previously he had floated ideas of reducing sessions, but we had always been able to discuss it and keep to four times per week. This time I knew he was telling me our work was over. He explained he had been feeling much better. Medication sufficed to control his now considerably lessened depression. Working on a creative project (quite new for him), he sought video footage of the "Christ of the Abyss." When I asked what that image was about and its place in his project, he refused to elaborate. He was taking the summer off to work well into the fall. "But don't think of this as my ending analysis," he said. "I will see you again." These last words were expressed with some warmth. I believe he meant them. At the same time, I think we both knew this was in all likelihood the last time we would meet. He was quite cheery as he left, too cheery in fact, while I glumly recalled Freud's last meeting with Dora.

### "Christ of the Abyss"

A week after our final session, I found a videotape in my waiting room. There was no letter. It was a video of the "Christ of the Abyss," a very tall, bronze statue of a submerged, underwater Jesus, feet encased in concrete, arms outstretched, head thrown back, straining toward the sunlight shining above through the ocean surface. It is a silent, eerie tape, taken by divers, slowly panning the figure.

What was Mr. M trying to tell me? Looking at those outstretched arms "buried" under 55ft (17m) of water, I think of Jesus abandoned on the Cross, crying out to his father for solace that never comes. I wonder if the image resonated for Mr. M as a visual metaphor expressing his own condition, abandoned, "s/mothered," not able to breathe, reaching for the surface, for air and light, but never making it, feet weighted down in the concrete, knowing he will not escape, destined to drown in a fate sealed by a traumatic past from which he longed to be free, yet to which he needed to cling. I often felt he was trapped in a searing dialectic of desire and despair, wanting to live, but "knowing" he was fated to die, existentially or physically, perhaps all the same to him.

### Discussion

I think Mr. M reached out for me, longing for contact, to be held and seen, to have a place in my mind. When he felt close, he drew back into the depths of himself, scared. Love wounded him. Even his mother left him – the ultimate maternal failure. With her suicide, he lost his "protective shield" (Khan, 1963) and, thereby, the opportunity for healthy development.

For Mr. M, I was the loving, supportive mother as well as the persecutory, seductive mother ("s/mother") who might treacherously abandon him at any moment, shattering his happiness and security. Perhaps I threatened to "replace" his mother, thereby leaving him bereft of any traces of her that remained deep within his heart. We were caught in a repetitive dialectic of often, but not always dissociated, disavowed hate and love, hope and despair that, despite our best efforts was, in the end, impossible to negotiate. I like to think that, in time, we might have.

According to Mr. M, the only moments of safety and care he ever experienced, however tentatively, were with me, in my consulting room, his "cocoon." Safety and care threatened him. He fought against trusting me. My smile was filled with potential treachery. My concerns about his health betrayed professional standards.

Thinking about why he left, I am reminded of Winnicott's (1975) story of the boy whose running away was an unconscious act of "saving the inside of his home and preserving his mother from assault, as well as trying to get away from his own inner world, which was full of persecutors" (p. 199). Mr. M might have been doing something similar. Leaving preserved his "cocoon," his haven of safety, and his analyst/mother from further assaults, and protected himself from newly emerging feelings and a changing self which excited and terrified him. Mr. M might protest that this is the "positive interpretation."

Christopher Bollas's (1987) writing about "conservative objects" helpfully illuminates this case. Mr. M's unresolvable trauma constituted an "inevitable part" (p. 111) of his identity. The possibility of transforming those traumas from perpetual reliving to remembered past threatened his sense of self and psychic stability. He was not merely *traumatized* – he *was* the trauma. Trauma constituted his core self. As he began to feel emerging attachment to me, he became terrified of losing his attachment to punitive, internal, bad objects that represented his only connection with his family. He needed to preserve a "being state" where traumatic childhood experiences and relationships are "conserved" rather than "transformed (symbolized)." Early parental loss, emotional and physical abuse became "self-defining event[s]." "Giving up" his depression would have meant relinquishing a crucial part of his identity that was "defining of life itself." Depression allowed him to maintain contact with a "true self experience" that prevailed "just at the moment when [he] felt he lost contact with [his] parents." Bollas's observation that "a conservative object preserves the child's relation to the parents at the moment of a breakdown in the parent-child engagement" (1987, p. 113) may help explain Mr. M's intense resistance to relinquishing his illness.

The severe pathology of Mr. M's early life and attachment relationships resulted in what Seligman (1999, p. 151) calls a "pressured" transference that is robustly immune to reflection. Cognition, perception, and fantasy were indistinguishable for Mr. M. What he imagined, he knew to be truth. His attributions about me were unquestionable facts that excluded all alternative explanations. Seligman describes this transference-countertransference situation as one in which the analyst feels "repeatedly pressured to agree with impossible positions that compromise [her] feeling of personal integrity (i.e., within which we cannot be true to our analytic self) with the result that [she is] often pushed to experience [herself] along the particular forms of relational rules that characterize the patient's internal object world" (p. 151).

Stability and self-preservation were purchased with the illusion of control and mastery that would be destabilized and undermined in the give and take of genuine relationship. Mr. M therefore preferred the isolation afforded by working in his room on solitary projects. Whenever he needed others to pursue his work, those relationships usually ended in irreparable rupture, most often precipitated by Mr. M. He was invariably baffled when people left him, unable to "mentalize" their intentions and feelings, or his impact on them. He could only experience their actions as punitive. Early relational traumas and continuing, cumulative traumas undermined his reflective capacities and sense of self (Fonagy et al., 2002; Liotti, 1999, 2004).

Why did Mr. M leave analysis? His history of relational trauma most likely resulted in a disorganized attachment system (Fonagy, 2000; Fonagy et al., 2002; Liotti, 1999, 2004). He was trapped in a "drama triangle" (Karpman, 1968) in which he and others shifted rapidly and incoherently between roles of victim, persecutor and rescuer. To protect himself from further trauma, he adopted a strategy of domination and submission. When he felt threatened by emerging, caring attachment, he became the punitive dominator, exercising control through humiliation. When he felt vulnerable and hurt, he became the pleading victim. When he was with others whom he felt to be at least as depressed as himself, he enacted the role of rescuer. As the frozen structures of his pathological attachment system began to thaw in analysis, the pain was unbearable. The safer he felt with me, the more terrified and ashamed he became, both that I would leave him and of his need for a relationship with me. He could only bear attachment to punitive, degraded objects. Thus, in the second year of analysis, he resumed the role of persecutor with a vengeance.

While Mr. M played out the persecutor role in which he felt powerful, possibly "evil," he felt himself to be a victim as well because of his helplessness and vulnerability (Liotti, 1999). He treated me increasingly the way family members treated him. I believe he was aware of this on some dissociated level. He thus created a situation where, from his perspective, both of us were in danger of being destroyed. Believing he was doomed by fate, it was only a matter of time. Perhaps he left for both our sakes.

I remain uncertain as to how things might have turned out had he stayed. Perhaps there was no psychoanalytic therapy that could satisfactorily address his conflicting needs. If his traumas were resolved, would he continue to exist? Certainly not as he was, as he had always known himself to be. Was the risk of dissolution in one form worth the risk of reconstitution in another? In leaving, Mr. M made his decision. Had I been able to resolve my own fear of his committing suicide and addressed the dissociated, unspoken enactments and feelings between us more thoroughly, could I have helped him more? Or, might I have precipitated the very thing I so feared? This question must remain unanswered, yet it is one that many analysts must deal with from time to time, in various ways.

Patients like Mr. M push us to our emotional limits, threatening our analytic identity. In the pressure chamber of sustained suicide threat, analysts can gain invaluable experience about themselves and these most difficult patients if they are willing to confront their feelings of anxiety, helplessness, and shame, finding the courage to address these feelings in the analytic relationship. If this is possible, the analyst *may* be able to liberate herself from the paralyzing fear that one misstep will nudge her patient toward suicide.

I remain uncertain about just why Mr. M broke off our work. Perhaps his leaving was a protective gesture toward us both. If so, I am deeply touched. I am thankful to him for having taught me much, however painfully, that has no doubt helped me become a better analyst. I am also moved, because I think he glimpsed a possibility that, ultimately, he could not allow himself to pursue. Maybe that is what he wanted to convey to me in the image of the "Christ of the Abyss."

## Note

\* My thanks to Stuart Pizer, whose sensitive reading of this chapter helped me formulate my thinking about the case with greater clarity, and to the members of the Clinical Dialogues seminar of the Institute for the Advancement of Self Psychology for their supportive, insightful comments.

1 Using the term "hate," Winnicott may be somewhat misleading in his description of the complex, contradictory feelings a mother has toward her baby, and an analyst toward her patient, that may at times include feelings of hatred. "Hate" does not accurately describe the complex feelings I had toward Mr. M.

## References

Bollas, C. (1987). *The Shadow of the Object: Psychoanalysis of the Unthought Known.* New York: Columbia University Press.

Bromberg, P.M. (1995). Resistance, object-usage, and human relatedness. *Contemporary Psychoanalysis*, 31: 173–191.

Fonagy, P. (2000). Attachment and borderline personality disorder. *JAPA*, 48: 1129–1146.

Fonagy, P., Gergely, G., Jurist, E.L. & Target, M. (2002). *Affect Regulation, Mentalization, and the Development of the Self.* New York: Other Press.

Gabbard, G.O. (2000). Hatred and its rewards: A discussion. *Psychoanalytic Inquiry*, 20: 409–420.

Gorky, M. (1962). *The Autobiography of Maxim Gorky.* New York: Collier Books.

Karpman, S. (1968). Fairy tales and script drama analysis. *Transactional Analysis Bulletin*, 7(26): 39–43.

Khan, M. (1963). The concept of cumulative trauma. *Psychoanalytic Study of the Child*, 18: 286–306.

Laing, R.D. (1965). *The Divided Self: An Existential Study in Sanity and Madness.* Harmondsworth: Pelican.

Laing, R.D. (1968). *The Politics of Experience & The Bird of Paradise.* Harmondsworth: Penguin.

Laing, R.D. (1969a). *The Politics of the Family and Other Essays.* New York: Pantheon Books.

Laing, R.D. (1969b). *The Politics of the Family. Massey Lectures.* Toronto: The Hunter Rose Company.

Loewald, H.W. (2000). *The Essential Loewald: Collected Papers.* Hagerstown: University Publishing Group.

Liotti, G. (1999). Understanding the dissociative processes: the contribution of attachment theory. *Psychoanalytic Inquiry*, 19: 757–783.

Liotti, G. (2004). Trauma, dissociation, and disorganized Attachment: three strands of a single braid. *Psychotherapy: Theory, Research, Practice, Training*, 4: 427–486.

Pizer, S.A. (1998). *Building Bridges: The Negotiation of Paradox in Psychoanalysis.* Hillsdale: Analytic Press.

Seligman, S. (1999). Integrating Kleinian theory and intersubjective infant research: observing projective identification. *Psychoanalytic Dialogues*, 9: 129–159.

Winnicott, D.W. (1975). *Through Pediatrics to Psychoanalysis*. London: Hogarth Press/ Institute of Psychoanalysis.

Winnicott, D.W. (1990). *The Maturational Processes and the Facilitating Environment*. London: Karnac Books.

# Part V

# PROFESSIONAL FAILURE IN THE CONSULTING ROOM AND ON THE CAREER PATH

# 12

# WHATEVER HAPPENED?

## A clinical evaluation of the relationship between Humpty Dumpty and the wall

*Frances M. Clark*

By placing the nursery rhyme "Humpty Dumpty" in historical context, this chapter draws attention to an actual event and its consequences. Over time, the event itself has become forgotten. It remains traceable if one is interested enough to look behind what has become a familiar chant in nurseries and playgrounds in many English-speaking countries.

I will use that historical event to explore the psychoanalytic concept of enactment. Using the relationship between Humpty Dumpty and his wall as a metaphor for the interdependence of two minds in therapeutic relationship (analyst and patient), I illustrate through clinical material how the unconscious of each has consequences for the other and, thus, for the success, or failure, of treatment.

I will present clinical material in which therapist failure to hold the frame is seen as repeating within the dyad (thus revealing) central, preverbal experiences belonging to the patient. I explore how the therapist understood her actions which, by their failure to hold firm the skin of the analytic frame in terms of time and place, produced a repetition of the patient's unsafe, potentially catastrophic, early experiences. The gap between the intention to provide a safe container for the patient and the failure to do so will be looked at with reference to the work of Ester Bick (1967) on "second skin," Bion (1962) on container/contained, and Winnicott (1985) on empathic holding.

As a therapist, I recognize how much we clinicians need to have freedom, first within ourselves, then with each other, to explore experiences of failure in our work. We need to be able to think and play thoughtfully together so we can survive and learn from these experiences. Often we fail to do this because of shame or fear of being attacked and losing respect in others' eyes when we expose limitations and mistakes.

In "Enactments in the countertransference," Gerrard (2007) makes an important point about processing enactments in psychoanalysis: "As long as I can free myself from the punitive superego that says 'You shouldn't have done/said that' then I can find the curiosity and wish to understand so that I can ask myself the question, 'I wonder why you did/said that?'" To be able to turn the question from "why" as a superego response to "why" as an enquiry requires freedom to play with one's "mistakes" and offers possibilities for growth.

Most English-speaking people are familiar with: "Humpty Dumpty sat on a wall / Humpty Dumpty had a great fall / All the King's horses and all the King's men / Couldn't put Humpty together again." What people are not so familiar with is the story behind it. "Humpty Dumpty" was, in fact, the name given to an unusually large cannon, which in the time of the English Civil War (1642–1651) was mounted on the protective wall of a church in Colchester, England, that was controlled by Royalist forces. A shot from a Parliamentarian (opposing side) cannon damaged the wall, causing the cannon to fall. The Royalists (all the King's men) attempted to raise Humpty Dumpty onto another part of the wall. Even with the help of their horses, they were unable to do so. Thus, Colchester fell into the hands of the Parliamentarians.

Humpty Dumpty came to mind when thinking about failure in relation to my clinical work. There is an interrelationship between wall and cannon. In the nursery rhyme, one was not effective without the support of the other. The wall had to be able to bear the weight imposed on it. Like the mother-infant dyad, patient and analyst function in an interrelated way. The analyst's job is to bear the emotional weight of the patient without collapsing. Analysts constantly address and rebuild failures of understanding, empathy, and insight.

This chapter is not about a treatment that was itself a failure, but about an aspect of treatment that was conducted in the initial years in an atmosphere of impending doom. Both participants feared treatment would fail. The patient stated it and I, as analyst, often felt that the battle to help him find an internal space in which things could be thought about and related to his history, where he could come to recognize and own feelings as his, might be lost due to the weight of his needs that threatened to blow apart the very wall from which he sought support.

Paul, a middle-aged lawyer, had tried different therapies over the years. He arrived in my consulting room in a state of distressing need, preoccupied with the question of why things had gone so badly in his treatments. What was it about him? Or was it everybody else who created mayhem in his life and relationships? This mayhem left him feeling both failed and a failure, in spite of professional successes.

From the start, I was struck by Paul's need to constantly intuit my state of mind. As he described interactions, I became aware of how skilled and perceptive he was at registering weak points and frailties. I knew I was being watched, judged, and assessed in the same way. Not surprisingly, given what I was later to learn of his upbringing, he needed to feel in control through constantly monitoring others' moods, intentions, and actions.

The world was perceived as a potentially attacking space, containing as it did the massively projected chaos of his internal world where nothing felt safe. From Paul's perspective, to survive he had to be aware and ready to strike first. In the initial years of treatment, I nearly always felt alert to incipient attack, never really sure if what I saw in front of me was the mouth of a cannon or the mouth of a hungry, needy infant seeking connection, or a mixture of both.

It was difficult to feel secure with any connection made with Paul because of the wall he had built to protect himself from exposing his loving feelings, as he was so afraid of being exploited and abused, then blowing things apart out of rage and despair. His internal world was structured around expectations of being failed, attacked and blamed. In dealings with others, these possibilities were noted, while other experiences that did not fit this framework were given little or no attention. In vulnerable states, Paul's paranoid perceptions gained ground. To survive perceived attacks, he often failed to take in insights or to see others' actions in a light that he could address and so prevent the abandonment and attack he dreaded.

I eventually understood why so much of what I said to Paul was often played back to me with almost the same words, but with a meaning so different from the original. His internal objects stripped the music from my words, distorted and confused them, robbing them of previously felt experience when with me of something potentially warm and understood between us.

One evening, after Paul (my last patient of that day) left, my phone rang. At the other end was Paul saying, "I am in the railway station. I am too early for the train I usually get because you have sent me away from our session early." Astounded, I looked at my watch. I had, indeed, sent him away early. I said, "You are quite correct, I do apologize. We can speak about this tomorrow." Putting the phone down, I struggled to make sense of what had happened. Paul's session on that day always ended at a time that was out of the usual pattern of my appointments, but that did not seem enough to explain my behavior. I reviewed what had been spoken about in the session, one in which I was beginning to hear something of the family background, particularly regarding his parents' relationship. I had no sense of having had any strong, stressful feelings that might have prompted ending early. Only much later did I understand that my absence of feeling had been what was important.

On working with my failure to hold the time boundary by tolerating Paul's anger at my sending him away early, I became aware of his need to see if I could acknowledge that I had made this mistake. I came to realize this was of prime importance to him. Would I admit I had made a mistake, tolerate and survive his anger about it? Only later did I learn that, prior to my ending that session, Paul had been aware that if he continued with what he had been saying, he might stumble into revealing to me an incident that had taken place within the family business. His father, panicked by what what his partners were wanting from him, attempted suicide, a scene witnessed by Paul.

Two years later, another experience of failure to hold the time boundary on my part occurred – this time a more extreme failure with more extreme consequences. Paul had asked for a slightly later time to allow him to attend a wedding. I agreed. In the week in question, a former acquaintance's partner died. I wanted to attend the funeral. I would be able to if I left at my usual stopping time, at the end of Paul's *usual* time. Surprised when Paul did not turn up for his session, I left for the funeral. Returning home, I played my voice messages. Among them was Paul's tightly controlled message asking where I was. He had turned up at the time arranged and my house had been closed. I had failed to note what was written in my diary. My horror at what I had done was matched by my bewilderment about how I could have let this happen. Fortunately, there was also a spark of curiosity about why it happened. Overall, though, I feared what damage I had done and how deadly this might be to the therapy.

The effect on Paul was devastating. Initially, he plunged into a state of shock and numbness. He operated on automatic pilot for the first hours, his frozen state somewhat broken by my contacting him to register my awareness of what had happened. He was curt, but polite, on the phone. We agreed to speak about it the following week. He spent much of the weekend in a state of rage, venting anger on those with whom he was in contact.

In the weeks that followed, Paul's feelings of distress, rage, despair, and abandonment caused by my action almost brought about a total collapse of the wall, the cannon, and the city they were intended to protect. I had to fight valiantly to keep alive a thinking space in which his anger and despair could be allowed expression, heard and felt by me in their full force, without destroying me or our alliance.

In the weeks of struggle following this event, I learned something I had to hold onto, as I knew that confronting Paul would be perceived as an attack. He had been aware of my not having mentioned the time change in the sessions preceding it – something he recognized as unusual – but chose not to mention.

These two events within the transference relationship are connected to failure to want to remember, seeing yet not seeing. They are located in the psychic structure and experiences of both participants, in both the wall and the cannon.

For Paul, these failures of mine served specific purposes relating to his previous analytic relationships. At the same time, they revealed, repeated, and began the process of working through the unbearable, almost catastrophic aspects of infant Paul's relationship with his mother. For myself, they linked me to a period in my life in which I had been faced with the possibility of physical death and a need to let go of an external structure that I had seen as fundamental to my way of being.

In his first important analytic relationship, Paul had found a helpful analyst whose job was made almost impossible once Paul's experience of rejection and abandonment was activated by the analyst's hospitalization. This prepared-for break coincided with a time of great anxiety in Paul's life. For several days after their last session, Paul found himself almost unable to form words to express his thoughts. He experienced himself as alone, speechless, helplessly at the mercy of his terror of having been dropped and left. Compounding this state was overarching fear that he had caused his analyst's illness.

The analyst's return did little to alleviate that experience. In Paul's mind, the analyst had damaged Paul's capacity to trust, confirming his internal world as littered with failed pieces of potential connections to a good breast mother. Paul's need to escape the analyst was immense. The therapeutic experience he had imbibed like mother, was now a failed accusing object inside. The analyst, in her seeming inability to bear the weight of his fears and love, confirmed him as too weighty in his needs to be lovable. The expanding family business gave Paul an excuse to leave that therapy, gripped by a conviction that he had no other option.

Paul's first need in choosing to take the risk of starting with myself was, I came to realize, for me to prove I could be reliable, meaning I could be experienced by him as thinking about him and about what I was doing to him. This had to be felt by him very concretely. I had to be seen to be fallible, to make mistakes and survive them without attacking or blaming him. This was not something expressed verbally. My unreliability was acted out within our relationship by my sending him away early. My lack of relationship to aspects of my own defense system maneuvered me to take in his projections in the only safe way possible for him, in the seen experience of both of us that it was my failure that had prompted his rage and attacks. It was me who was bad, not him.

The second piece of acting out on my part, the missed session, took that first experience between us to a much deeper level, exposing us to a repetition of the extreme abandonment he had experienced with the ill therapist. In the weeks following, there were many sessions in which I experienced myself as inarticulate. I was empty of the capacity to reach a state where articulation of anything remotely resembling a thought seemed possible. What saved the day was that this inarticulate experience was occasionally surmounted by my capacity, in desperation, to recall images that had been part of previous experiences between us. These images acted for both of us as transitional objects, creating a truce in the relentless anxiety that had been generated between us – a possibility of the mother me being able to confirm infant Paul's spontaneous gesture. It was the engagement of struggling to survive this battlefield that opened a new path toward understanding Paul's infantile experiences in which he had been at the mercy of a mother whose mind was not able to attune to her infant, whose fear of what was ahead in terms of external circumstances presented her infant with an absence of a mind on which he could depend. Paul's infant self often seemed left unheard, unheld, and flooded with residues of his mother's battles.

Two papers illuminate these powerful enactments. In "The experience of skin in early object relations," Bick (1967) discusses how the internal function of containing parts of the self depends on introjecting an external object, mother, experienced as able to sustain this function. Until the containing functions have been introjected, space within the self cannot arise. If mother is not able to do this in a good enough way, constructing an object in an internal space is impaired. In its absence, projective identification will continue unabated and confusions of identity will manifest.

In "The language of absence," Gurevich (2008) describes a continuum of environmental non-attunement and non-responsiveness in the stage of absolute dependence. Extreme external absence causes such shock and fear that the automatic survival response is dissociating parts of the self, an inner absence, and the infant experiences nameless dread that lives on within the psyche. For this to be repaired, the analyst has to be engaged in an encounter that allows and survives expression of that fear and the rage and protest it engenders.

This chapter is about a wall, a cannon, and the impact of each on the other. What Paul did not know was that I, too, had a wall. I failed to connect in those early years of his treatment with a period in my life when I had lived in a war zone and experienced the incredible anxiety and stress that life and death situations produce. I failed to see behind my defensive wall to remember my reaction on two occasions when the village I was in came under attack during the night. On the first occasion, I was asleep when the firing started. Though wakened by noise and seeing tracer fire from weapons, I fell back asleep. In reality, I blanked out from terror. On the second occasion, when a further incursion was feared, I could not be awakened to take my turn on watch, so was left to sleep on.

It was this response, absenting myself in the face of terror, that Paul unconsciously tapped into. For me, this was the extreme end of a spectrum of how I react in the face of physical or psychic danger or emotional hurt, a spectrum that ranges from "going out to play with friends" (the funeral) to blanking out in sleep. We both had to find a language and capacity to turn something potentially damaging (his aggressive attack) and my defensive turning away from it into something manageable, with potential for the future.

Paul's alertness to frailty in his analysts, and his inability to hold onto any good in internal objects, raised the possibility of engaging in the battle to turn his inner world from a graveyard into a place where battle could take place and he could feel strong enough to engage internally with keeping good experiences alive. For this to happen, I had to be awake and prepared to fight for him.

That we survived is due in no small part to the help of all the King's men, in that I was supported by colleagues – from the holding of supervision, to the putting me together again that informal meetings and chats with colleagues provided. It was this wall of insightful support that allowed me think about my experience of failing in this treatment and survive the necessary enactments that interacting with Humpty Dumpty Paul engendered.

# References

Bick, E. (1967). The experience of skin in early object relation. *International Journal of Psycho-Analysis*, 49: 484–486.

Bion, W.R. (1962). *Learning from Experience*. London: Karnac.

Gerrard, J. (2007). Enactments in the countertransference. *British Journal of Psychotherapy*, 23: 217–230.

Gurevich, H. (2008). The language of absence. *International Journal of Psycho-Analysis*, 89: 561–578.

Winnicott, D.W. (1985). The maturational process and the facilitating environment. In *Studies in the Theory of Emotional Development*. London: Hogarth Press.

# 13

# FAILURE TO CONTAIN UNBEARABLE AFFECT

## Rupture and e-repair

*Linda S. Bergman*

For ten minutes, Carol ranted about how abusive members of her therapy group had been, and how she "told the whole group the truth about themselves." It surprised me when she added that she had quit the group to which I had referred her. I did not know what I was actually feeling as I listened to her comments, except that I was apparently having a strong reaction.

As Carol continued on about that last group session, I broke into her tirade, and shouted, "Other people have had lives like yours and they got better! Get over it!" When she looked up, and asked why I was yelling, I denied it. She shouted back, "I'll never trust you again. I'm leaving and never coming back!" Storming out of my office, ten years of treatment exploded into the air. I sat in my chair, finally aware of my feelings: shattered and overwhelmed.

This interaction grew out of years of analytic work with Carol. She had a history of chronic, brutal physical and sexual abuse by several family members. Her parents were alcoholics. She earned some support and approval from mother by beating up kids in the neighborhood at mother's behest. As an adult, Carol had difficulty in most interpersonal situations, including marriage, church, and workplace. Not too much time elapsed before any group morphed into her family-of-origin. Depending on her self-state, Carol would then become paranoid, withdrawn and compliant, or confrontational and aggressive.

Carol rejected her family, primarily because parents and siblings had not validated her experience of abuse and sexual exploitation by an older brother. A caring, passive, slightly older man rescued her from her family when she was 18, paying for an apartment for her to live in prior to their marriage.

When we began, Carol was 30, married ten years, with a preschool child. Throughout treatment, she struggled with issues of shame around the sexual abuse, including sadomasochistic and self-destructive fantasies. Several years passed before she could articulate some of these feelings and begin talking about the experiences. Rage at men kept ambivalent feelings in control. It was easier if she only hated them.

Much of our work prior to the enactment related to Carol's preoccupation with self-destructive thoughts and fantasies, including suicidal ideation, and ongoing descriptions of her victimization and the malicious behavior people directed toward her. My countertransference experiences were complex and varied (primarily compassion mixed with annoyance, impatience, and fear). Although I was horrified by her family's behavior, I was also frustrated with her harangues and paranoid worldview. She attended online chatrooms in which there were detailed discussions of sexual abuse and victimization of various types. Eventually, some women in the chatroom would begin victimizing one another. Carol would perceive plots against her on the part of some participants or administrators, and would fear being attacked, either online or physically, even though it was highly unlikely that anyone knew where she lived. I witnessed the cycle of attraction, fascination, and terror as Carol became drawn further and further into these sado-masochistic relationships, feeling both annoyance and concern about her behavior.

We were both becoming aware of Carol's tendency to position herself so that those around her would inevitably exploit or attack her. I was reluctant to point out these behaviors or challenge her, lest I join the rank of the attackers. I was committed to containing her painful affects, using Bion's (1962) container-contained model. On a wishful thinking, almost fantasy level, I experienced myself as a completely understanding, benevolent mother, able to accept, absorb, and metabolize Carol's pain and negative affects – a perfect container. I was not going to retraumatize this fragile woman. This seemed to work for a few years. She was grateful for my acceptance and understanding, dubbing me Mom, "the good one," but I was also becoming aware of the squealing tires before her car would slam into my parking area.

Benjamin (2009) describes awareness of her failures in recognition and her internal struggle with self-regulation, shame, and guilt, while in the presence of patients monitoring signs of her internal state. Carol examined my face for signs of anger or disgust, but I kept my anger and frustration at bay. Neither of us broached the subject of her anger or "Carol of the squealing tires." Occasionally she asked if I was angry with her. I always answered no, afraid of how she would react.

Carol and I had made a tacit, unconscious agreement to keep difficult issues outside in the parking lot, or confined to her chatrooms. Mostly dissociated, I experienced my anxiety and rage only fleetingly, and would most often be affectively constricted and tense. Believing I had been doing a pretty good job managing affect and projections, we inexorably marched toward the culmination of our ongoing enactment.

Carol had been seeking admittance to a support/therapy group for women who had been sexually abused, but was unable to find an opening. We discussed attending a psychoanalytic group instead. She speculated and fantasized about what that might be like. Although fearful there might be men, she decided to try it. I referred her to a seasoned colleague, recently trained in group therapy. She believed Carol would fit her group.

After about a month, Carol began reporting that the therapist showed favoritism and the group was protective of the one male participant. Carol became increasingly critical and hostile toward each group member. As she became more agitated by the group, I found myself growing more angry and impatient. It had been my hope that group therapy might help us work on Carol's retraumatization experiences.

As Carol's demonization of group members increased, I, in addition to feeling bored and impatient, began to question whether I had made the correct decision by encouraging her to participate and referring her to someone other than the most experienced group therapist I could find. I was feeling incompetent and hopeless about Carol's treatment and the possibility of any change.

When Carol announced that she quit the group, I was not aware of precisely what I was feeling or doing. Soon I became very conscious of what I had said, and thought deeply, with remorse and concern. Shouting "Get over it!" I not only failed to contain her painful affects, but also expressed my uncontained rage, disgust, helplessness. I was neither the good mom nor the good therapist!

Over the last few decades, much has been written in the psychoanalytic literature on enactment, once considered acting out on the part of the analyst. Jacobs (1986) used the term "countertransference enactment," although he may not have been the first. There have been differing opinions on whether enactment, assuming the behavior is not unethical, could be a positive occurrence, or is categorically negative.

In the past, enactment was thought of as a one-person act. In 1989, Chused (in Chused et al., 1999) states, it was redefined as a two-person event in which each participant's behaviors were unconsciously motivated by different psychic conflicts that together led to an interaction which had specific, different meanings for each. With analyst and patient as recipients of the other's projection, enactment appeared to be interpersonal, but was more likely a symbolic interaction with different unconscious meanings and motivations for each.

Practitioners of traditional, one-person psychologies lean in the direction of caution, warning of possible negative outcome following enactment. Renik (in Chused et al., 1999) suggests that traditional analytic theory regards analytic technique as impersonal and believes countertransference enactment contributes to bad technique. Renik believes countertransference enactment is continuous and does not distinguish good technique from bad. Interpersonal and intersubjective perspectives view enactment as helpful and believe it can reveal chronic collusion in analytic work (Cassorla, 2001). Enactments may offer a road to unconscious aspects which might otherwise be left unexplored (McLaughlin & Johan, 1992). This viewpoint supports the notion of enactment as a true interpersonal event in which both analyst and patient are unconsciously enmeshed.

Ten years ago, unfamiliar with the enactment literature, I thought of what happened between Carol and me as projective identification. I was not entirely incorrect. In viewing the interaction from that perspective, however, I believed I was playing a role ascribed to me by Carol (Steiner, 2000). She may have "made me do it," but I believed I behaved badly nevertheless.

The morning after I shouted at her and she stormed out of my office, Carol phoned to tell me she was through with therapy. I expressed regret that I had caused her so much pain, acknowledging that I was working hard to understand what triggered my uncharacteristic behavior.

I reviewed the entire range of our transference-countertransference dynamics. Carol and her mother had bonded over her success at beating up neighborhood kids. How had Carol dealt with the unarticulated experiences of love and hate from and to her mother, and how had she been conflictually shaping me to fill those maternal shoes? I thought about the violent projections she had to endure from her mother and, consequently, the violent projective identifications from Carol that I had been unable to metabolize. What was being played out between us as I "sent" her to the kids in group therapy?

In spite of my devastating feelings of failure, of being a bad therapist, wearing my shame like a shroud, I reminded myself of Carol's habit of jokingly calling me "Mom, the good one." Recalling this idealized transference, the symbol we had chosen to represent nurturing and positive aspects of our connection, helped me sustain remnants of an analytic position. I told Carol I believed that, if we continued to work together, we could repair our relationship break. Apparently, I had so strongly desired to be the "good mother" that I was out of touch with much of Carol's experience. Refusing to continue, she threatened me with a lawsuit and physical harm.

Carol was so enraged she clearly could not tolerate face-to-face sessions. I suggested she consider emailing me her thoughts and feelings. She could write whatever she wanted. I would not respond.

Reading and writing were active interests we shared and valued, interests which linked us. In my reverie, the emails were an umbilicus, keeping us connected, providing a holding environment (Winnicott, 1960). My intention was to provide Carol with a safe venue with the space, albeit cyberspace, to express what she needed to express, allowing me the same safe space to metabolize what I apparently could not bear in real time. Parker (2007) discusses cyberspace as offering an opportunity to operate somewhere between solid, everyday perception and cognition and fantasy states that appear when ego censors are lifted. I felt a sense of unbearable loss at the thought of Carol leaving treatment because of my untoward words and affect, a sense of "miscarriage." Having Carol communicate via email kept the dreamlike connection between us alive, and allowed me to continue to "hold" her.

During the next few days, I was terrified. I did all I could to not call a malpractice attorney just in case. My clinical self knew the terror was not mine alone. Somehow, Carol and I both managed it, and her writing began.

Carol's first letter, sent by snail mail, stated:

> You won't let me be afraid and you won't let me be angry. Why is that? Why can't I let my crazyness [sic] out? I'm sick and I'm tired and I'm afraid and enraged and horrifying things are going through my head and

I can't tell anyone. Why won't you let me be sick? You always refuse to allow me to be sick … Has 10 years blinded YOU? Do you want me to "succeed" so much that you won't let me show you the horror that I have? I think you helped me bury it. We played some game, a dance, a Freudian [sic] jig that we both enjoyed because it was easier.

Why is it not okay? Don't say it is, because it hasn't been okay. Every time I say something that begins to broach that area, you say something condescending. When do I get to feel it? Why does my anger have to be clapped up? Why can't I yell about stuff? What is the matter with you that you can't hear it? Are you there? Can you be there? If it's too fucking much, let me know, because I can't risk beginning this without knowing that you can take it, Make dam [sic] sure you can hear this. Make dam fucking sure you're strong enough. Regular people trigger too, you know. And believe me. This is some sick fucking shit, not only about what happened to me, but what is going through my head.

Are you ready? Really, really ready? For me? For what is? Details, the whole nine yards? Be sure, don't just leap because I'm going to off myself. That won't do. It won't work.

I'm so scared of it that I don't think I could do it in person. I'd have to do it in email. I guess that makes it easier for you, but sooner or later, we'd have to meet.

Initially I was shocked. After reading Carol's letter again, it was clear she experienced me as not only failing to tolerate her rage, but also failing to hear her "crazyness [sic]" and the horror of her experiences. Was I dissociating from difficult material? Carol had been reluctant to verbalize experiences of abuse as well as the contents of her inner life. If that was resistance, it belonged to both of us. Carol and I sought ancillary support, going outside the relationship, perhaps in an attempt to strengthen or avoid a containing function in which neither of us had much faith. I felt relief when she began group therapy, then felt hopeless again when she abruptly left. Reading and rereading her words, I acknowledged to myself that I had avoided parts of Carol's inner life and experience that were less easily contained. I rejected and abandoned those parts for a seemingly healthier, but *ersatz* Carol.

In the next segment, Carol mocked and berated me as foolish and naïve, underestimating the murderous rage within her, or perhaps within us:

Linda, there is nothing you can do for me, and I want you to stop pretending that there is, or hoping that there is. This carrot that you dangle in front of me is a mirage, or at best, just a carrot, even if you hope that it isn't. If I can't "fix" me, what makes you think you can? And you've been in practice a long time. It seems we're beating a dead horse.

My anger now is too huge to see you, and I don't want to bury it the way I have in the past to not scare or hurt you (with words). Whether the anger be at you or others, I think I would bury it if I saw you. You really have no idea, hell; I had no idea what it was. And I don't want to hear you lie to me, saying things designed for just that … soothings, affirming … stupid things that I can see right through and would just make me madder. It would be too much of a lie to go there from where we were and I think that is what you had in mind for the future.

I don't trust you now … not just because of the yelling, but because of everything (I'm not blaming you … I'm just saying it hasn't worked for me and that really, you can't help me, much as you may want to), and I think you would say anything now to keep me from hurting myself and that would be another lie. Don't say you wouldn't lie … you're scared now too and you couldn't help it.

I know you don't want it to end this way. But I have to stand on my own feet. Every move I make I want to call you about … everything that's happened in the last few days that came about because of my unbelievable confusion, I want to tell you … and I can't. Because then I'm still running to you, and I have to stop it, maybe it's all about not thinking for myself … always wondering what you would say in a given situation.

I don't know if I'm willing to hear whatever else you may have to say, because I'm concerned about being swayed by you. This is my ball now … let me do the bouncing. I'm struggling with not calling you. Don't violate my struggle. I have to do this alone. Whether you think so or not, you can't hear my pain/rage. So let me hear it, without intrusion.

Thanks anyway.

I had invited Carol to vent her thoughts and feelings. She did, aware I would not reply. Several days later, she wrote: "I would like to know that you received them (because I'm scared of sending it to someone else … just a 'got it' will be enough)." This resonated with my visceral sense of connection, with a primitive, symbiotic holding, containing, rhythmic quality induced by the ritual we had established. I was reminded of Ogden (1989) writing of primitive modes of sensory experience (autistic-contiguous position) that include the quality of rhythmicity in the "dialogue" between infant and mother.

The third letter began:

You're a fucking liar. I hate your fucking guts. You're letting me believe that there is hope and there is no fucking hope … it's a fucking lie. And you do it just because you want to believe it. 10 fucking years and nothing. Blame it on me I was a "child"? fuck you, you were the "parent" – you MADE me the child. Look at what the fuck happened the first time I let you have it. You can't take it … and you don't want it. We're gonna sit down and have nice little chats? No fucking way. To hell with you. Stringing me along without the slightest fucking idea whether you can help me or not. It's all just a game to you ... a wonderful Freudian dilemma ... meanwhile I'm writhing. Fuck you?

You don't know what the fuck you're messing with and you better not fuck with me. You ain't never seen anything like me and my fury. I nearly threw a chair after I got off the phone with you ... You wouldn't be safe with me in that room. You'll get hurt, you idiot. Why the hell can't you see that? Keep saying you're available? What the hell is the matter with you? You don't know what the hell you're offering ... what the hell it is.

Well sister, if you're sure you're ready for the beast, you better think again. You had a lily white life, and where I'm coming from is beneath the gutter. If you fucking do this, you dam [sic] well better not fucking run ... or send me away before I'm done. I swear to god. If you chicken out on me before I'm exorcised, I will sling your name through every bit of mud I can find, newspapers, magazines, anything. I'll scream to the world about your abandonment when the going got tough, you better make dam fucking sure ...

A week later, overwhelmed with suicidal and violent fantasies, Carol feared I would hospitalize her. She struggled to reject any life-affirming, loving connection with me. "2:40 AM fuck that shit u take this u fucking bitch why should I live just for u ... but not fair!!!! Shit fuck want out now fuck her I ain't seeing her no more bitch."

The writing continued for two weeks. Carol experienced cathartic relief after each letter. Her emails detailed the abuse she suffered as well as her fantasies and memories. Other than the "got its," I responded only once. When she asked if I would hospitalize her, I answered that I would not.

During treatment, I *had* tried to avoid Carol's rage as well as the awfulness of her experience. Based on what she wrote, her experience of treatment and me recapitulated past invalidation and abandonment. The treatment container, brittle, false and leaky, made enactment inevitable, and both of us felt helpless, without hope.

Carol's writing was explicit and painful. There came a point when I realized I was calm and contained. Carol sent an email one morning full of rage, abuse and self-loathing, but she sent me a postscript later letting me know she felt much better. The note signaled to me that she was experiencing being understood and held, and I felt she wanted to communicate that to me. Her writing became less fragmented and things began to shift. Although Carol had been using quite a bit of alcohol at the beginning of this episode, drinking became less frequent. Our treatment alliance did not seem so fragile. She freely expressed her ambivalence toward the treatment, and me, but with more thought and fewer fireworks. She wrote about joining a writing program, perhaps getting an MFA. Carol was using our writing link in the service of growth and differentiation. She soon suggested we resume meeting in person twice weekly. Regular treatment continued for four more years.

My dramatic outburst marked the beginning of the end of play-acting and stultifying collusion that had become embedded within the treatment. As a result of the enactment, Carol and I began a dialogue in which we attempted to be as honest as we could. Carol admitted that she had been desperate to hold on to a good mother at any price. I explored my wish to rescue her and my need to nullify her experience of madness. Together we unearthed the collusion that had been flourishing for several years.

With both of us taking responsibility for our contributions to the faltering treatment, over time we created something similar to the space of the third (Benjamin, 2004) in which we were able to connect differently, respect our differences, and share rather than vie for position. Ellman (in Chused et al., 1999) postulates that therapeutic enactment involves patient and analyst allowing the other to enter their world in an intense, relatively uncontrolled manner and survive. After a period of narcissistic disequilibrium for one, or both, survival creates an inhabitable, transitional space. This space seems similar to that described by Benjamin.

Carol ended treatment when she moved a distance away from my office, making regular sessions difficult. She had divorced her husband, purchased a small home, and worked in a real-estate office. Occasionally she had difficulties with co-workers, but no fireworks.

After living on her own for three years, Carol sold her house, purchased an RV, and set out for New Mexico. She settled in a camping community populated by couples and single men. She wrote a blog which had a nice following. She developed some good friendships in the community. There were misunderstandings, hurt, and a little paranoia. She would email me to vent, but basically handled her pain in solitude with self-reflection while hiking, fishing, and enjoying nature. She had a brief, caring relationship with a man.

Eventually, Carol began to feel land-locked. Relocating to Florida, she purchased a two-family home in which she plans to live with her son and his wife. She has been unemployed since leaving her job. Fearing working for someone else, I believe she is trying to figure out what sort of business she can own. She is resourceful and has the capability to be successful if she can feel safe enough.

Carol graciously granted permission for me to reproduce her writings.

# References

Benjamin, J. (2004). Beyond doer and done to: An intersubjective view of thirdness. *Psychoanalytic Quarterly*, 73: 5–46.

Benjamin, J. (2009). Psychoanalytic controversies: a relational psychoanalysis perspective on the necessity of acknowledging failure in order to restore the facilitating and containing features of the intersubjective relationship (the shared third). *International Journal of Psychoanalysis*, 90: 441–450.

Bion, W.R. (1962). *Learning from Experience*. New York: Basic Books.

Cassorla, R.M.S. (2001). Acute enactment as a "resource" in disclosing a collusion between the analytic dyad. *International Journal of Psychoanalysis*, 82: 1155–1170.

Chused, J., Ellman, S., Renik, O. & Rothstein, A. (1999). Four aspects of the enactment concept: definitions, therapeutic effects, dangers, history. *Journal of Clinical Psychoanalysis*, 8: 8–61.

Jacobs, T.J. (1986). On countertransference enactments. *Journal of the American Psychoanalytic Association*, 34: 289–307.

McLaughlin, J.T. & Johan, M. (1992). Enactments in psychoanalysis. *Journal of the American Psychoanalytic Association*, 40: 827–846.

Ogden, T.H. (1989). On the concept of an autistic-contiguous position. *International Journal of Psychoanalysis*, 70: 127–140.

Parker, I. (2007). Psychoanalytic cyberspace, beyond psychology. *Psychoanalytic Review*, 94: 63–82.

Steiner, J. (2000). Containment, enactment and communication. *International Journal of Psychoanalysis*, 81: 245–255.

Winnicott, D.W. (1960). The theory of the parent-infant relationship. *International Journal of Psychoanalysis*, 41: 585–595.

# 14

# REFLECTIONS ON THE FAILURE
# TO BECOME A TRAINING ANALYST

*John A. Sloane*

Fifteen years ago, in 1995, I failed to meet standards required of a training analyst in Toronto. That failure provided me with much food for thought – as I hope it will for others. I described the experience and what I had learned from it in an unpublished paper, "Psychoanalytic Identity, A View from Purgatory," which I presented to the Canadian Psychoanalytic Society in 2003 (Sloane, 2003). Over the years since then, I have gone on learning in several directions.

One of those areas concerns the *trauma of failure*, specifically the failure *to be* or *live up to* what's required in the eyes of another who matters deeply to us, whether that be parent, patient, colleague, or an institution – whoever or whatever embodies our "god-representations" (Rizzuto, 1979). This is a hugely important area of study that can be looked at from many angles, including what Paul Finnegan (2007) wrote about as "chronic recurrent maternal decathexis," elaborating on Furman and Furman's (1984) notion of "intermittent decathexis," a withdrawal of interest (Freud, 1915, 1926) on the part of essential others that leave children feeling worthless, annihilated, or non-existent.

Another direction of learning is about the process of healing, reparation, or "new beginnings" (Balint, 1968) made possible through analysis as well as through other forms of dialogue, including prayer and meditation (of which analytic listening could be considered a variant). A third area of learning concerns the basic assumptions, ideals, and authority of the psychoanalytic community and how they are preserved, or in danger of being destroyed, by different systems of training analyst selection. In a brief presentation, I can only touch on these interweaving and far-reaching themes in hopes of sparking further discussion.

My attempt to become a training analyst after about a dozen years of analytic practice was something I had put off longer than some do, partly as a result of prior failure *in my own eyes* – and in the eyes of some patients – by falling asleep in the countertransference. That is another area for discussion, about which I and others have written (Dean, 1957; Dender, 1993; Dickes & Papernik, 1977; Eshel, 1998, 2001; Grotstein, 1990; McLaughlin, 1975; Sloane, 1993, 2010). Very briefly, my falling asleep was experienced by some patients as a deeply disturbing "decathexis" (Freud, 1915, 1926) or failure, on my part and/or on theirs, that caused or reopened narcissistic wounds. *I* experienced it as a shameful – and sometimes harmful – inability to remain awake, consciously attentive, present, and knowledgeable, not only about the person for whom I cared, but also about what *I* was doing. Instead, I felt utterly ignorant of what was going on between us in the moment, annihilated by it, powerless to alter or address it, but nonetheless responsible for it. In an effort to understand and overcome that vulnerability, I went back into analysis, and wrote about the experience for discussion among colleagues. I came to see it as a powerful relational enactment, the multiple meanings of which have roots in both members of the analytic dyad. In brief, I consider it to be a *loss of self* in the temporary absence of the person to whom I am attending, or an *introjective identification* with a psychic deadness or buried aliveness that requires its own cocoon (Winnicott, 1963) that I can sense, but cannot grasp, close to the surface in my patient. As such, it activates a core identification with my father's deadness. It constitutes a repetition and opportunity for reparation for both parties that is *sometimes* realized, sometimes not. It requires careful, but occasionally explosive working through of essential desires, defenses, and self-object needs on *both* sides (Bacal & Thomson, 1996). It took me several years to reach a point of confidence that I had ways of working with it, whenever it occurred, that met the standards of a good-enough training analyst, *even in my own eyes*, let alone in those of external powers-that-be.

The training analyst selection process, as it existed in the Toronto Institute of Psychoanalysis at the time, required detailed presentation of process material to three different training analysts who reported to a Committee on Institute Membership to which I also submitted reports on all my analytic cases (which included several instances of falling asleep and its working-through). That committee reported to the local Training Committee, which reported to the National Training Committee, which reported to the International Psychoanalytic Association, the "highest power" in that psychoanalytic world. My work, including ways I worked with empathic failures inherent in falling asleep, met with the unanimous approval of those who observed my work first hand. But the Committee, whose questions about my competence were not answered sufficiently to recommend me to the next level in the hierarchy, overruled their consultants' recommendation that I be accepted. There was an intra-systemic conflict in the institution.

I was officially judged "defective in ego mastery, with a lack of access to, and capacity for fantasy elaboration of my aggression, unanalyzed defenses against knowing, and a lack of a consistent theoretical position." There is truth to all that which I have come to appreciate more over time. But it was not the whole truth – nor is it one that renders me, or others like me, categorically less capable than those who are more masterful, aggressive, or certain of their position. Each analyst has biases, faults, limitations, and excesses potentially harmful to some patients. Do we have nothing to learn from each new patient? Is our psychoanalytic identity or theoretical position so fixed that it cannot be touched and reshaped by close encounters with *each* Other? Do we not *all* have issues of which we are unconscious until they are, sometimes forcefully, brought to our attention? The key, for me, is not to be free of fault or always in the know, but to be ready to regress in the service of the process, and to recognize, acknowledge, and accept responsibility for what we do unconsciously. It is *that* which affects (emotionally enlivens) the process and triggers transference-laden reactions requiring recognition, validation and analytic understanding.

The Institute's characterization of me is painfully true in relational contexts that activate a dissociated and intractable self-state associated with the psychic disappearance and death of my father when I was a boy. In that state, I was, and still am, powerless to access someone whose disappearing emotional presence is essential to my aliveness, although it can usually be worked through productively with each person in whose presence (or emotional absence) I "lose myself." In the eyes of the Committee, those defects rendered me untrustworthy as a training analyst, just as some patients concluded I was untrustworthy as their analyst. For the Institute, I might embarrass it, putting it at risk at a time when it was already reeling from the very public failure of a founding father of the Toronto Institute to live up to ethical standards – through repeated, aggressively sexual violation of his patients. That was a traumatic experience for the whole analytic community, one that threatened its existence, one that we are still working through and, hopefully, will always remember and learn from.

That view of me as dangerously untrustworthy and unacceptable to an authority I looked up to and depended upon was made official by an almost unanimous vote of the Training Committee – which included many I considered personal friends as well as admired mentors and colleagues with whom I had previously enjoyed much mutual respect. Suddenly, I was an outcast, unworthy to be included among those who had, until then, valued my contributions to the life of the Society. Although I thought I was prepared for that possibility, it hit me with far more force than I had expected. It reactivated regressive affects from being ignored, judged, rejected, and punished by my father for failing to be what *he* needed me to be. I had not measured up, as a boy, to the manliness he demanded – increasingly irrationally – as he was dying of a brain tumor. On the other hand, when I finally voiced my all-out aggression at him for *his* failures and excesses of authority as *I* saw them, the light went out of his eyes. My authoritative aggression seemed to visibly hasten his death. That experience left me with lifelong guilt, and profound mistrust of my authority and aggression (infantile omniscience and destructive omnipotence). It also left me with deep sensitivity to others' vulnerability to intrusion and with respect, perhaps reverence, for that which I don't-yet-know (the Unconscious, broadly speaking). Like many of us, I have an abiding need to make symbolic reparations (rooted in benevolent omnipotence) by means of this impossible profession.

The result of being judged unacceptable by those who collectively re-presented my father was profound narcissistic injury that unleashed psychosomatic regression that included not only mortification and depressive affects, but also a malignancy that required radical prostatectomy.[1] As you might imagine, that tumult involved working through considerable castration anxiety, among other things. One of those things was being shunned by a senior member of the Committee, who, when he passed right by me on the street, ignored my greeting as though he had neither seen nor heard me. I felt stunned. Was I no longer even human in his eyes? Or, was *he* ashamed of himself in *my* eyes? Did he feel guilty about what he had done to me in the name of Analysis?[2]

Meanwhile, others (including my wife) were quite angry on my behalf – some even more than I was. I could understand where the Institute was coming from. It was the same place I had been earlier, doubting myself. It was the same painful, endangered place that some of my patients found themselves in, face-to-face with an 'impaired', then psychically dead mother or father whom they experienced as betraying their trust, abandoning them, or being bored to death *by* them, not recognizing or "cathecting" (Finnegan, 2007; Freud, 1915, 1926; Furman & Furman, 1984) them as existing, mattering, one way or another.

Where *I* felt most pain, anger, and betrayal was with those I had considered friends or theoretical allies, including self-psychologists who *ought* to understand, I felt, the inevitability and necessity of working through empathic failures. With two of those friends, I made a point of meeting to voice my anger and disillusionment about *their* failures, making room for mutual understanding and progressive repair of *those* relationships. There was still an enormous amount to be worked through in relation to Something far greater than any particular person, some nonthing that shaped my view of what I considered to be "my father's world." For that purpose, I needed to express my day-to-day dreams, self-experience, and countertransference feelings in a self-analytic journal. That practice set the stage for uncanny, synchronistic (Jung, 1952) experiences of responsiveness from many directions including poetry, the Bible, and our evolving professional literature, all of which spoke to me of an underlying Omnipresence. I wrote about that sense of a transpersonal, collective unconscious in "The Loneliness of the Analyst and its Alleviation through Faith in 'O'" (Sloane, 2012).

My thoughts turned to what might be wrong with the system – to system failure in which trauma can easily be re-enacted, but remains unattended and uncontained in ways that do more harm than good, not only to individuals but to the psychoanalytic community itself. The basic assumption of mainstream training programs has been that, in order to ensure preservation of what is essential to analysis, the process must be "controlled" by those who "know" – a vestige, I believe, of infantile omniscience and omnipotence. Those who analyze and supervise candidates in IPA institutes must be specially chosen for that purpose by powers that be, resulting in a centralized hierarchy, fraught with power struggles and political splits among those who view the "pure gold of psychoanalysis" from different angles. "Ordinary" analysts get devalued, or caught in the crossfire, or self-select to stay out of the fray – leaving training to those who are characterologically inclined to climb the ladder of power and authority to define what is and is not analysis, and to regulate the borders of a field they believe *belongs* to them. Another way of looking at those who rise to positions of power and responsibility within Institutes is that they highly value our discipline, care a great deal about its future, and are willing to make it a priority, even when there is a choice to be made between the wellbeing of the institution and that of some individuals.

A climate is thereby created where it is not safe to be open about how we work. The fear of being judged and exiled from our professional home can cut us *all* off from the kind of down-to-earth collegial discussion that provides relevant, constructively critical feedback. Such silencing happens not only with those quiet souls who don't dare "come out" into the open, but also with others who openly disdain and loudly depart from the Society, from the psychoanalytic community, or even from their own psychoanalytic identity (Leonoff, 2002). We, and the next generation of analysts, lose (access to) many excellent clinicians that way, as well as losing the opportunity for open discussion of innovative clinical experience that is pre-judged to be idiosyncratic or heretical – much too risky to expose until one is firmly established through compliance or identification with *existing* authority. Even then, training analysts acquire special status that must be defended by secrecy that can, unfortunately, breed emotional, relational malignancy.

Shortly after I had been judged unacceptable as a result of my politically imprudent openness about countertransference experiences I (and others) thought were worth talking about, I attended an "Annual Day in Psychoanalysis" put on by the TPS. At that meeting, those who had rejected me praised the visiting speakers for their courage and openness about otherwise shameful countertransference lapses similar to what I had acknowledged. At that point, I had the peculiar experience of simultaneous feelings of vindication (I was not the only analyst who sometimes falls asleep) and vindictiveness toward what I saw as hypocrisy. My rage erupted internally, then crystallized into the kind of cold contempt that leads many in our community to turn up their noses at one another, causing deep splits. I realized I had been victim of my own naïve trust in the Institute, partly out of my arrested developmental need for acceptance as I was, warts and all, and partly as a result of my experience with two unusual training analysts. One was my own analyst, the other a supervisor, both of whom were humble enough to be open about what they learned from their failures. It's one thing, though, to do that from a position of recognized power and authority – quite another as an ordinary analyst aspiring to become a training analyst.

Although I was encouraged by some to try again, for me the cat was already out of the bag and could not be put back in. I could not be other than what I am: vulnerable to the emotional absence of, or exclusion by, a significant Other. Until the theoretical or political climate changed, it would have been masochistic to "go there" again. Fortunately, I have found more congenial "homes" and opportunities to teach and analyze candidates in the self-psychology institute (IASP) and the contemporary institute (TICP).

Recently, I made a point of presenting an updated paper on sleep in the countertransference for discussion at the Toronto Psychoanalytic Society (Sloane, 2013). I had reached a point where there was no longer trauma in adversarial selfobject functioning in an open forum in which no final, official judgment is passed, nor punitive sanctions imposed. I was met, there, by animated discussion and respectful, even illuminating critique of my views. Incidentally, I was seen by the discussant to have failed to recognize or interpret what he was convinced were unconscious sadomasochistic forces at work in the transference and countertransference (a view for which there was some evidence). I was also approached by someone after the meeting who voiced *secretive* words of agreement with my relational perspective that more benign forces were at work, despite their apparent destructiveness.

On the basis of all that, I think what needs to happen is the elimination of centralized decision-making about who is and is not acceptable for analyzing and supervising candidates. Such centralized judgmental power is contrary to the spirit of analysis – which is one of *openness to that which is not-yet-known*. We need institutions whose ambience is consistent with the process they seek to facilitate – one of mutual respect, empathic enquiry, emotional honesty, and open reflection on the meaning of things (and non-things) from different points of view.

In my view, and in that of many contemporary training programs, the selection of personal analysts for trainees is better left to *natural selection* or *mutual selection* on the basis of reputation and responsible exploration of a wider range of possibilities than is available when candidates are restricted to an arbitrarily engineered gene-pool. Such an open system is more likely to result in "good fits" between analysts and analysands.

That process could be facilitated by a voluntary rite of passage in which analysts with five years of experience could present their work to two consultants, as I did, and perhaps as a paper to the Society – not for official judgment, but for open discussion from which all could learn. Quality assurance, I am convinced, is best served in the long run by open discussion of complex issues at all levels. It is not something that can be controlled without running the risk of serious side effects of unrecognized trauma, maladaptive defenses against it, creative inhibition, and perverse abuses of authority.

As Freud (1921) wrote, "The problem consists in how to procure for the group precisely those features which are characteristic of the individual and which are extinguished in him by the formation of the group" (pp. 86–87). What that would require, I think, is for those in positions of power to voluntarily surrender (Ghent, 1990) some of it by taking a leap of faith in the analytic process as it manifests in the evolving analytic community. While I realize that such a leap would require letting go of something solidly established and time-honored, my hope is that open discussion of these issues will make that change possible.

Narcissistic injuries and political power struggles occur in any academic training program and human institution, no matter what its structure. Tough decisions must sometimes be made that require a measure of ruthlessness, as one very gentle analyst once said – tempered with careful, conscious, responsible consideration of the destructive consequences for all concerned. Every remedy has side effects. Each person has faults. "Everyone is much more simply human than otherwise" (Sullivan, 1953). When one group is chosen by a "higher power" as having *permanent special status* – even though that may be a necessary developmental phase in a new discipline's evolution – that sets the stage for troublesome, disavowed feelings of inferiority and superiority inside and outside the group, where the "narcissism of minor differences" (Freud, 1930) plays a powerful, dysfunctional role. Such judgmental discrimination amplifies forces that play havoc with what might otherwise be more respectful, cooperative, and *constructively* critical or competitive relationships. The lack of containment of those forces that lead to narcissistic injury, alienation, and behind-the-scenes splitting within and between individuals and groups could be considerably reduced.

Failure is part of being human. So, too, is learning through experience that leads to mutual understanding, and to reconsideration of basic assumptions. Forgiveness is said to be divine – which it may be. But the capacity for forgiveness is also biologically *inborn*. Children are naturally trusting and forgiving – to their own detriment, at times. Forgiveness is implicit in understanding – including that which analysts come to with the help of patients and colleagues. It also tends to occur spontaneously, if unconsciously and unspoken, when we, as analysts, acknowledge our empathic failures to our patients. Forgiveness, then, works *both* ways in the healing of what Balint called "the basic fault" – wherever we locate it (Balint, 1968).

## Afterthoughts

It seems relevant to include, here, my experience of presenting this paper to the Fifth Joint International Conference in 2010. Just as traumatic enactments occur as part of the group-processing of the unconscious forces that bring us into this field in the first place – and get powerfully reawakened by our clinical work – so, too, there are reparative possibilities within the group that are worth making conscious.

Although I had reached a place of confidence that I had something of value to offer a wider audience, in the days preceding the conference I experienced a welling up of old feelings of failure and inferiority as I approached those I know to be more knowledgeable and accomplished. That feeling was alleviated, to some extent, by the memory of having been well received when I presented to the same group two years previously. As it happened, there were two people present at this meeting who had played a part in the failures of which I would speak. Although I knew in advance that one would be on the panel, I did not know what, if anything, either might have to say about *their* views of what I would describe.

The fellow panelist, before making his presentation, found it necessary to voice the feelings stirred up in him by hearing mine. He disclosed the fact that he had been "one of those patients on whom John fell asleep." He made it known that he had experienced my doing so as a traumatic breach of trust that caused an irreparable rupture of the therapeutic relationship. From his point of view, the Institute was right in their decision.[3] The other person, who had played a part in the events fifteen years ago, was a colleague whose work I cited on the effects of "maternal decathexis." In the course of the discussion, he disclosed the fact that he had been one of the non-training analysts on the Committee on Institute Membership![4]

He commented that, instead of citing him, I might just as easily – and angrily – have pointed him out to the group as "one of the S.O.B.s who did that to me." He went on to outline some of his personal dynamics, as well as his thoughts on the politics of the group process, both of which played a part in the judgment against me, thereby validating not only my perceptions and recollection of the events but feelings associated with them.

Those unexpected disclosures galvanized the group in a way that constituted a dramatic enactment! It brought the issues to life and made them real in a way that generated much valuable, visceral discussion, and ongoing reflection for all concerned. "For when all is said and done," Freud (1912) wrote, "it is impossible to destroy anyone in absentia or in effigie." Similarly, it is impossible to repair what has been destroyed in the absence of those who represent the Other (others) involved.

Here was a person I injured, as well as one who injured me. One judged me unacceptable as his personal analyst, the other decided, with the group, that I was unfit to become a member of a select group of analysts considered superior. Here, too, was a group of knowledgeable, accomplished, and critically discerning analysts who not only found me acceptable, but who appreciated and freely associated in very animated, thoughtful ways to what I had to say. It is worth noting, too, that the third presenter on our panel described an enactment in which she had impulsively and angrily judged a difficult patient in a way that caused a traumatic rupture of their relationship. That "failed" treatment was also repaired, over time, by extended email correspondence prior to resuming a productive analysis. In addition to those participants, there was a non-analyst in the audience, a journalist with a lifetime of experience and reflection on the best and worst of human nature, who voiced his response to *all* the presentations this way: "Although I had not expected to be able to relate to psychoanalytic papers, I found myself experiencing several stabs of self-recognition." None of us was alone, in other words, in our appreciation of the co-created opportunity to speak openly and reflectively of our *personal* experiences of failure, and the complex dynamic circumstances of their occurrence and recovery.

As I mentioned to some of the conference organizers afterwards, we don't really know some things until they are gone. In my case, it was a profound, pervasive, and timeless sense of shameful insufficiency. Suddenly, that "absence" of something essential to my self was no longer there under the surface, nor was it in the wings, nor in the air. I felt joyfully free, but grounded and present in a way I had never imagined possible. This was not just a bipolar mood swing – even if I did feel like pinching myself to see if this "new me" was real! In other words, not only was the discussion professionally valuable for me and others, but it was also surprisingly healing – even though I know it will require ongoing working through.

I am not suggesting that the Institute made "the wrong decision" any more than it is wrong for a patient to decide that a particular analyst is not right for him or her. Decisions that are right or necessary, from one point of view, may be wrong from another, depending on one's point of view. What I *am* saying is that when such decisions are made, officially and authoritatively, on behalf of the analytic community, especially when that community is valued and essential as a professional home, there can be deeply destructive effects, not only on individual analysts but also on the group. The psychoanalytic group exists, after all, for the wellbeing of individual human beings. Somehow, the group needs to recognize, learn from, and accept responsibility for its own destructiveness, on the way to transforming itself.

One member of the audience asked me what had helped me contain the damage and recover as much as I had. My answer surprised even me. "I went home," I said, "to my wife and children." They welcomed me into *their* world (*our* world), thereby taking me out of (or into a different part of) myself. I also mentioned my self-analytic journaling in which I find words for the otherwise inchoate undercurrents and up-wellings of affect, dreams, etc. (Stern, 1997), as well as the synchronistic (Jung, 1952) responsiveness that I experience with patients and others (Sloane, 2012). It was also very helpful to be able to find a new professional home in other institutes, as well as meaningful companionship in the Christian (Anglican) Church. It is, after all, a community that revolves around one man's survival (so the story goes) – not only of the same kind of hatred or all-out aggression (Winnicott, 1969) that I had directed at my father, but also his excruciating betrayal, abandonment, judgment, and rejection by those he loved. I am not alone in taking comfort, encouragement, inspiration, and food for thought from such emotional resonance with, and reflection on, many dimensions of my own experience. *All* those things helped me survive, *but none in quite the same way as this face-to-face meeting did.*

At this point, then, I want to express my deep gratitude (which seems to have the power to overcome envy (Klein, 1975), shame, resentment, mistrust, contempt, etc.) to those who provided such a receptive, responsive, respectful holding environment. I also want to voice my conviction that the analytic process, with all its pitfalls and possibilities of genuinely corrective emotional experience, is not confined to our consulting rooms, but has parallel processes (Searles, 1955) in our psychoanalytic community and beyond. As such, the analytic process, broadly conceived, is worthy of faith – and is very useful to speak openly about. It is, I think, part of an ongoing, multidimensional process of wording – by which we find ourselves in the mind of "the Other," and multiple others in our own hearts.

## Notes

1  I realize that my subjective sense of a causal connection between the traumatic blockage of a life goal, integral to my identity, and the onset of prostate cancer, has not been scientifically proven beyond a shadow of doubt, according to the U.S. National Cancer Institute. It was, however, validated as a possibility in *Getting Well Again* (Simonton et al., 1980, p. 63) which cites studies of exactly that correlation. It is beyond the scope of this paper to review relevant literature on this as yet unsettled question about mutual influences between mind and body.

2  At a recent social gathering honoring a retired, much-admired training analyst, I noticed this man and how much he had aged. I tried to catch his eye, but could not. I was not sure whether he was avoiding my gaze or simply caught up in the joyful, generous, and thankful spirit of the evening. As I was leaving, he was ahead of me, lending a hand to someone to whom I wanted to say goodbye. It felt natural to greet him and ask how he was doing, extending my hand as I did so. He had a surprised look on his face, but took my hand, shook it warmly and firmly, and said with a good deal of feeling in his voice, "How nice of you, John, to shake my hand!" I was strangely touched by that encounter – as, apparently, was he. It confirmed my sense that he might have felt badly about the impact of his decision on me, and that those feelings were still with him, years later. It also seemed that something had come full circle in a way that felt very good – inclusive of the bad – thanks to the spirit of the evening, generated by the much-appreciated presence of the person for whom it was held. Another colleague, who has remained at the center of our conflicted analytic community, and has suffered her own wounds in the process, commented as she was leaving, "An evening like that gives me hope for our Society."

3  The assumption, here, is that such decisions about particular analysts must be made by the institution itself, not left to individuals in relation to one another. The question was raised whether I (assuming it were up to me) would make someone who fell asleep with patients a training analyst (assuming that category to be necessary). My answer would be "Yes" – as long as that person was able to recognize it as a failure or fault *in himself*, reflect on its relational triggers, functions, and meanings, and accept his share of responsibility for the effects it has on each patient with whom it happens.

4  This was a joint committee, with "ordinary members" of the Society as well as training analysts.

# References

Bacal, H.A. & Thomson, P.G. (1996). The psychoanalyst's selfobject needs and the effect of their frustration on the treatment. In A. Goldberg (ed.), *Progress in Self Psychology*. New York: Guilford Press, vol. 12, pp. 17–35.

Balint, M. (1968). *The Basic Fault*. London: Tavistock.

Dean, E.S. (1957). Drowsiness as a symptom of countertransference. *Psychoanalytic Quarterly*, 26: 246–247.

Dender, J.M. (1993). The phenomenon of sleepiness in the analyst. Unpublished presentation at the 16th Annual Conference on the Psychology of the Self, Toronto, October 30, 1993.

Dickes, R. & Papernik, D. (1977). Defensive alterations of consciousness: hypnoid states, sleep, and the dream. *Journal of the American Psychoanalytic Association*, 25: 635–654.

Eshel, O. (1998). "Black holes," deadness, and existing analytically. *International Journal of Psychoanalysis*, 79: 1115–1130.

Eshel, O. (2001). Whose sleep is it anyway? Or "night moves." *International Journal of Psychoanalysis*, 82(3): 545–562.

Finnegan, P. (2007). Towards a Fairbairnian understanding of multiple personality. Master's thesis, University of Sheffield, Sheffield, UK.

Freud, S. (1912). The dynamics of transference. In J. Strachey (ed. and trans.), *The Standard Edition of the Complete Psychological Works of Sigmund Freud* (vol. 12, pp. 97–108).

Freud, S. (1915). Mourning and melancholia. In J. Strachey (ed. and trans.), *The Standard Edition of the Complete Psychological Works of Sigmund Freud* (vol. 14, pp. 243–258).

Freud, S. (1921). Group psychology and the analysis of the ego. In J. Strachey (ed. and trans.), *The Standard Edition of the Complete Psychological Works of Sigmund Freud* (vol. 18, pp. 65–143).

Freud, S. (1926). Inhibitions, symptoms and anxiety. In J. Strachey (ed. and trans.), *The Standard Edition of the Complete Psychological Works of Sigmund Freud* (vol. 20, pp. 75–176).

Freud, S. (1930). Civilization and its discontents. In J. Strachey (ed. and trans.), *The Standard Edition of the Complete Psychological Works of Sigmund Freud* (vol. 21, pp. 57–146).

Furman, R.A. & Furman, E. (1984). Intermittent decathexis – a type of parental dysfunction. *International Journal of Psychoanalysis*, 65: 423–433.

Ghent, E. (1990). Masochism, submission, surrender. *Contemporary Psychoanalysis*, 26: 108–136.

Grotstein, J.S. (1990). Nothingness, meaninglessness, chaos, and the black hole* II: the black hole. *Contemporary Psychoanalysis*, 26: 377–407.

Jung, C.G. (1952). Synchronicity: an acausal connecting principle. In R.F.C. Hull (trans.), *Collected Works*, Princeton: Princeton University Press (Vol. 8, pp. 520–531).

Klein, M. (1975). *Envy and Gratitude and Other Works 1946–1963*. New York: Delacorte Press/Seymour Lawrence.

Leonoff, A. (2002). Psychoanalytic identity. Unpublished manuscript. Presented to the Toronto Psychoanalytic Society, February 13, 2002.

McLaughlin, J. (1975). The sleepy analyst: some observations on states of consciousness in the analyst at work. *Journal of the American Psychoanalytic Associuation*, 23: 363–382.

Rizzuto, A.-M. (1979). *The Birth of the Living God: A Psychoanalytic Study*. Chicago: University of Chicago Press.

Searles, H. (1955). The informational value of the supervisor's emotional experiences. *Psychiatry*, 8: 135–146.

Simonton, O.C., Mathews-Simonton, S. & Creighton, J.L. (1980). *Getting Well Again*. New York: Bantam.

Sloane, J. A. (2003). *Psychoanalytic identity, a view from purgatory; Reflections on the experience of being judged unacceptable as a training analyst.* Paper presented at the Canadian Psychoanalytic Society, Vancouver.

Sloane, J.A. (2012). The loneliness of the analyst and its alleviation through faith in "O." In B. Willock, L. Bohm, & R.C. Curtis (eds), *Loneliness and Longing: Conscious and Unconscious Aspects*. New York: Routledge.

Sloane, J.A. (2013). Sleep, death and rebirth: A relational perspective on sleep in the countertransference. *Contemporary Psychoanalysis*, 49: 509–535.

Stern, D.B. (1997). *Unformulated Experience: From Dissociation to Imagination in Psychoanalysis*. Hillsdale, NJ: The Analytic Press.

Sullivan, H.S. (1953). *The Interpersonal Theory of Psychiatry*. New York: W.W. Norton & Company.

Winnicott, D.W. (1963). Communicating and not communicating leading to a study of certain opposites. In *The Maturational Processes and the Facilitating Environment*. Madison, CN: International Universities Press, pp. 179–192.

Winnicott, D.W. (1969). The use of an object. *International Journal of Psychoanalysis*, 50: 711–716.

# 15

# THE BLAME GAME

## Finding attributional balance in failure

*John V. O'Leary*

It's not whether you win or lose, it's how you place the blame.
(Oscar Wilde)

I describe myself as an interpersonalist by virtue of training and experience, yet cognitive and neurological fields have always fascinated me. As a shameless eclectic, I draw from social psychology and philosophy to round out my approach to the complex problems we face. Having long been intrigued by the contribution that Attribution Theory might make to psychoanalytic puzzle-solving, I welcomed a recent opportunity to speak on its relationship to failure. Preparing this talk led me to see how Attribution Theory might support my efforts to alleviate psychic pain associated with profound failure experiences.

Attribution Theory is about the ways people view causality and assign responsibility to themselves or others. Drawing from concepts rooted in cognitive and social psychology, it posits that people ascribe personal failure in highly subjective ways. While obvious to others, their bias may be utterly unclear to themselves. For example, a faculty member complains to colleagues about his failure to get tenure. While he claims the Dean lined up cronies against him, his peers quietly agree that the problem was this professor's failure to publish. This illustrates an "attribution error" on the professor's side in which he ascribes a negative outcome to others, whereas a successful one would have been credited to himself.

Attribution Theory suggests that, when convinced we have caused a failure, we can react in powerful ways. Self-blame can affect self-esteem, professional performance, and significant relationships. Likewise, being certain that someone else is responsible can set the stage for further distancing from others, paranoia, even revenge.

As an assistant professor at a small college many years ago, I was notified (along with four other faculty) of contract non-renewal. Financial reasons were cited in a letter circulated to the entire faculty. We felt publicly humiliated and disbelieved the fiscal excuse. Some bit of personal background made each of us unholy. It was political activism in my case; one man was openly gay. I became angry and depressed. I blamed the school's narrowness of mind and myself for not having achieved academic stardom. For some time, preoccupation with failure dominated my life and negatively affected my work. It would have been better had I not assumed the budgetary issue was a ruse and, instead, recognized it as a legitimate factor beyond anyone's control. Indeed, the college invited me back a few years later when their financial position improved. I was promoted and stayed on for four years.

Whether a perceived failure is personal or not, we all spend much time and energy determining blame. For example, consider your effort to locate responsibility for some big external disaster, like the Gulf of Mexico oil spill, or the mortgage crisis. Or, reflect on the recent breakup of a significant relationship. How much time was devoted to finding fault? Figuring out who did what to whom fills endless hours with anxiety, anger, and pain.

Attribution error can go to pathological extremes. I suspect, however, that the ubiquitous, often unsavory blame game is a vital human activity. It may serve larger evolutionary purposes as part of the mechanism meant to protect us from repeated mistakes. It may help us sort out possibilities, learn from them, develop the capacity to move on, not dwelling on what cannot be changed. We appear similarly protected by an innate capacity to accept fate's blows with a philosophical shrug.

Since the late 1950s, attribution theorists like Heider (1958) and Kelley (1967) have demonstrated powerful connections between attribution of causality and self-esteem. Attributing success to internal factors enhances pride and a sense of accomplishment, whereas attributing failure to internal factors diminishes self-esteem.

One of the most robust findings in the attributional literature is that depression and paranoia have serious core attributional distortions (Candido & Romney, 1990; Kinderman & Bentall, 1997). From a psychoanalytic perspective, paranoids project aspects of themselves onto others. Depressives have harsh superegos and, consequently, are self-critical. It is, however, simplistic to say paranoids blame others while depressives blame themselves. Cognitive theorists have elucidated a more complex understanding by outlining two additional concepts that play a role in attribution: stability and globalness.

Stability refers to continuity and predictability over time. For example, saying one is congenitally bad at math expresses a stable cause, as a biological unsuitability for the subject would affect every math exam one takes. Saying one failed a math exam because one was up all night partying constitutes an unstable cause, since there's no guarantee one will party before every exam. Even the most dedicated party-lover can be distracted by chance events, say, a flat tire or a bout of flu.

Globalness refers to expanding perceived causes for failure beyond one's power to change or control. For example, one might declare, "I am just not college material." A considerable element of stability creeps into these internal attributions, as when a depressed individual globalizes: "I am a failure. *Nothing* I do *ever* pays off." Paranoid individuals are also inclined toward a mix of stability and globalness, as in the external attribution: "They always do that. They are all out to get me."

Stability and globalness pique my curiosity, especially regarding external attribution. These concepts acknowledge possibilities of larger forces at work, beyond individual control, perhaps deeply cultural. In a *Wall Street Journal* article, Lena Boroditsky (2010) asks us to consider how different languages influence our world-view. She cites recent work in cognitive science strongly attesting to this possibility. How we put words together changes what we perceive. In English, we might say, "John knocked over the vase," whereas a Spanish or Japanese speaker's causality would be expressed as "The vase fell over." English speakers appear prone to conceptualize agents, and are thus more likely to place blame. Cultural bias may bind us to a particular attributional construction. Americans are inclined to overlook or deny the importance of fate, while people in many other cultures see it as the most powerful determinant in life's events (see Hewitt, this volume, Chapter 11).

While we may underappreciate the role of happenstance because of cultural emphasis on individual determinism, there is broad agreement in our profession that things outside anyone's control – including the unconscious – play a huge role. When we accept the Freudian imperative to make the unconscious conscious, do we not anticipate a shift of attribution, sometimes from happenstance (say, an early death in the family) to responsibility (or, should I say, the self-blame role), which comes with personal awareness? This enormously rich area of enquiry invites exploration.

I have observed that paranoid individuals assiduously avoid attributing cause to luck or chance. One such patient ascribed calamities to God's genius. Any problem, large or small, was seen as part of a perfectly conceived plan, the purpose of which we might comprehend if our minds were better developed. This patient's extreme rejection of any *other* causality is interesting. Including chance as a valid cause suggested new possibilities for dealing with his sense of failure. Believing this approach might mitigate harsh aspects of the blame game with other patients as well, I began considering the importance of happenstance and the need to understand the role it plays in attributing fault.

This chapter proposes a simple heuristic for psychotherapists – an application of Attribution Theory that should be tested. My simplified attributional model acknowledges dual possibilities of external causation in a dynamic triad. In my view, failure, non-achievement of a desired end, or lack of success, might be ascribed as:

1 My fault (I was refused tenure because I didn't publish)
2 Someone else's fault (The Dean told all his pals not to vote for me)
3 The fault of happenstance (In the midst of the recession, the school could not afford to offer tenure).

I begin with a basic assumption that there is an optimal balance for internal and external locus of control that might be considered healthy. Proposing more or less equal distribution of blame, I dub this "Balanced Attribution Theory." In my heuristic, a wholesome balance is generally achieved when bad outcomes are ascribed roughly 1/3 to self-blame, 1/3 to fault of others, and 1/3 to happenstance. Of course, these fractions are somewhat arbitrary and subject to wide variation. Very different weightings would be appropriate, for example, in a case of natural disaster, or armed robbery. Subtle shadings will certainly apply in each individual circumstance. The purpose of my heuristic is to reduce the experienced sense of failure by focusing on the need for attributional balance.

Let's consider a purely hypothetical example from the political arena. In the first year of his presidency, President Obama might have said: "I acknowledge three broad causes in the failure of our employment initiatives. First, I could not have foreseen the financial collapse of certain European countries, which hindered the growth of our exports. Second, I fault people who lobbied extravagantly to block our work-stimulus initiatives. Finally, I acknowledge being distracted by details of Health Care Legislation. In retrospect, I lingered too long on finishing touches and lost track of priorities." This imaginary confessional illustrates balanced ownership of failure with roughly equal distribution of responsibility (one internal attribution and two external). This sturdy triad sets the stage for undamaged self-esteem, ability to rebound politically, and room to think about what action to take next.

Now, let's take the model into the consulting room and see how it might apply in treating a patient dealing with a profound sense of failure. Tay was a 27-year-old Korean patient. For five years, he worked as a day trader for an independent New York City firm that earned its profit from thousands of trades that Tay and others, many of them Ivy Leaguers like himself, registered in a day's work. The company provided high-speed computers and work space. Tay provided the money he wagered. In a single year, he earned an astounding $900,000. Around 2007, his – and Wall Street's – luck ran out. Three years of straight losses led to my office. Tay felt he had made a horrible mistake. His years of day trading were a stain on his resume, making it unlikely he would ever find a position among "respectable," mainstream traders. He envisioned a bleak professional future.

Tay also considered himself a failure in relationships. Extremely shy, he had not dated since his college girlfriend broke up with him. He was currently living with friends, but resisted socializing with them, saying he felt he had nothing to say to strangers.

Slowly, hesitantly, Tay disclosed he had been bullied and physically abused by an older brother, Kim. It took months before Tay could bring the full burden of these experiences into our conversation. These painful, humiliating episodes had never been shared.

Despite success in a laundry business and purchasing several tenement buildings, Tay's parents never learned to speak English. They failed to raise their son with sufficient mastery of Korean to converse with them. The measure of alienation between them was Tay's refusal to learn their tongue and their refusal to learn his. Small wonder he felt others had no desire to talk to him, and that he felt at fault for this.

Uncomfortable among male peers, Tay was also awkward with authority figures – asking them for nothing, and expecting nothing from them. He could not bring himself to solicit a recommendation from an old professor who liked him and gave him an A. In sessions, Tay was often tongue-tied and self-conscious. He never asked for help from me. His low expectations of authority figures were buttressed by the shame (a form of self-blame) of even "having to see a shrink".

Tay was a serious self-blamer. When I began working with him, he was shouldering at least 80 percent of responsibility for his interpersonal and economic problems. Abuse he suffered innocently at his brother's hand damaged his ability to trust anyone, including himself. A language barrier of his father's making had hampered normal paternal identification, isolating Tay to the point where he now chose to identify with isolation, loneliness, and failure. Tay could not shift fault from himself to the financial crisis in which thousands of others lost their jobs and "shirts." His deep anger was largely appropriate. Turning that anger inward reified it, held it in place, making it even more difficult to stop blaming himself. Bringing Tay into a more balanced state of attribution would require sorting out where the blame actually lay.

As a first step, it seemed important for Tay to confront his brother about the beatings. When he summoned the courage to do so, Kim surprised him by acknowledging how cruel he had been, sobbing with regret. The positive dynamic in an interaction like this is exponential. Their relationship improved. As a more reasonable attributional balance was achieved with respect to the source of Tay's difficulties in life, he began to forgive Kim, and himself. Since it was now possible for Tay to grasp that he did not choose to have Kim for a brother, a few points could also be added to the "happenstance" column in my proposed heuristic.

Regarding causation outside anyone's control, I felt it would be expedient at this point to deal with the professional issue that brought Tay to me. I asked for a primer on day trading, his specialty. Working the day markets profitably requires a huge volume of trades, making many small investors essential to market performance, rather than large, institutional investors whose operations are more closely governed by rules and formulas. Tay's early success in this field was due to an uncanny ability with math, the kinds of algorithms used in speculative calculation, during one of history's greatest bull markets. For a brief, golden age, much money could be made if you were in the right place at the right time, willing to take risks.

Tay's troubles began with the market unhinging – the so called "sub-prime crisis." Small investors rapidly fled the scene. With billions of dollars drained from the market, risk was concentrated in fewer, larger, more regulated trades. Tay was unable to keep pace with these developments. Financial losses undermined his last bastion of self-esteem.

Tay cast himself as the culprit in this mess. While external factors clearly played a major role, he blamed himself, even as co-workers, managers, and CEOs tanked along with him. During the good old days, Tay compared the success of his wagers only to those in his group whose results were better. Now, he focused on himself as the lone loser, at the bottom of a greatly diminished heap. To deal with these contradictions, I gave some thought to what Attribution Theory calls "attribution bias." It comes in several flavors.

Attribution theorists identify several biases common in our society. In the case of the "fundamental attribution error," people are more likely to attribute outcomes of other's actions to their personalities whereas they attribute their own outcomes to the situation. In Tay's case, there was a strange reversal of this error. He overvalued personality-based explanations, discounting temporal and situational factors. His inadequate personality was at fault. Refusing to see the economic downturn as central to his predicament, Tay's distortion might also fall under the category of "fallacy of the single cause." Feeling abjectly responsible for his losses, he took the event that affected the entire economy very personally.

A "self-serving bias" could also be pried out of Tay's construction of his problem. While self-blame does not appear to be self-serving, it is in fact egocentric. For my patient, secondary gains accrued with this posture. Why push himself when it could only make things worse? The solid belief that he was a failure justified distancing himself from others. Tay was comfortable with isolation.

Secondary motives raise the possibility that unacknowledged aspects of personality may properly belong in the circumstantial category of my heuristic. Until they become conscious, truly hidden motivations and actions cannot be attributed to self. I emphasize *truly* to underscore that the line between conscious and unconscious is sometimes difficult to draw and is – hopefully – subject to change.

What was the therapist doing to improve Tay's attributional balance? Initially, I posed questions to move discussion away from narrow concern with self-criticism. Mindful of the absence of parenting figures, listening empathically and providing mirroring feedback was a central strategy. I tried to build a new narrative. It had to be plausible, comprehensive enough to take in Tay's major life experiences, and clear enough to support demystification.

Because of Tay's wariness and shame about therapy, I stayed close to his biggest worries and concerns. I learned to monitor my own attributional style. This seemed especially important with a patient so different in cultural background. For example, in Korea there is little tolerance for criticizing members of one's family, whereas Americans do this rather casually.

When Tay began to realize he was both creator and victim in his narrative, the pieces of his story fell into place. He had faced with his sibling the issue of childhood abuse, and come to terms with parental indifference. He could acknowledge complicity with the family directive to go it alone, suffer in silence, and rely exclusively on intelligence and a narrow range of professional skills at the expense of interpersonal needs. He did bear some responsibility, but not all. He was especially a victim of larger circumstances in the decline of his fortune. While he might have made more prudent choices (along with a lot of folks), the economic collapse so many suffered lay completely outside his ability to control. It became plausible to Tay that responsibility lay in roughly a 33 percent split between himself, others, and the Universe.

Gilbert et al. (1992) suggests attribution of cause for failure passes through three stages. The first determines categorization (Who did what to whom?). The second is characterization (What trait does the action imply?). Finally, correction (What situational constraints may have caused the action?). Distortion occurs when the process terminates at whatever stage some psychologically satisfying conclusion has been reached. To achieve optimal attributional balance, it is desirable to keep questioning and not abort the attribution process prematurely. My approach invites patients to scan their environment to locate multiple causes, viewing their situation dimensionally. Additionally, in treating patients with a powerful sense of failure, psychoanalytically oriented psychotherapists might consider the following:

1    To assist a patient to achieve more balanced attribution, listen for, "It couldn't be helped" and "What could I do?" Support for attribution to "powers beyond control" can ameliorate a sense of personal failure, and offer opportunities to empathize with the patient's experience.

2    It is essential to examine one's attributional tilt. As Lewis (2009) reminds us: "Attribution Theory research demonstrates that it is precisely in ambiguous situations, in which the cause-effect links are not quite so evident, that attributions may be primarily determined by the observer's (i.e., the therapist's) own needs, wishes, and preferences." A therapist may say, "That sounds like your mother talking." Investigating parental responsibility for a patient's difficulties is important. As an attributional bias on the part of the therapist, however, it can result in collusion with the patient in a merry chase to bury the parents.

An interesting angle on self-serving bias has been studied by Murdock, Edwards, and Tamera (2010) in the context of premature terminations. They found that when patients abruptly end treatment, they disliked the therapist or felt "stuck." Their therapists, when asked to explain the termination, may cite external causes, such as loss of insurance. Therapists are also far more inclined to shift responsibility to patients' deficiencies, e.g., "reluctance to dig deeper." When these same therapists are asked to review the work of supervisees or other therapists whose patients terminated, they are more likely to make attributions to a dysfunctional therapy.

3    There is something to be said for getting rid of the blame game altogether. The flipside of blaming oneself is responsibility-taking. The flipside of blaming others is positive self-assertion toward the other. It is absurd, however, to think we could abolish negative attribution, internal or external. It probably would not be healthy. It is more reasonable to become more aware of how we attribute fault, and more thoughtful about the impact blaming mechanisms have on ourselves and others.

4    Listening for an even-handed attribution style, or its absence, might help decipher transference-countertransference reactions and enactments. For example, the diagnostic label the patient bears may mitigate against the analyst taking seriously complaints about, or negative reactions to the treatment.

The therapist has the convenience of blaming the patient's behavior on a quality perceived as relatively stable in the patient. This might prevent serious consideration of the therapist's contribution to a negative state of affairs.

Tracking your feelings can also lead to uncovering attributional systems, both yours and the patient's. I remain on the lookout for my anger, guilt, and shame because I believe there is an intimate tie-in between these emotions and attributional mechanisms, but that is fodder for a future essay.

## Conclusions

Balanced Attribution Theory might help clinicians in cases where the sense of failure plays a pivotal role. While attributional bias and distortion tend to halt constructive criticism and contribute to general paralysis, attributional balance supports continued reflection and appropriate action.

Good affect regulation occurs when the person's emotional life is goal-directed, integrated, and under control. Affect storms (overwhelming sadness, helplessness, or rage) may be less likely when a multidimensional attributional style is at work. Balanced attribution is correlated with better control over emotional life.

The concept of attribution has high explanatory power. It is easily understood by patients. It can be communicated readily to therapists of diverse persuasions.

Finally, the idea of attribution with a more balanced inclusion of happenstance might appeal, especially, to psychoanalytically inclined practitioners. By granting more legitimacy to events and forces that lie outside personal control, my theory offers new opportunities for dialogue and new gateways to unconscious process. It encourages analysts to attend to their own attributional biases, thereby gaining a deeper understanding of countertransference. We need to remain open to all such possibilities.

## References

Boroditsky, L. (2010) Lost in translation. *Wall Street Journal*, Culture section. July 23.

Candido, C.L. & Romney, D.M. (1990). Attributional style in paranoid vs. depressed patients. *British Journal of Medical Psychology*, 63: 355–363.

Gilbert, D.T., McNulty, S.E., Giuliano, T.A. & Benson, J.E. (1992). Words and fuzzy deeds: the attribution of obscure behavior. *Journal of Personal and Social Psychology*, 62: 18–25.

Heider, F. (1958). *The Psychology of Interpersonal Relations*. New York: John Wiley & Sons.

Kelley, H.H. (1967). Attribution theory in social psychology. In D. Levine (ed.), *Nebraska Symposium of Motivation*, 15. Lincoln: University of Nebraska Press, pp. 192–238.

Kinderman, P. & Bentall, R.P. (1997). Causal attributions in paranoia and depression: internal, personal, and situational attributions for negative events. *Journal of Abnormal Psychology*, 106: 341–345.

Lewis, J. (2009). The crossroads of countertransference and attribution theory: Reinventing clinical training within an evidence based world. *American Journal of Psychoanalysis,* 69: 106–121.

Murdock, N.L., Edwards, C. & Tamera, B. (2010). Therapists attributions for client premature termination: are they self-serving? *Psychotherapy: Theory, Research & Practice,* 47: 221–234.

# Part VI

## INTEGRITY VS DESPAIR
Facing failure in the final phase
of the life cycle

# 16

# THE CHALLENGE OF OBSOLESCENCE

*Michael Stern*

Four young guys are sitting around, contemplating life. The past appears fairly carefree, trouble far away. But when they imagine being old, very old, say 64, they worry: "Will you still need me, will you still feed me?" What was it that the Beatles worried about? What do people fear when they think of aging? Death is certainly a concern, but way before that there is fear of uselessness and irrelevance, being unneeded, a burden rather than an asset, being obsolete.

Obsolescence has its widest current use in manufacturing and marketing. Objects are manufactured with a specific lifespan in mind that affects their design and materials used. Unlike Roman aqueducts, built for the ages, modern products are expected to have limited longevity. As the saying goes, the genius of modern technology lies in building things to last twenty years, making them obsolete in two, not only in anticipation of improvements but also in the service of continued production. That is where marketing comes in, creating a perceived need for the "new and improved," declaring last year's model, even if still perfectly functional, obsolete. A new consumer culture beats the drums of change, touting benefits of the new, declaring it incompatible with the old.

Anything that sticks around long enough – be it an object, a theory, or an individual – stands the chance of becoming obsolete. Willock (2007) offers a cogent analysis of the rather violent process in which the old has to fight for its life under a relentless, continuous attack from the new, especially in an age "favoring freely mobile cathexes, instant gratification, death wishes, and other manifestations of primary process, rather than reflection and cultivation of more enduring, complex commitments" (p. 57). As individuals live longer, the struggle to remain up to date starts earlier and earlier within one's expected lifespan. Fear of obsolescence precedes, and sometimes supersedes, fear of dying.

Obsolescence has been referred to as slow death, gradual draining of life's energy. Unlike death, of which we are aware on some level from an early age, obsolescence does not enter our consciousness till young adulthood. Even then, it appears avoidable, or at least negotiable. Unlike death, which is an all-or-nothing event, obsolescence is a multifaceted process. Since it is at least partly defined by the environment in which we live, encounters with it come gradually. We become increasingly aware of new developments that we are unprepared for, tasks we find hard to perform. Who among us has not been reminded, repeatedly, by our children that, as dinosaurs, extinction awaits? Threats of obsolescence appear from different directions. One may respond by surrender and depression, or continued adaptation to changing circumstances.

On the biological level, the journey toward obsolescence starts almost at birth. Women start losing eggs from the get-go. Physical stamina starts dwindling after the first quarter. By halftime, comfort and preservation of energy trump exertion and expansion. There is no clearer expression of biological obsolescence, at least Darwinially speaking, than menopause and impotence. Unlike the wishful saying that life begins when the kids go to college and the dog dies, the loss of procreational and nurturing functions, which tend to occur in rapid succession, is a significant loss with definite implications for our sense of self. "The aging body is an enfeebled friend of the self, a friend who increasingly fails to reciprocate affection" (Esposito, 1987, p. 69).

Analysts and therapists are fortunate to be able to continue working productively into advanced age. There are many, however, who are measured by "sociological age," for whom age is the critical determining factor for retirement. However a society defines old age, being old invariably means being less useful to society than one once was. The association of age with perceived ability often has the effect of making people feel weaker and less competent that they are. Societal criteria for age and competency often lag behind individual perceptions, giving rise to claims of age discrimination and backlash protestations such as "60 is the new 40." For men in particular, crises of aging can turn into narcissistic crises "when old men are no longer able to look upon themselves, or are being perceived by others, as those into which they have made themselves. Idealizations and misconceptions of reality can no longer be upheld" (Teising, 2007, p. 1337).

On a social/familial level, we are threatened with obsolescence when our roles within the structure are curtailed. We need to be needed and to have people around whose needs we seek to gratify. Society's attitude toward its older members has a profound effect on their place in its hierarchy. In traditional social structures, the relatively few elderly served as storytellers, healers, teachers. Their life experiences were invaluable for historical information and knowledge. That changed in the industrial age, when the social value of the elderly began to decline as younger workers proved more productive. The capitalist system has always admired the productive consumer who is engaged in the marketplace, responsive to trends, bringing up a new generation of consumers, and who, in time and as a reward, will be secure in old age.

The drift has been further and further away from admiration, or even respect for the elderly, who, by and large, shy away from trends and reckless spending (see Martin, 1992). The definition of old age as the point in life when individuals become irrelevant to primary social discourse makes people old at an earlier age now than ever. As Yogi Berra would say, "It gets late early out there." This situation produces a greater challenge for maintaining self-esteem and sense of belonging for an ever-growing portion of the population. Social stereotypes of the aging process further discourage both young and old from expecting continued vigor and productivity beyond a certain age.

Working with an older population presents therapists with the challenge of helping individuals face narcissistic and realistic injuries. Among these are fear of diminution or loss of sexual potency and its impact on relationships, threat of redundancy and displacement at work, marital anxieties arising after children have left home, awareness of aging, and inevitability of death before goals have been achieved (King, 1980). People regret getting old no matter what glories of heaven they may expect to follow.

While biological aging must be viewed as a blameless, non-negligent process, the same cannot easily be said about psychological aging. That individuals feel old and useless cannot be attributed entirely to nature. Physical deterioration no doubt contributes to growing inactivity, but more likely the phenomenon of experienced decline and marginal living is affected by social forces as much as it is inherently biological.

Robert Butler (1975), who coined the term "ageism" to describe the stereotyping of old people, akin to sexism and racism, pointed out that as a group older people actually become more psychologically diverse with advancing years. Similarly Cath and Miller (1986) stated that the elderly "remain as curious, adventurous, creative, gifted and well motivated for psychoanalysis as in any other phase of life" (p. 164). Yet society expects older individuals to sit back, sum up, and often shut up.

By the time people get to nursing homes, issues of physical decline and increased isolation appear almost universally. Even then, remarkable individual differences exist in how residents perceive their situation. In my work at one such facility, I asked people about their take on aging and loss of functions. These individuals are between 85 and 99 years old, long retired, lost spouses, use walkers or wheelchairs, and are on an average of 12 daily medications (the industry average). What was striking is that their attitudes toward loss of functions did not dovetail with objective factors such as degree of physical incapacitation, presence or absence of relatives, etc.

Mr. A, a retired lawyer with a sharp mind and varied interests, nevertheless described his life as in "a desolate place." What bothered him most was "the failure of creativity," no longer being able to create a future or even imagine a desired future. He liked books on history. I am not sure he recognized the irony of reading, at the time of our conversations, a book on the demise of empires. He was eager to offer fellow residents help and advice about living well, but found few takers. He became increasingly frustrated by what he called "a throwaway society." The notion of just existing filled him with dread. He was determined to find ways to remain relevant.

Ms. N also found that few around her were interested in her input, but she was content to "dispense wisdom even if they don't need it." She refused to get discouraged by her advice being ignored and, helped by creeping dementia, presented herself as the mother hen who still needed to hold the family together.

Ms. F positioned herself differently; "The best I can do for my children now is to die." This belief was stated not in a depressed or angry manner, but rather as cool assessment of what she had left to do. She viewed her life's mission as raising a family. Nothing in current options appeared relevant or justifying continued existence.

Mr. S is a paradox. At 99, his body is beat up and failing, though not in an imminently life-threatening manner. His mind remains quite sharp, allowing him to articulate his nihilistic take on life. "Obsolete?" he growled. "One is always obsolete. It's smarter not to be born in the first place." He can see no way and no point to look into the future with any hope, since nothing will change the final outcome. He dismisses all that medical and nursing staff have told him, except one doctor's confirmation that he will indeed die within the foreseeable future: "He is the only honest doctor here!" In our conversations we go nose to nose. As he fights tooth and nail to prove the meaninglessness of life, he becomes passionate and related, in other words – alive.

Ms. T had always viewed herself as a helper and rescuer. Now that she depends on others for help, she cannot tolerate the change. She was the child assigned to take care of ailing parents. She did not go to college. She had to settle for what was left after siblings took what they needed. At the nursing home, she views fellow residents as she viewed her privileged siblings – spoiled, snobbish elitists who look down upon her. She reacts by staying in her room, trusting only a few aides, identifying with their place in the professional hierarchy.

Finally Ms. L, a youngish mid-eighties woman, still working part time when she drove home one day, blacked out, hit a tree and broke 14 ribs. She met the physical rehab challenge with characteristic determination. The prospect of giving up driving, on which her children insisted, filled her with dread, even though her well-to-do son arranged for a personal driver. "It's not the getting there," she said. "It's how you get there." Even as she winced in pain with each breath, she refused to give up. "I am not going to stop and feel sorry for myself today because then I will wake up tomorrow and realize I lost yesterday."

What these individuals present can be summarized as the "Now what?" challenge. They are acutely aware of life's approaching end, but also of still being alive and needing to fill the spaces created by declining capacities and loss of family, friends, homes, and functions. The obsolescence they experience is not unlike industrial obsolescence. It is not primarily the object's dysfunction, but rather the perceived loss of its utility in a changed environment by which its value is assessed. That perception is often created by one's sense of temporal being, of belonging to a particular generation or historical period. When individuals say, "In my time …" or "In the old days …," they refer to when the world first became their own. To them there is just one style of art or music, one way to be married, one way to live. All other options are variations on the major chords, but are mere approximations at best.

Valenstein (2000) speaks of the need to live life where it can be found: in old age people tend to focus on times when life was meaningful and productive. He suggests people's tendency to repeat the same old stories are not necessarily indicative of forgetfulness, but an effort to maintain a sense of vitality and agency.

The most frequent accompaniment to a sense of obsolescence is depression. Weiner and White (1982) defined depression as a narcissistic disturbance in which the self is unconsciously expected to accomplish grandiose expectations and is regarded as a failure when it does not. These omnipotent fantasies include prevention of object loss and triumph over death. When that fails, as it always does, depression is a risk.

Is obsolescence failure? The simple answer is that it sure feels like it. On a subjective level, obsolescence represents structural collapse, failure to hold what was built up, layer upon layer, throughout life. It leaves one questioning past accomplishments, doubting earlier success, and suffering a slew of successive narcissistic blows. Yet obsolescence does not necessarily fall on the success-failure continuum. Rather, it occurs when continued fulfillment is no longer attainable. It is determined not by objective criteria of success or failure, but rather by subjective experiences of having no purpose.

Self-blame and the assumption of failure may be part of anyone's inability to maintain health, relevance, and usefulness. It does not appear directly related to objective personal accomplishments. In fact, becoming obsolete may be significantly more challenging or devastating for individuals whose lives were marked by self-motivation and reliance on their own resources rather than by professional or financial success.

In considering the place of failure in obsolescence, one must go beyond the individual. We age in a social environment, affected by its beliefs. One can argue that current society fails many older people by viewing them through the lens of stereotype, depriving them of opportunities, commanding them to adhere to rules of "appropriate aging."

Philosophers and sociologists, more than psychologists, have increasingly pointed to the need for individuals and social institutions to change as the population gets older, and to envision changes akin to environmentalism and conservation in their focus on the larger picture. Esposito (1987), a philosopher, imagined conceptual and social changes that would address old age obsolescence. He felt the work ethic that defines the value of persons by what they do, intrinsically devalued the very young and the very old, and was no longer appropriate for a world in which people live way past their working years. Life's meaning had to include intellectual stimulation, happiness of fellowship, love, passion, and work for a better future. He similarly envisioned a change in the meaning of death. The ancient stigma of death as punishment for sin, or the more modern view of death as nature's way of sacrificing the old for the young, must be replaced by a new perspective that enables one to choose between living and dying, formulating one's death scenarios and refining them as life goes on. A similar emphasis on changing criteria for self assessment in older age was proposed by Per-Einar and Geir (2005).

What has psychoanalysis to offer the study of obsolescence? At first glance – not much. Freud's belief that aging brings about a loss of mental elasticity, thus limiting intrapsychic reorganization and making psychoanalytic technique less effective, discouraged the application of psychoanalytic theory and technique beyond middle age (see Limentani, 1995; Nemiroff & Colarusso, 1985; Wagner, 2005). Death has been studied in the context of psychological development (Razinsky, 2007; Willock, Bohm, & Curtis, 2007). The term "obsolescence" does not, however, appear in psychoanalytic literature. Hints of the phenomenon appear in writings about narcissism. Some ideas in the literature seem to have limited utility. For example, the belief that old age is a regression to bodily preoccupations is quite an oversimplification considering the vast differences in the form and meaning of bodily concerns in infancy and in old age.

Like the world in which it is practiced, psychoanalysis, in an effort to avoid its own obsolescence, changed over the years to accommodate evolving social sensibilities. Newer theoretical branches were not necessarily based on new, objective, scientific discoveries, but may have evolved as approaches more in line with current societal trends. (See Willock, 2007, for an extended review of how changes occur in psychoanalytic theory.)

Theoretical and practical expansions allowed reaching out to the growing percentage of the aging population that traditional psychoanalysis viewed as over the hill. The question has shifted from who can fit into the firm boundaries of psychoanalysis to how psychoanalysis must change to accommodate the changing population.

On the basis of clinical experience, Cath and Miller (1986) suggest the following characteristics serve as positive prognostic indicators for working with older individuals: "the person's sense of reconciliation to his or her achievement level; wisdom, born of experience in living; a relatively low level of defensiveness; and a perspective indicating some degree of clarity concerning individual values" (p. 164). These are close to criteria Karl Abraham stated in 1919 (quoted in Pollock, 1982): "Prognosis of psychoanalysis in advanced age is favorable if the neurosis has set in its full severity only after a long period has elapsed since puberty and the patient has enjoyed for at least several years a sexual attitude approaching the normal and a period of social usefulness" (p. 277).

It is said that old age is like everything else – to make a success of it, you've got to start young. One implication may be that, as analysts, we should balance our almost exclusive preoccupation with people's past with a richer exploration of their understanding of, and preparation for their future, especially their decline and mortality: "One of the things we have to listen out for is the future itself, because it has a habit of creeping up on us so softly that we don't see it coming" (Holloway, 2004, p. 138).

One aim of psychoanalysis, regardless of age, is to enable the patient to accept the anxiety associated with having limited influence on the course of events (Hoffman, 1998). Each phase of life, particularly in transition periods, presents specific variations of such anxiety with implications for attachment and support considerations on the part of analysts. Work with older individuals, for whom such anxiety is an ever-growing companion, presents phase specific challenges.

One adaptation made by psychoanalysis as new insights were incorporated and applied in clinical work with all age groups was the loosening of norms regarding the relationship between analyst and patient. It is now understood that it is the intensity, form, and content of the transference-countertransference analysis of older persons that is likely to vary from that of the younger (e.g., Lipson, 2002). For the older patient, transference serves reality-based attachment needs no less than psychic organization. The ability of the analyst to stray from neutrality, to push for action when the patient appears to either pull back into passivity or to view him/herself beyond a viable future, offers both participants the use of energy that would otherwise remain dormant. The willingness of the analyst to gratify attachment needs, to become "more" than an analyst, invites the patient to become "more" than an old person.

Herzog (2007) similarly advocates flexibility in dealing with the old: "The requirements of the patients and the capacity of the therapist determine the opti-mal response of the therapist. This kind of intuitive approach improves the flexi-bility of the therapist, who, not being constrained by any predetermined technical position, can engage in therapeutic actions that can be highly spontaneous, making use of the therapist's interpersonal strengths to make powerful, beneficial inter-ventions" (pp. 254–255).

Long (2007) wrote on adapting relational principles of mirroring, holding, and mutuality to therapeutic work with older individuals, when language has lost some of its power, and coming to terms with dying has taken center stage.

Above all, it is important, writes Wagner (2005), to resist such stereotypes as: "What is future when so much is past; don't rob the elderly of their good old days; and, where there's age there is no longer fuel for fire" (p. 83). Past experience does not sever the desire to bond with the future.

Wisdom has been defined as the realistic, empathic understanding of the human condition tempered by acceptance of finiteness of time and personal death (Settlage, 1996). Martindale (1998) wrote on the importance of changing the con-cept of time with aging. Psychoanalysis, he stated, can help develop the "capacity to be able to mourn many of one's youthful ideas and ambitions that is a central key in defining personal creativity in later life, a life that is adapted to the confines and realities of finite time" (p. 261).

When introspective engagement with one's personal history is applied to reas-sessing what's really important and lessening needs for approval, there is potential for wisdom and for giving up narcissistic delusions. The goal is not ecstatic embrace of aging, but rather an ambivalent, tolerable relationship with it.

Frommer (2005) suggested that anticipatory dread of meaninglessness can actually enhance the meaning of current existence, and that psychoanalysis can make use of this perspective in helping patients confront life's realities. Awareness of getting older may serve to motivate one to make better use of time before choice and active living are preempted by further decline.

"The goal of psychoanalytic treatment is to make more of people available to themselves for present and future creative and satisfying life experiences. We all know that psychoanalysis is a humanizing force which allows an individual to be in touch with parts of himself or herself that have been forgotten, neglected or pushed away and yet continue to exert important influences upon the individual" (Pollock, 1982, p. 279). Under the threat of obsolescence, the goal is to redefine meaning, develop an active concern with life itself, and find small pockets of engagement that are admittedly less intense than past attachments but, nevertheless, maintain a tie to what life is left. Ideally, says Holloway, "having had our place in the sun, we should rejoice that others are now replacing us" (2004, p. 203).

An essential element in treatment is redevelopment of healthy narcissism and substitution of grandiose fantasies with more realistic ones. An honest, open look at a diminished existence does not have to be defeatist: "A bell with a crack in it may not ring as clearly, but it can ring as sweetly" (Ackerman, 2011, p. 302).

As is the case with any psychoanalytically oriented endeavor, searching for dynamics and meanings is a self-reinforcing process, diametrically opposed to surrender and obsolescence. Life can still be considered worth living when one is helped to face its progression with courage and determination.

# References

Ackerman, D. (2011). *One Hundred Names for Love: A Stroke, a Marriage, and the Language of Healing*. New York: W.W. Norton & Company.

Butler, R.N. (1975). *Why Survive? Being Old in America*. New York: Harper & Row.

Cath, S. & Miller, N.E. (1986). The psychoanalysis of the older patient. *Journal of the American Psychoanalytic Associastion*, 34: 163–177.

Esposito, J.L. (1987). *The Obsolete Self*. Berkeley and Los Angeles: University of California Press.

Frommer, M.S. (2005). Living in the liminal spaces of mortality. *Psychoanalytic Dialogues*, 15(4): 479–498.

Herzog, B. (2007). Love and death: affect sharing in the treatment of the dying. In B. Willock L.C. Bohm, & R.C. Curtis (eds.), *On Deaths and Endings: Psychoanalysts' Reflections on Finality, Transformations, and New Beginnings*. London and New York: Routledge, pp. 247–256.

Hoffman, I. (1998). *Ritual and Spontaneity in the Psychoanalytic Process: A Dialectical Constructive Point of View*. Hillsdale, NJ: Analytic Press.

Holloway, R. (2004). *Looking in the Distance*. London: Canongate.

King, P. (1980). The life cycle as indicated by the nature of the transference in the psycho-analysis of the middle aged and the elderly. *International Journal of Psychoanalysis*, 61: 153–160.

Limentani, A. (1995). Creativity and the third age. *International Journal of Psychoanalysis*, 76: 825–833.

Lipson, C. (2002). Psychoanalysis in later life. *Psychoanalytic Quarterly*, 71: 751–775.

Long, S.W. (2007). A relational perspective on working with dying patients in a nursing home setting. In B. Willock, L.C. Bohm, & R.C. Curtis, (eds.), *On Deaths and Endings:*

*Psychoanalysts' Reflections on Finality, Transformations, and New Beginnings*. London and New York: Routledge, pp. 237–246.

Martin, C. (1992). The elder and the other. *Free Associations*, 3: 341–354.

Martindale, B. (1998). On aging, dying, death, and eternal life. *Psychoanalytic Psychotherapy*, 12: 259–270.

Nemiroff, R.A. & Colarusso, C.A. (1985). *The Race Against Time: Psychotherapy and Psychoanalysis in the Second Half of Life*. New York: Plenum Press.

Per-Einar, B. & Geir, H. (2005). Balancing losses and growth: a relational perspective on identity formation in the second half of life. *Journal of the American Psychoanalytic Associastion*, 33: 431–451.

Pollock, G.H. (1982). On aging and psychopathology. *International Journal of Psychoanalysis*, 63: 275–281.

Razinsky, L. (2007). On the strange case of the attitude of psychoanalysis toward death. *Contemporary Psychoanalysis*, 43: 149–164.

Settlage, C. (1996). Transcending old age. *International Journal of Psychoanalysis*, 77: 549–562.

Teising, M. (2007). Narcissistic mortification of aging men. *International Journal of Psychoanalysis*, 88: 1329–1344.

Valenstein, A.F. (2000). The older patient in psychoanalysis. *Journal of the American Psychoanalytic Association*, 48: 1563–1589.

Weiner, M.B. & White, M.T. (1982). Depression as the search for the lost self. *Psychotherapy: Theory, Research & Practice*, 19(4): 491–499.

Wagner, J.W. (2005). Psychoanalytic bias against the elderly patient: hiding our fears under developmental millstones. *Contemporary Psychoanalysis*, 41: 77–92.

Willock, B. (2007). *Comparative-Integrative Psychoanalysis: A Relational Perspective for the Discipline's Second Century*. New York: Analytic Press.

Willock, B., Bohm, L.C. & Curtis, R.C. (2007). *On Deaths and Endings: Psychoanalysts' Reflections on Finality, Transformations and New Beginnings*. London and New York: Routledge.

# 17

# FAILURE OF THE BODY

## Perseverance of the spirit

### *J. Gail White and Michelle Flax*

David Hume, the great Scottish philosopher, in 1775 uttered these words: "We are placed in this world as in a great theater, where the true springs and causes of every event are entirely concealed from us; nor have we either sufficient wisdom to foresee, or power to prevent those ills with which we are continually threatened. We hang in perpetual suspense between life and death, health and sickness, plenty and want" (1775/1976, p. 33).

Psychoanalysts have long understood the body as theatre (McDougall, 1989). Our bodies are writ large with conflicts and unconscious phantasies. Concurrent with this psychological process is a biologically based aging process that involves bodily breakdown. There is ongoing tension between "life forces" and "death forces"[1] within each individual, forces that are both biologically and psychologically driven. As our bodies fail, death forces take us in their grasp, becoming stronger at the expense of life forces. When death forces hold sway, we are caught in a psychological tomb where no thought is possible; only circular rumination leading to apathy and despair.

How do we make our destiny thinkable and bearable? Through imagination, we can find solace through symbolization, thereby attending to the soul's needs. As Wordsworth said in "The Daffodils": "Though nothing can bring back the hour of splendour in the grass, of glory in the flower; we will grieve not, rather find strength in what remains behind."

Freud's (1916) "On Transience" captures the spirit of our argument: the bloom is no less beautiful for its imminent demise. In fact, it is the transience of beauty and life that raises its enjoyment. Creativity, with its life affirming qualities, can bring to bear the beauty of the ephemeral and the "in-between," the living on of meaning through objects, ideas, and symbolic space.

Our work with elderly patients illustrates the powerful seduction of death forces as aging and illness set in. What is truly lost is the sense of self as strong, effective, lively and mobile. This can be experienced as a narcissistic loss depleting the self. For some, self-reflection and expanding awareness allows them to utilize their life forces to hold on to the possibilities in "what remains behind"; for others, illness, aging, and the inevitable progression toward death usher in apathy, "giving up" and melancholia. Depressive anxiety against the experience of helplessness and fragmentation staved off in early childhood can return as the finitude of life is realized (Jacques, 1965). Anticipation of agony can form a concrete core fear of death (Ricoeur, 2009).

The Kleinian paranoid-schizoid position and terrors therein are useful in conceptualizing aging. In particular, the idea of destructive forces being turned onto the body evokes the helplessness and hopelessness felt in relation to death. Suffering individuals can be helped through annihilation terrors by making reparation to the "destroyed self" through creativity and imagination. Facing death can become a creative, ego-integrative experience, if we encounter the tragedy of personal death with appropriate grief (Anshin, 1985). Creative mourning of our deaths can further our capacity to tolerate conflict and imperfection. Hate turned inward is not denied, but is mitigated by love.

De Masi (2004) attributes the persistence of infantile annihilation fantasies and psychotic disintegration terror to the lack of integrating those fantasies into the "symbolic order." Terror of self fragmentation follows from the lasting absence of the other and the loss of the experience of care. It returns as the Real (i.e., as concrete), unmitigated by elaborations of language and creative arts. The will to live, through the creative endeavor, can diminish these frightening feelings related to death and destruction.

"Only those who mourn shall be comforted" (Ricoeur, 2009, p. 4). How does one mourn lost aspects of self?[2] Does one succumb to loss so that the entire self is consumed, or is one able to retain enough libido to enliven remaining aspects of self? Do death forces prevail, or is there a way to "mourn" the lost part that allows for the vitality of life forces? Freud (1917) suggests our way through mourning is by processing memories of the other, slowly decathecting such memories to the point where a substitute may be found to compensate for loss. When aspects of self are lost in aging, no real substitutes can be found. The loss can be represented only in symbolic form.

All of us must grapple with failure of our bodies and the impact on our minds. As analysts, we work with tortures of the soul, allowing for life-affirming symbolization of terror-filled losses. What is needed is full contemplation of the tragic, and successful working through of the depressive position. The thought of death can then be carried in thinking, and not predominantly in projective identification (Jacques, 1965). The paralyzing fear of death can be turned into productive, symbolic rendering of the Real. The realization can come that we can live on through loved ones and our work, if we can move beyond persecution and chaos within. The creative arts are a symbolic area in which the life and death forces have a theatre in which to play and intertwine, without the reality of either becoming negated.

Our role as analysts when the death forces are strong is to seduce patients back into the life forces, and to make tolerable in thought real bodily failures. This is done through the intensity and power of therapeutic relationships and mobilization of creativity. The unconscious is not confined to the individual psyche, but appears in the relation between subjects (Lacan, 2008). Our bearing witness, in an affective environment, to the overwhelming losses involved in bodily failures enables patients to begin bearing "nameless dread."

In *On Death and Endings*, Long (2007), Kaplan (2007), and Herzog (2007) all talked movingly about the importance of the analyst's affective presence in helping those dying. Kaplan talked of letting go of language to see where the non-verbal mind goes, co-constructing "bodymind" experiences and using imagery and the "generative unconscious" to connect affectively. Herzog talked of the importance of deep "affect sharing" that can convert tragic, lonely processes of dying into more comforting, humane experiences. This is Long's goal, as well, as he talks about the analyst's mirroring, holding, and reciprocation in establishing and maintaining relationships with the terminally ill.

We add to this literature the belief that the use of creative forms within a soulful, holding environment is a way to make the unsayable speakable. This is a place where analyst and analysand implicitly acknowledge the inherent pain and struggle of human existence, allowing for a mediated "third" dimension. It is here in the "third space" that sensory, generative, and creative life forces can liberate a melancholic standstill, allowing the contemplation of death within the culture's symbol systems. We present below our work with three patients illustrating these themes.

## Clinical illustrations

### Elizabeth

Elizabeth, a beautiful, cultured, 90-year-old, has been in analysis three times a week for seven years. She had a penchant for art, poetry and photography, but as her body failed these passions waned. Her mobility became compromised. Requiring a walker assaulted her aesthetic sensibilities. She complained about lesser things, her decline being too much to contemplate. Elizabeth's limitations began with two serious falls, hospitalization, and the diagnosis of spinal stenosis, which left her frail and afraid to move. The past few years have been reduced to their selling homes to which she and her husband can no longer travel.

Elizabeth's dominating husband refused to accept her growing limitations. After 65 active years together, he had great trouble facing her decline. Trying in vain to uphold his standards of fitness and perfection left her feeling like she was only a piece of art in his vast collection. With no emotional attunement between them, Elizabeth felt empty. He pressed her to attend social functions as they had always done. This was difficult for her, physically and mentally. She had no space or permission to mourn the loss of her agile, worldly self. Losing the spark and play of symbolization, there was no boost for her sagging spirit. She felt no optimism that the world still had something to offer her. There was nothing to look forward to. Unlike Wordsworth, who was still able to "dance with the daffodils" while lying on his couch in old age, Elizabeth was unable to use memories to find joy and strength.

Every day she made her way, well put together, to her chair in the drawing room next to the phone, maintaining the image for others. Her nails were done, hair was styled, makeup applied by staff. There she spent much of the day, "bored, discombobulated and discouraged."

I, too, became very discouraged. There was a "goneness" about her, a lack of connection between her self and the outer world, and even worse, her deep innerness. She experienced a constant melancholia for that which would never return. We were both deadened. There was no therapeutic progress. I could join her in nothingness or find a way out of the impasse.

A sliver of hope came one day when I mentioned that my grandmother, on hearing of my father's death, recited a line from a poem that I did not recognize: "let there be no moaning of the bar when I put out to sea." Sharing my grieving experience emerged from a strong desire to enliven her, to keep her from the powerfully active death forces. Elizabeth immediately recognized Tennyson's poem, "Crossing the Bar," named it for me, and delightedly recited the whole piece.

This "death" poem brought us both from the tomb, giving us in-between space where we could "dance with the daffodils" again. At our next meeting, Elizabeth brought me lines from Swinburne's "The Garden of Proserpine":

> Pale beyond porch and portal,
> Crowned with calm leaves, she stands.
> Who gathers all things mortal
> With cold immortal hands...
> …
> She waits for each and other,
> She waits for all men born.

Now we were talking about death – the thing that could not be named – but we were talking about it in a bearable way, through poetry's symbolic space. Elizabeth's liveliness was returning. We began a search for more poetry that applied as we made our way out of the "dead" concrete back into the "lively" symbolic.

Elizabeth seemed present again. I was reminded how William Blake (1982), close to the end of his life, observed in a letter that he had been near death and returned "very weak & an Old Man feeble & tottering, but not in Spirit & Life not in The Real Man The Imagination which Liveth for Ever. In that," he said, "I am stronger & stronger as this Foolish Body decays" (p. 783). Elizabeth was surely feeble in body, but the "Real Woman" in her was coming back to life. Her rejuvenation was based on symbolic acceptance of death through poetry.

I knew that her soul was finding peace many months later when she tearfully read me this stanza from Swinburne:

> From too much love of living,
> From hope and fear set free

We thank with brief thanksgiving
Whatever gods may be
That no life lives for ever;
That dead men rise up never;
That even the weariest river
Winds somewhere safe to sea.

## Jane

Jane, a 72-year-old retired academic, within one year of retirement, developed cancer. Three years later, metastases were found. Treated with radiation, she is in remission, closely followed. Despite health scares, she is doing well, calling her cancer "this precarious music," this "change of key."

Jane is in a second marriage to Robert, recently diagnosed with dementia. She was referred to me when he began to decline 18 months ago. Her first marriage was to Martin, who died after 20 years of marriage, when Jane was in her mid-fifties. Her mother died within a year of Martin's death. Her father died shortly afterwards.

Unlike Elizabeth, Jane resided more vividly in the uncertainty of her life, grateful for the days. And yet, while it was subtle, she had lost some of her life force. The two bouts of cancer, the loss of her first husband and parents, and the rapid decline of her second husband, left her shaken. She found herself, at the start of our work, in that indeterminate space between life and death forces. She felt haunted by the losses, yet was able to draw great pleasure from intellectual and musical pursuits. Jane had always looked forward to retirement, envisioned it as a new beginning where she could explore new territory, focusing more on personal growth. She often talked about the Victorian concept of "a good death" and wanted one for herself. Yet her suffering stalked her and she would take to a glass of wine and bed midday, sometimes in despair. Her sadness seemed unbearable at times, especially in the middle of the night. She would briefly talk to me about this sadness from a safe distance. She said she felt unworthy of psychoanalysis, with its focus on the self, but maintained the sessions, and our relationship deepened.

Jane approached analysis as if it were a seminar. She was task-oriented, arriving with her daily journal and handing me a copy. She was very interested in psychoanalytic ideas, reading voraciously. It was difficult for her to immerse herself in her feelings. She enjoyed sorting things out intellectually. I tried to seduce her out of the cold comfort of ideas into the vitality of relating and into a deep emotional engagement with her own feelings. It was very easy for me to be vitally present with her. She was the older, courageous woman missing in my life since my mother and aunt's death, and she was highly intellectual, which delighted my academic self.

Jane faced her illness as she lived her life. She went to the library and learned all she could, immersing herself in the death and dying literature. Working with Jane, I sometimes felt her no-nonsense, Calvinist approach to life's harsher events to be somewhat hollow, with little emotional texture. Dreams echoed this approach. In many, she saw water from a distance – tumultuous water overflowing its banks.

She was often on a cliff looking down, or safely on dry land. She thought of herself as T.S. Eliot's "village explainer," observing and describing the turmoil below.

One day, while she was discussing her meditation practice, I spoke of the consolation that could be found there, as in therapy. She did not like the word "consolation": "I guess I don't approve of consoling," she told me. "One can be stoic and courageous, or one can collapse and let someone take over. I want truth, not consolation."

I queried gently whether a third possibility could be entertained. Could she allow for feelings to knock on the door of her mind, the way Rumi describes in "The Guest House"? Could she invite them in? Could the sadness find its way in so that it could be worked through and symbolized? I invited her to share her feelings with me, adding that feelings were half as heavy if shared.

Jane was receptive to this third possibility, especially as it was presented through poetry. As with Elizabeth, poetry provided a medium for making feelings bearable. Jane had found that Amy Clampitt's (1997) "A Hermit Thrush" represented for her a therapeutic journey to a border area, a "healing place." She told me the border in this poem lies between two realms: one more-or-less hospitable to human life (life); the other indifferent, potentially deadly, and profoundly unknowable (death). The poem is about an anniversary picnic. The people have had a low-tide picnic on this isolated, wind-raked spot every year for a decade. Each time, they've been relieved to find island flora and fauna have survived the winter's gales:

> Still there,
> The gust-beleaguered single spruce tree,
> The ant-thronged, root-snelled moss, grass
> And clover tuffet, underneath it,
> Edges frazzled raw
> But, like our own prolonged attachment, *holding*.

Jane tells me the poem's meditation is on attachment, the healing attachment of the island plants, shrubs, and trees by tiny delicate threads to their soil, and the picnickers' attachment to each other and the place. The picnickers cannot know in advance whether the delicate threads of roots will have survived winter's battering. The attachments "are under many kinds of threat, beleaguered, broken, and much-mended, yet they appear to be as dependable as anything is likely to be in human experience."

Throughout this poem is the unspoken uncertainty as to whether there will be another picnic next year, reflecting Jane's uncertainty about her own life holding another year. She told me she didn't have any guy wires (ropes anchoring tents to the ground), but was thinking how a poem – this poem in particular – is one of those things of our own devising that anchor us, at least temporarily, to our uncertain world.

Through our working relationship, with the help of the symbolizing function of poetry, Jane connected to a feeling self. Her dreams became more important to her, less intellectualized. They indicate that Jane's avoidance of psychic pain has diminished considerably, and she is able to contemplate death.

Recently she told me a dream that brought together her grief for lost loved ones and her ability to grieve her own potential passing. There was no fear or suffering, just restfulness and joy in being with loved ones. In light of the dream, she said: "Death doesn't seem so frightening anymore."

Jane has allowed for the sadness and grief that had remained outside the guest house of her conscious mind, keeping her stuck in a "middle position." Her unfelt grief for her husband, parents, and herself kept her from truly feeling and symbolizing. Analysts, sharing the weight of these powerful feelings, mediated through poetry and dreams can render patients' feelings bearable, and usable for symbolization.

## *Theresa*

Art, another expression of creative imagination, allowed Theresa a symbolic channel for powerful, unintegrated feelings. She is an 80-year-old retired schoolteacher whose body began to slowly deteriorate over the past year. Nothing was life-threatening, but gastrointestinal difficulty, osteoarthritic knees, and a frozen shoulder all descended on her around the same time. When she was briefly admitted to hospital for shoulder surgery, it became apparent to both of us that her life force was weakening. She lost the will to get out of bed, or to resume any of the activities that had so enlivened this spirited woman. She also set aside her art, which had sustained and defined her in these latter years. Her understanding of her loss of will was limited. She had no words for it and temporarily withdrew from our work. As her shoulder began to recover, I spoke with her by telephone and asked her to paint her experience of her body's failure. Painting had helped me recover through a particularly difficult period in my own life. My patient's artistic proclivities encouraged me to think this activity might be useful for her, too.

Two weeks later, she agreed to see me and brought three paintings, depicting the pain she had experienced, and the accompanying shock and depression. The vivid colors and rich textures spoke of the depth and intensity of Theresa's trauma. Painting freed her to begin thinking about what she had gone through. We were able to resume our work, putting words to her experience of bodily failure.

Recently, Theresa reported that she was required to fill out a "Do not resuscitate" form, stating whether she wanted to be resuscitated in case of cardiac arrest and, if so, whether she wanted this resuscitation to be aggressive or palliative. She completed the form with little hesitation, indicating she wanted aggressive resuscitation. "I have a good deal of life left in me yet," she said firmly. "God and I have an agreement, and it is not my time yet."

For psychoanalysts, "man's last enemy" is not death, but the thought of death (De Masi, 2004), and the very real fact that our bodies fail. Contemplating death and failure of the body with patients through symbolic cultural forms allows for access to soulful psychological resources that can make death contemplatable. Poetry and art facilitated the therapeutic process with our patients, but in the end, as we all know, it is relatedness that saves and consoles. The intimacy and grasp between two connected souls renders these symbolic forms so powerful. In turn, it is creativity, with its life-affirming, generative potential, that allows the related-ness to take hold. Creativity within the human connection awakens the spirit and allows for its perseverance in the face of bodily failure. Tennyson's words from *In Memoriam* reverberate: "Let love clasp grief, lest both be drowned."

## Notes

1 The notion of the biological in the death force is given support by the work of molecular biologists (e.g., Ameisen, 1999; Clark, 1998). Ameisen points out that our cells have, at any given moment, the capacity to destroy themselves in a few hours by triggering an endogenous program of cell suicide. Their daily survival relies on signals from other cells that allow them to repress the onset of their own suicide.
2 Talking of parts of self implies a cohesive self, a notion widely challenged in recent years. We could talk of "multiple selves" and the "selves" that are lost, but to do so complicates the narrative, calling forth other contentious assumptions.

## References

Ameisen, J.C. (1999). *Al Cuore della Vita: Il Suicidio Cellulare e la Morte Creatrice.* Milan: Feltrinelli.

Anshin, R.N. (1985). Omnipotence and self-fulfillment: Key issues in analytically-oriented psychotherapy with older persons. *Journal of American Academy of Psychoanalysis,* 13: 247 258.

Blake, W. (1982). *The Complete Poetry and Prose of William Blake,* ed. D.V Erdman. Berkeley and Los Angeles: University of California Press. (Poem originally published in 1827.)

Clampitt, A. (1997). *The Collected Poems of Amy Clampitt.* Toronto: Random House.

Clark, R.W. (1998). *Sex and the Origin of Death.* Oxford: Oxford University Press.

De Masi, F. (2004). *Making Death Thinkable.* London: Free Association Books.

Freud, S. (1916). On transience. In J. Strachey (ed. and trans.), *The Standard Edition of the Complete Psychological Works of Sigmund Freud* (vol. 14, pp. 305–307). (Original work published 1916.)

Freud, S. (1917). Mourning and melancholia. In J. Strachey (ed. and trans.), *The Standard Edition of the Complete Psychological Works of Sigmund Freud* (vol. 14, pp. 243–258). (Original work published 1915.)

Herzog, B. (2007). Love and death: affect sharing in the treatment of the dying. In B. Willock, L.C. Bohm, & R.C. Curtis (eds.), *On Deaths and Endings.* London: Routledge, pp. 247–256.

Hume, D. (1775). *The Natural History of Religion,* ed. Wayne Colver. 1976.

Jacques, E. (1965). Death and the mid-life crisis. *International Journal of Psychoanalysis,* 46: 502–514.

Kaplan, S. (2007). Lessons from the hospice: when the body speaks. In B. Willock, L.C. Bohm, & R.C. Curtis (eds.), *On Death and Endings.* London: Routledge, pp. 217–236.

Lacan, J. (2008). *My Teaching,* trans. David Macey. London: Verso.

Long, S.W. (2007). A relational perspective on working with dying patients in a nursing home setting. In B. Willock, L.C. Bohm, & R.C. Curtis (eds.), *On Death and Endings.* London: Routledge, pp. 237–246.

McDougall, J. (1989). *Theatres of the Body.* London: Free Association Press.

Ricoeur, P. (2009). *Living up to Death.* Chicago: University of Chicago Press.

# 18

# BRIEF CANDLE

*Robert Langan*

Tomorrow and tomorrow and tomorrow
Creeps in its petty pace from day to day
To the last syllable of recorded time.
And all our yesterdays have lighted fools
The way to dusty death. Out, out brief candle!
Life's but a walking shadow, a poor player
Who struts and frets his hour upon the stage,
And then is heard no more. It is a tale
Told by an idiot, full of sound and fury,
Signifying nothing.
     (Shakespeare, *Macbeth*, 5.5.17–28)

The Scottish king's bitter lament upon hearing of the death of his queen bemoans our common fate, our shared failure. We fail to obliterate obliterating death. Our posturing is hollow. We cannot live forever. All our wishes cannot make it so. Wishes fail. Hopes for certainty and permanence evaporate. All those around me, you and I myself, change and disappear. We find ourselves, in fact, alike, in a like predicament before the swishing scythe of time.

*Children sing to one another about it:*

The worms crawl in, the worms crawl out,
The worms play pinochle on your snout.
They eat your eyes, they eat your toes,
They eat the boogers inside your nose.

The children laugh uneasily at the grossness of it all. They turn carnal death into a joke. But they cannot forget the last laugh is the joke's.

 Another children's song, this one a dashing tango, ends with our existential riddle:

Lep-ro-sy is crawling all over me.
There goes my eyeball
into your highball.
There goes my fingernail
into your ginger ale.
Catch me quick,
there goes my upper lip.
I have no nose to pick.
Where can I be?

Some children can comfort themselves with prayer:

Now I lay me down to sleep.
I pray the Lord my soul to keep.
But if I die before I wake,
I pray the Lord my soul to take.

Yet for those who put away prayer with childish things, little comfort is left. No leap of faith can cross the void.

Parents sing:

Rockabye baby, in the tree tops.
When the wind blows, the cradle will rock.
When the bough breaks, the cradle will fall,
And down will come baby, cradle and all.

The lucky thing for baby is in not being able to understand the lullaby's ominous words. Soon enough, all boughs break. The baby, however, need pay no attention. The baby is swaddled in the present moment, in the gentle comfort of mother's lulling voice, in the gentle letting go of sleep. Letting oneself go, it seems, is key.

Letting oneself go opens the timeless *nunc stans*, the ever-standing now of the present moment, the stepping aside from sequential time into the moment which endures forever. Past and future are flitting thoughts, much like oneself, in the presence of what is now occurring in the now of forever.

We get through childhood, most of us, with a convenient fiction that others may die while I shall live forever. The recollection of an experienced forever is strong. With luck, there's no time to think about death. No need to worry. Each success-fully succeeding day proves it can't happen to me. Here I am, growing then all grown up, leading my life, *I*, the indomitable center of my world.

Then, for some of us more than others, the world erodes indomitability. We cannot easily face it. No longer am I the master of my fate. Life leads my I through anger and despair, hope and disappointment, through sickness and aging, suffer-ing and loss, intractable problems in living. Life, in time, makes failures of us all.

Life confronts us with the problem of how, in the face of our human frailties, we best may live. Some few of us, in these our times, seek answers in psychoanalysis.

Psychoanalysis holds an appeal for those who are willing, or driven, to seize their time to reflect on the nature of how it is that *I* am this living, onflowing experience of becoming my not-to-be-forgotten self. Some few sign on for several sessions a week for several years. Even fewer sign on for the training to become psychoanalysts. Here we are, the practicing few.

To give so much time to this reflective endeavor can lend itself to childhood's illusion that time is forever. In psychoanalytic time, in those twosome hours in our scattered consulting rooms, an empty hollow cups our words and musings, our struts and frets, our itches and scratches and unthinking glances towards the clock. We protect ourselves with the assumption that there shall be – don't give it a thought – our next session. And the one after that. Yet lurking in the shadow is the sometime none after that, when my now shall be no more.

This background small-print guarantee of failure, the inevitability of mortality, whether explicit or implicit, informs the fundamental nature of the psychoanalytic endeavor. From this perspective every patient – indeed, every analyst – presents an idiosyncratic variation of the same problem: how to live a life signifying something, however fleeting, in the face of oblivion. And the psychoanalytic process, the therapeusis, becomes a letting go of the fortress castle of a well-defended self oblivious to termination, and an opening to the bare-faced meeting of one another in our shared brief time and common plight. Instead of buttressing what *is* or what *should be* in a vain attempt to make the monument of the imperious *I* last forever, the process potentially reveals timelessness and unbounded spaciousness in the moment's gift of presence of you and me, me one and you other, me your other, you my one.

Here in the now we rest, while we cannot remain. We continuously arise and pass away, our living experience both separate and co-created, both *data* given and *capta* chosen and all soon forgotten.

We rise and fall on waves of onflowing experience in which we can dare to meet, and to find significance through one another. We are holding hands while letting go.

A couple who did not know one another met at an open window on the top floor of a burning skyscraper. Smoke and flames drove them out. He took her hand, she his. They helped each other to the sill, no going back. Still holding hands, they leapt. The banshee shriek of rising wind against their falling bodies sucks screams from their expiring lungs. Yet they grip each other's hands, their terror of falling touch-comforted, known and unknown together. And you and I, hearing and speaking, see them now in mind's eye, feel wind blast on our falling faces, clench together our white-knuckled hands, know the final impassive explosive impact of letting go.

Is letting go death? Yes, but no. Letting go entails an acceptance of death which is an actively chosen letting, not a passive surrender. There may be no necessity to "Rage, rage, against the dying of the light," but rather an equanimous acceptance of sunset's concomitant nightrise over a still, reflecting lake, the eye of ourselves. The rage, perhaps, appears, with the urge to go down in battle like a valiant warrior, but the rage is only part of it. There is also longing more for the sweetness of life, for love and beauty, for the dearness of others; regret for opportunities lost and mistakes made, work unfinished; fear of the unknown, and pain; addled confusion, paranoid blame; and just perhaps, a measure of relief at being finally released, undone, in fact: free. The feelings and thoughts are ripplings on the surface of this bottomless lake, unborn and undying, in itself no thing but a fluid transparency embracing the universe in emptiness. The letting go, then, is not only death, but simultaneously a disappearance and an expansion, a stepping outside of time, beyond form and place. The struts and frets of life matter, because they are the forms in which we find one another. We are pleased to meet one another, forms in time and place. Our forms change, girl body to woman, boy to man, both to dust. Living through life's forms while more and less open to the letting go of form allows the freedom to live one's dying – that is, to be no thing.

*Another king, Richard II, knew this well:*

Thus play I in one person many people,
And none contented
… but whate'er I be,
Nor I, nor any man that but man is,
With nothing shall be pleased till he be eased
With being nothing.
            (Shakespeare, *Richard II*, 5.5.31–41)

Let me proceed with a clinical example of someone who, I believe, found in the course of her dying an ease in being no thing.

When I first met J she was 44 years old, single, working as a corporate executive secretary, and sober five years in Alcoholics Anonymous after decades of alcohol, cocaine, and barbiturate abuse. Our therapeutic work would continue off and on for fifteen years.

What troubled her initially was a difficulty relating to others. Not being included in an office party invitation prompted an upsurge of paranoid suspicions, and the vivid re-emergence of childhood feelings of isolation. Her earliest memory came up: She is an infant, lying on her back in the middle of a large bed, feeling from the window a warm wind, trying very hard to notice the details of the room, trying with great effort to be present. No one is there with her.

Expectably, much of the ensuing therapeutic focus was on how she and I were, or might be, together. Was I genuinely present, or just a paid-for-services comforter? Could she dare to be herself with me? What self? She felt split between her mousy sober self, the organized capable secretary, and the flamboyant party-girl drinker she had been as the right-hand manager, and lover, of the rich European art gallery owner who toyed with her sixteen years, then dropped her. Her first dream was of her own face painted down the midline, half white, half black, with a tall crewcut hairdo that might be militarily severe or outrageously punk.

She would needle me, sometimes, insisting I drop my therapeutic stance. She could knock me off my perch, though now I have conveniently forgotten how. She pushed for what she wanted, an honesty about my thoughts and feelings despite anxiety, which allowed her to risk that honesty herself. She could disorganize me, and trust me to reorganize myself as her therapist. It was months before she could relax enough to put her feet up on the footstool in my consulting room.

Only then could she reveal the shameful memory she had occasionally referred to in our sessions, but never told anyone. She was perhaps 5, playing in the yard with her best friend. She thought to show her something she had recently discovered. They went under a bush, pulled down their underpants, and she was showing her how good it felt to rub when her mother screamed down from above, leaning out a second-story window. She ordered the other girl to go home, ordered my patient into the house, where she beat her, telling her over and over again how she was utterly disgusting. As she told me the memory she marveled at how innocent she had been, and at how very disgusting her mother had made her feel, and at how unashamed she felt to tell it now.

That house loomed large for her, and became a symbol of herself. She described how it looked fine on the outside, well maintained, lawnmowed, as prosperously respectable as any of its neighbors. But when she walked through the front door, it was "Cambodia!" – by which she meant the war-ravaged, blood-soaked place of screams, anger, and mayhem. She battled with her sister, feared her lashing tyrannical alcoholic mother, missed the traveling father, who, when he was home, confused her with compliments about how pretty she was, how he favored her over her sister, over her mother, how he wished it were just the two of them together.

So we looked at her history, at her struggles to accept herself against her inclination to obliterate herself, at her relationships, at our relationship, at how she was coming to value the life she was shaping for herself.

About the eleventh year of treatment, her breast cancer was diagnosed. She took it as a call to do her best to take care of herself. She read up on options, got second opinions, made sure her calls were answered. Her operation appeared successful. When she was discharged, I paid home visits so we could meet face to face. She was proud to show me that her neat and tidy apartment was not Cambodia.

After she returned to work she decided to take a break from therapy, feeling her life was going well enough. When her cancer recurred, she came back. It had spread to her brain. Doctors told her she had less than a year to live. She marshaled herself, doing what she could about medical decisions and her affairs, while she was able to attend to them. By this time her family was gone and her friends few. She talked about what she would like in a memorial service, joking that it was like planning her last party. When it was clear she could no longer leave hospitalization, she asked me not to call or visit unless she first called me, because she wanted us to meet only if she was having a good day. It put me in a parallel limbo. She never knew how she'd feel; I never knew if she'd call.

She called. She had been transferred to a different hospice. Could I bring cranberry juice? I arranged the time, remembered the juice. The nurses' station was like the hub of a wheel, patients' single rooms ringing round it. She was lying on a high bed, her window open to let in the breeze. She had made herself up, and put on a necklace and earrings, somewhat incongruous with her hospital gown. She greeted me warmly, thanked me for the juice, and complimented my suit. She told me she was on morphine, but that it was all right, she felt like herself. We chatted, about nothing of consequence. I don't think it was the morphine, but she seemed reconciled and content. It was as if nothing was of consequence, nothing pressing. She was happy to see me, then and there.

She asked me to help her get out of bed to go to the bathroom. I don't believe we'd ever touched before. She was frail, and shuffled. The bathroom echoed, and she was a little embarrassed when she came back for my help to get into bed. But not so embarrassed: simply there she was, stinky body, clear mind. She said she wanted to rest. We said our goodbyes, briefly holding hands and letting go. I left her lying on her back in the middle of her bed, feeling from the window a warm wind, very much occupying her time and place, present.

Without hearing from her, I did call the next week. The nurse at the station told me no information could be released, but that no one by her name was there.

Just so, she slipped away. The friend who was to organize her memorial never did. As I tell her story, this is my memorial. She rests in mind. Her goodbye was to pull herself together for our last visit, and to show herself to me eased, as it were, with being nothing.

## Bibliography

Becker, E. (1973). *The Denial of Death*. New York: Free Press.

Farber, L. (1966). *The Ways of the Will: Essays toward a Psychology and Psychopathology of Will*. New York: Basic Books.

Langan, R.P. (2002). Portals. *Contemporary Psychoanalysis*, 38: 477–484.

Pickering, W. & Whittingham, C., the Younger (1853). *The Book of Common Prayer, Ornamented with Wood Cuts from Designs of Albert Durer, Hans Holbein, and Others. In Imitation of Queen Elizabeth's Book of Christian Prayers*. London: Folio Society, 2004.

Shakespeare, W. (1606). *The Tragedy of Macbeth*, ed. A. Harbage. Baltimore, MD: Penguin, 1956.

Shakespeare, W. (1623). *The Tragedy of King Richard the Second*, ed. R.T. Petersson. New Haven: Yale University Press, 1957.

Thomas, D. (2003). Rage, rage against the dying of the light. In *Collected Poems 1934–1953*, ed. W. Davies & R. Maud. London: Phoenix.

# Part VII

# METAPHORIC BRIDGES
# AND CREATIVITY

# 19

# OTTO RANK'S NOTION OF THE NEUROTIC AS THE *ARTISTE MANQUÉ*

*Ann Baranowski*

I first heard about Rank when I read Ernest Becker's Pulitzer prizewinning book, *The Denial of Death* (1973), in the late 1970s. Becker hoped his encounter with Rank would "send the reader directly to Rank's books" (1973, xx). This is exactly what happened for me, and I ended up writing a Master's thesis on Rank. I wrote that thesis many years ago, before I began my clinical practice. I want to revisit his idea of the neurotic as *artiste manqué* now in order to think about the idea's clinical relevance. Before I address the value of this notion, I provide some background on Rank[1].

Many psychoanalysts today know very little or nothing about Rank (sometimes confusing him with Theodore Reik or Wilhelm Reich). His works have been sadly overlooked by most in the field. This is unfortunate since his post-Freudian writings are filled with remarkable theoretical insight and clinical wisdom.

From 1905 to 1925, Rank was a central member of the early psychoanalytic movement. Born in 1884, 28 years younger than Freud, they met in 1905, when Rank was 21 and Freud was 49. Rank came to the professor with a manuscript called *The Artist*, which he wrote when he was 20. Freud said the manuscript revealed "very unusual comprehension" (Lieberman, 1985, pp. 41–42). This essay, about the sexual psychology of the artist, pointed out that Freud's psychology could not explain the creative type. Rank's preoccupation with creativity and the artist continued in all his subsequent writings. Freud hired Rank in 1906 and, at the age of 22, he became secretary of the Vienna Psychoanalytic Society. He remained its secretary for 18 years. During this time, Freud nurtured Rank's prodigious talent and supported his education.

In 1924, Rank wrote *The Trauma of Birth*. This became his most well-known work which is unfortunate since it represents just the beginning of his creative efforts, but is far from the full statement of his mature views presented in later works. Near the end of his life, Rank said he wished he'd never written it (Lieberman, 1985, p. 225). In this book, Rank discussed the trauma of separation and how separation is an essential feature of the task of forming a personality.

He compared the creative drive with the individual's self creation. In other words, Rank likened human development to the creative process.

Rank came to the US that same year as ambassador for psychoanalysis. At the American Psychoanalytic Association (APA) meeting in 1924, Rank was awarded honorary APA membership. Over the next two years, he continued his break from Freud over growing differences in theory and technique. In *The Trauma of Birth*, which signified his own birth and separation from Freud, he said the mother-child relationship was primary. Most of psychoanalysis now accepts this premise, but at the time this notion was sacrilege.

At first, Freud praised the book, "accepting it as the greatest progress since the beginning of psychoanalysis" (Lieberman, 1985, p. 225). As Rank became a rising star, he began to be slandered by jealous psychoanalytic siblings, especially Ernest Jones and Karl Abraham. Their opinions of Rank influenced Freud to gradually withdraw from him. Rank eventually separated from Freud and his inner circle and went to live and work in Paris and the US. Since his ideas were diverging greatly from central tenets of psychoanalysis, he ultimately stopped calling himself a psychoanalyst, developing, practicing, and teaching what he called "will therapy."

Over the next few years, rumors spread that Rank was manic and psychotic. While he initially applauded the book, Freud later called *The Trauma of Birth* "the theory in which he deposited his neurosis" (Kramer, 1996, p. 36). At the 1930 Washington, DC APA meeting, president A.A. Brill, who regarded Rank's ideas as arising from a mental disorder, put forth a motion to remove Rank's APA membership. The motion was seconded by Harry Stack Sullivan, voted on, and passed. Those analyzed by Rank had to be reanalyzed to keep their APA membership. After his falling out with Freud and psychoanalysis, Rank did not fight the slander and hostility, but carried on writing and practicing in the US.

Rank went from being part of Freud's inner "Ring" committee, and perhaps the colleague who was the closest to Freud, to possibly the least known of Freud's disciples. There are several reasons for this. First, after his excommunication, Rank's works were rarely quoted since to do so would be to put one's own reputation at risk. Also, Rank's books are incredibly hard to read. His writing style is often overly academic, and he did not write about cases.

Many of Rank's ideas are now part of accepted contemporary psychoanalytic practice, but Rank is not credited with introducing them. In addition to being the first to emphasize the primacy of the mother, the notion of "denial" was first articulated, not by Freud or his daughter Anna, but by Rank. He was the first to use the term "preoedipal" and write about the significance of this early period. He wrote about separation and individuation before Mahler. His focus on the present therapeutic relationship, the therapeutic relationship itself as mutative, and his emphasis on new as opposed to repeated, old experience, anticipates important features of interpersonal and relational psychoanalysis. As I will show below, ideas we now associate with Winnicott, such as seeing therapy as play, are present in Rank's works. Winnicott's analyst said, "Winnie should be a Rankian, not a Freudian" (Solomon, 1998).

One of Rank's most valuable contributions is that he likens human life and growth to the creative process. In broad strokes, this process, as he saw it, begins with separation, an emergence from dependency brought about by pushing away from someone or something. We see this process in birth, weaning, and walking, but also in the psychological birth of the self that Rank called "self creation." To create or grow, we must first say "no" to some other, before we can say "yes." This "no" produces guilt, and how we respond to this guilt determines the *type* of person we are.

Rank proposed a typology. The main characters are the neurotic and artistic types. He also talked about the average type, but much less so. He did not restrict his understanding of "artist" to painters, poets, composers, etc. He used the term broadly to refer to the productive type, and regarded personality creation as the highest creative act. He recognized that there are no pure types. Each of us has aspects of each.

The neurotic is stuck in the negative expression of will that Rank called "counter-will." The neurotic is an *artiste manqué*, an artist who has not been able to express will positively. Neurosis in this sense is a perversion of creativity. One difference between neurotics and artists is that, while neurotics are unable to bear the guilt that comes with any expression of will, artists are *motivated* by guilt into further artistic expression, paying for guilt with creative acts which give back to life.

"Will" is the central concept in Rank's thinking. By "will" he meant the "creative aspect of the personality ... which distinguishes one individual from another" (Rank, 1938, p. 268). He had read Nietzsche and Schopenhauer and knew well their thoughts about will, but his notion differed both from Nietzsche's tendency to glorify will and Schopenhauer's tendency to vilify it. By will, Rank does not mean will power. Will, for Rank, is that which acts upon, not merely reacts to, the environment. The will of the individual, as Rank conceives it, is a first cause and produces something new. Rank did not deny that we are shaped by past experiences and that we have unconscious motivations. To focus on these exclusively, however, was to lose sight of the fact that we can also be motivated by conscious acts of will. Psychoanalysis, Rank said, recognized will, but never in its positive expression, calling it instead "resistance" and judging it as something to be overcome.

In an age of scientific determinism, Rank's focus on will was alarming to many. Jessie Taft, Rank's friend, translator, and first biographer, wrote about attending a seminar in New York dedicated to studying Rank's works: "I can still recall the sudden shock created by his use of the word 'will,' so long taboo in academic circles as a remnant of faculty psychology and therapeutically akin to quackery. Only someone with the force and brilliance of a Rank could have carried this medically oriented group through a change so sudden and complete" (Taft, 1958, p. xiv).

It is not uncommon to hear patients say things such as "It's just who I am. I can't do anything differently." Rank would view this as a beautiful example of what he called "counter-will." Patients' counter-will opposes the implicit "will" of the therapist whom they presume wants them to change, or perhaps demands they change. The neurotic is stuck in this negative will. "All neurotic reactions can be thus reduced to one Big No that men hurl at life" (Rank, 1935, p. 258). Neurosis, for Rank, is not about being ill, but about being caught in this initial phase of development. Neurotics live their lives in opposition to someone else. They view external norms as compulsions they must continually oppose.

Neurotics are typically viewed as weak-willed, especially because they often blatantly deny their will, most noticeably in the therapeutic context. In Rank's view, both the artist and the neurotic are strong-willed. Both have a creative urge. The artist is able to objectify this urge in works of art, while neurotics are unable to channel it positively.

Rank also differentiated the neurotic and the artist by how each responds to fear. We move, he says, between fear of life and fear of death. Fear of life is fear of becoming a separate person. If we manage to overcome this fear of life and experience our separateness, this can bring our mortality and fear of death into consciousness. Fear of death can lead to the desire to immortalize and perpetuate the self through creative expression. The self is created in the struggle with these two fears: fear of becoming a self through individuation and fear of losing the self through either merging with the other or dissolving into the whole through death.

If the creative life involves being able to master fear of separation on the one hand and fear of annihilation on the other, it is no wonder many of us fail! For the neurotic, these fears are experienced in the extreme, interfering with functioning and inhibiting self creation. As Rank sees it, life is a loan, death is the payment. The neurotic "refuses the loan (life) in order to avoid the payment of the debt (death)" (1929c, p. 126), a sort of "You can't fire me, I quit!"

Will for the neurotic is denied and projected onto fate, the gods, the id, the other, or the therapist. We can hear will projected onto fate in the following: "All I ever do is ruin things"; "I fail at everything"; "I'm doomed to be the person everyone uses." Will can be projected onto the therapist, as with a patient who worries, "What is she gonna want me to talk about this time?" Will is projected because it is deemed too dangerous to own, since to do so would not only bring about unbearable guilt, but also terrifying separation from parental introjects.

When Rank wrote about the neurotic, he was intentionally using Freud's term, but giving it new meaning. He understood neurosis, not in terms of internal conflict and repressed drives, but as miscarried creativity. He thought Freudian psychoanalysis misunderstood neurotics and their will problem and Freudian technique could only leave the neurosis more entrenched. The basic analytic injunction of free association, Rank says, "specifically states, eliminate entirely the little bit of will which your neurotic weakness has perhaps not yet undermined and resign yourself to the guidance of the unconscious, to the id" (Rank, 1929c, p. 11). Thankfully, he concludes, such "Buddhistic will-lessness" is impossible, since will is the therapeutic foundation of analysis, and indeed, for Rank, is its only therapeutic value.

Furthermore, in Rank's view, the Freudian focus on helping neurotics gain insight into their motives, seeing through their manifest thoughts, words, and behaviors to latent meanings, also betrays lack of understanding about neurosis. Many neurotics, he thought, had no trouble *seeing through*, but their insight was crippling or used as punishment. For many neurotics, seeking the truth of their motives can be destructive. "With the truth," Rank (1929b) says, "one cannot live. To be able to live one needs illusions." (p. 42). Jessie Taft, explains that by "illusion" Rank is not referring to something false, nor about deceiving the self. Rather, he means illusion (as Winnicott would later understand it) as play, making reality our own (Rank 1929c, p. 173 fn. 1). Illusions are those external worlds we create to live in, whether artistic, philosophical, religious, or scientific. Will and potency are inner illusions which ultimately, in face of mortality, are vital lies protecting us from death anxiety.

In his 1929 book *Will Therapy* (subtitled *An Analysis of the Therapeutic Process In Terms of Relationship*), Rank considers the therapeutic task to be liberation of the individual will. How exactly would Rank set about to do this? Again, because Rank gave no case illustrations, it is unclear.

Rank gave only a few examples of what he actually did clinically. In a 1929 Yale lecture, he shows how he invites positive expressions of will: "When I explain a mechanism or a symptom to a patient, the immediate reply is, 'All right, I see it, but what am I going to do about it?' I say, 'You must be patient, you must wait and see, I cannot predict anything, I can only tell you what you are doing, but not what you are *going* to do'" (Rank, 1929a, p. 240).

While Rank said very little about technique, he did have a lot to say about therapeutic action. He maintained that neurotic suffering is emotional and the curative agent is the therapeutic situation. Patients bring their old, well-worn ways of being into therapy, but they are also reacting to a new relationship. Rank thought patients' reactions to this unique relationship were the only therapeutic value of psychoanalysis. Therapy for Rank was an intense mutual emotional experience. He provided the setting, the playground where patients could find and feel their strength. He let himself be the stuff they used to develop positive will. As they expressed their will against his, and as Rank gave room to the expression of their will, they could come to feel their positive will. The goal of will therapy is not to conquer resistance, but to transform counter-will into creative expression. Patient and therapist interact, providing the treatment's therapeutic action.

One contemporary psychoanalytic writer is remarkably Rankian. While never referring to Rank or crediting him, Frank Summers' recent book, *Self Creation* (2005), proposes a very similar view of therapeutic action. Even the book title is a term Rank used frequently, since he thought that creation of one's personality was the highest creative act. Summers begins his book with the very same dilemma Rank spoke about in his Yale lecture in which the patient says: "Ya, I know that doc, but what do I do about it?" Summers even views patients as "failed artists," the term so central in Rank's thinking about neurosis. He refers to Adam Phillips (1998, pp. 3–4) as the person who gives us this "beautifully worded phrase" (Summers, 2005, p. 270). Neither Summers nor Phillips credit Rank.

Summers points out that every school of psychoanalysis understands therapeutic action as something the *analyst* does. Whether it is interpreting, empathizing, performing selfobject functions, optimally responding, performing holding or containing functions, the emphasis is on analysts' actions while patients remain in a passive role. Summers adds to Winnicott's notion of potential space, showing how it can be used by the patient to transform insight into creative self expression. Here Summers' understanding of therapeutic action is precisely what Rank advocated. Long before Winnicott, Rank saw the therapeutic situation as life lifted to an illusory play level (Rank, 1929c, p. 174). In this playground, therapists facilitate the patients' self creation.

Rank saw that neurotics typically have insight into the dynamics which leave them feeling so stuck, but this insight does not lead to change. We are most helpful, according to his vision of therapeutic action (and, currently, Summers') when we are able to enter into potential space, recognize, and welcome patients' unrealized potential, dormant capabilities, hidden agency, or even the faintest wisp of desire buried deep within their negative expression of will. The patient is invited to be the actor. It is Rank's vision of the patient as failed artist that helps me keep in the front of my mind my patient's creativity and will. Rank's will therapy also encourages the creativity of the therapist. He gives no formula, just a profound understanding of the relational nature of will and how it plays out interpersonally. He invites *us* to use this understanding creatively as we strive to recognize and relate to our patients' positive will so it need not be denied, buried, projected onto us, or abandoned to a cruel fate.

## Note

1  The background information comes mostly from Lieberman's (1985) excellent biography of Rank, *Acts of Will*, as well as Taft (1958), Menaker (1982), and Karpf (1953).

## References

Becker, E. (1973). *The Denial of Death*. New York: The Free Press.

Karpf, F.B. (1953). *The Psychology and Psychotherapy of Otto Rank: An Historical and Comparative Introduction*. New York: Philosophical Library.

Kramer, R. (1996). Insight and Blindness: Visions of Rank. In R. Kramer (ed.), *A Psychology of Difference: The American Lectures*. Princeton, NJ: Princeton University Press, pp. 3–47.

Lieberman, E.J. (1985). *Acts of Will: The Life and Work of Otto Rank*. New York: The Free Press.

Menaker, E. (1982). *Otto Rank: A Rediscovered Legacy*. New York: Columbia University Press.

Phillips, A. (1998). *The Beast in the Nursery: On Curiosity and Other Appetites*. New York: Vintage Books.

Rank, O. (1929a). The Yale Lecture. In *A Psychology of Difference: The American Lectures*, ed. Robert Kramer. Princeton: Princeton University Press, 1996, pp. 240–250.

Rank, O. (1929b). *Truth and Reality: A Life History of the Human Will*, trans. J. Taft. New York: Norton, 1936.

Rank, O. (1929c/1931). *Will Therapy: An Analysis of the Therapeutic Process in Terms of Relationship*. Trans. J. Taft. New York: Norton, 1978. Originally published in 2 vols.

Rank, O. (1935). Neurosis as a failure in Creativity. In R. Kramer (ed.), *A Psychology of Difference: The American Lectures*. Princeton: Princeton University Press, 1996.

Rank, O. (1938). Modern psychology and social change. In R. Kramer (ed.), *A Psychology of Difference: The American Lectures*. Princeton, NJ: Princeton University Press, 1996, pp. 264–275.

Solomon, S. (1998). Just Say No? Humans Make the Unreal Real! Lecture at the Ernest Becker Foundation, with discussions by Tom Pace and Eugene Web, Ernest Becker Foundation, Seattle, March 19.

Summers, F. (2005). *Self Creation: Psychoanalytic Therapy and the Art of the Possible*. Hillsdale, NJ: Analytic Press.

Taft, J. (1958). *Otto Rank: A Biographical Study Based on Notebooks, Letters, Collected Writings, Therapeutic Achievements and Personal Associations*. New York: Julian Press.

# 20

# STANDING TALL

## Bodily metaphors in a case of self-defeating personal failure

### *Christopher A. McIntosh*

We often come to understand our psychic life through metaphors (Lakoff & Johnson, 2003). Metaphors can help us deal with diffuse, abstract concepts, bringing them into focus. They also offer a nuanced way of communicating something that may be difficult to express directly, which is likely why their use is ubiquitous in psychoanalysis.

This chapter discusses how bodily metaphors enriched the psychoanalysis of Scott, a man who, by his mid-forties, had suffered a series of medical, occupational, and personal failures. These failures took him from a privileged position as a well-regarded graduate student, thought to have a promising career ahead, to being destitute, unemployed, and living in a hostel room strewn with garbage. The fact that this protracted fall began with bodily failure (the onset of chronic lower back pain) may explain why, as analysis progressed, metaphors about the body were key in the development of Scott's capacity to be more self-reflective.

Scott's proficiency in a school of Japanese martial arts, Aikido, also became remarkably fertile ground for self-understanding. We explored and worked through Scott's significant challenges with affect and bodily regulation, assertion and dependency, fear of success, and management of relationships via metaphoric reference to the bodily skills and positioning in this martial art.

The development of Aikido, as well as its underlying philosophy, are meaningful to understanding this case. Aikido was created by Morihei Ueshiba, a former soldier and martial arts teacher, who lived in Japan from 1889 to 1963. The son of a farmer and local politician, Ueshiba was a weak, sickly child but was encouraged by his father to pursue athletic activities to become stronger. He took to strengthening his body after his father was attacked by the thugs of a rival politician. Ueshiba had a lot of "nervous energy" and struggled in school and jobs because of boredom and distraction. He discovered an affinity for martial arts and pursued military training. After leaving the military, he continued training and instructing in martial arts.

A series of spiritual experiences in his early forties led him to become a pacifist. He therefore developed his own distinct martial arts and religious philosophy, Aikido, translated as "the way of the harmonious spirit." Aikido was a melding of Ueshiba's martial arts training in ju-jitsu with his religious philosophy of universal peace and reconciliation. In practice, the defender, called *Nage*, must protect himself from the assault of the attacker (*Uke*), by using a series of throws that blend with the movement of *Uke*. Of utmost importance is that *defensive maneuvers must neutralize the attack without harming the attacker*. As we shall see, this central philosophy of Aikido comports well with what Scott needed to learn in relating to people in his life outside of Aikido and analysis.

About a year into our work, Scott decided to resume practicing Aikido. At that point he was failing in most areas of life. Surgery to repair his back injury failed, leaving him in chronic pain. His wife asked him to leave the home they shared with their two daughters. His attempt to resume the practicum component of his advanced engineering degree, from which he had been on medical leave due to his back injury, failed. He lost his remaining income source after a researcher terminated Scott's part-time work contract. After he and his roommate were evicted from their apartment, he lived in a hostel. These failures left him feeling defeated, with no motivation to clean his room, which, as a result, was strewn with garbage.

During the first year of analysis, Scott expressed little affect. The work had an intellectualized quality. In his life and analytic work, it became clear that anger was an emotion about which he was highly conflicted. This problem began to shift in an incident with his roommate, Tanya, after she refused to pay any more than $100 for the final month's rent. "I thought about how it just wasn't right that people stay rent-free. I knocked on Tanya's door and said 'People don't stay in apartments for free. I don't want $100, I want the whole amount you owe me.' She started to say that $100 was all she was comfortable paying. I'm not proud of myself, but I got really angry at her. I felt so badly, but I was yelling at her, this is something that I *never* do [Scott's emphasis]. She went and got a cheque and wrote it out for the whole amount. She asked me why I hadn't said something earlier."

"You said you felt really badly."

"I work so hard at trying to be understanding, to be the nice gentle guy."

Indeed, this was something Scott worked very hard at since his teens. Like Morihei Ueshiba, Scott grew up on a farm, and had "nervous energy" to spare. In fact, Scott first presented to my general psychiatric practice wondering whether he suffered from Attention Deficit Hyperactivity Disorder. He gave a compelling "Dennis the Menace" narrative of a hyperactive, impulsive, inattentive child who frequently failed to adequately perform farm chores. By his teens, his family characterized him as an oddball screw-up, to which he responded with furious expressions of property damage and self-abuse via heavy drinking and careless accidents. At a certain point, he, like Ueshiba, had a spiritual experience. He decided he would turn things around by taking to heart the Fifth Commandment: "Honor thy father and mother." Almost overnight, things changed. He quit drinking and stopped hanging out with his shady friends. He tackled his studies with renewed vigor and devoted himself to his Evangelical Christian church. He graduated with high marks from high school and went on to study engineering, receiving accolades from teachers. At university, the boorish, obnoxious behavior of some students challenged his defenses against anger. He recounted an episode at the residence where, in a fit of rage, he bodily lifted a hefty floor-mate and threw him down the hall. Around the same time, he became involved with martial arts. After trying several schools, he settled on Aikido.

Scott and I have often returned to a bodily metaphor that emerged from an event some months after his wife asked him to leave. Scott, who is nearly 2 metres tall, has a somewhat slumped, slouching posture that causes him to appear shorter. One day while Scott was back at the family home, helping with household chores and childcare, he decided to stand taller and not slouch. He immediately noticed his wife looked at him differently, with admiration or respect, instead of her usual derisive expression. This was eye-opening to Scott and was the first of a series of metaphors of posture or body positioning that we made use of in our work. However, a cautionary signal from Scott's unconscious appeared in the form of a dream a few months later:

> I am walking with my daughter, Tracy, and we enter this park. In the park there is a dog … or a wolf. From the distance, another figure comes running toward us. It is a dog running on its hind legs! It has googly, cartoonish eyes and teeth. From behind the park's trees, more dogs are coming out to surround us, running in circles around us. Just as a dog tries to bite at our legs, I wake up.

The dog running on hind legs (standing tall) is a frightening image of naked, undisguised aggression. Scott's description of the running figure's cartoonishness led me to picture it as an amalgam of The Road Runner and his nemesis, Wile E. Coyote, from the classic Warner Brothers cartoons. The Coyote is a predator who is perpetually foiled attempting to obtain what he wants despite ever-more-elaborate plans to entrap his prey. Over time, the audience develops sympathy for the hapless bumbler and irritation with the smugly superior Road Runner. Who is truly the aggressor in the cartoons?

In the dream, Scott is walking with his daughter and there is immediately an issue of correctly perceiving an aggressor. Is the first animal a harmless dog, or feral wolf? This could represent difficulty distinguishing between whom one should trust and of whom one should be wary. It is also a depiction of Scott's ambivalent self-representation: "Am I a lovable, loyal pet, or a wild, ferocious beast?"

Scott's functioning began to improve as he continued to participate in mutually reinforcing Aikido and psychoanalysis. Regular exercise improved his physical strength and endurance, which led to less back pain. As Scott's chronic pain eased, he became more able to self-reflect. He began to comprehend his contribution to his situation rather than thinking about it exclusively from a paranoid, victimized position. With this greater sense of agency, Scott began to feel he could re-engage with his family and pursue academic work as well as the testing and advancement process of Aikido.

The *sensei*, or Aikido teacher at Scott's *dojo*, was a small, elderly woman whom Scott greatly admired. She encouraged him to test for the next level in the progression toward black belt status. Scott felt honored she asked and committed to doing so. As the test date approached, I became more anxious about it than he (at least consciously). Scott regressed in his ability to set boundaries on his wife's intrusive, demanding behavior. He was missing Aikido sessions to perform chores at the family home (from which he was otherwise barred). In the first session that followed the test, I was almost afraid to ask how it went. Scott passed. His body knew the forms required for this test well. This time, his body had not failed him, despite his unconscious mind's attraction to repeating a failure pattern.

When Scott began practising in earnest for the next level, he began to notice another self-defeating pattern. When he was defending against an attack by *Uke*, his form was impaired because he paid overly intense attention to his attacker's welfare. He was not just concerned about not harming *Uke*, which is a requirement of Aikido's philosophy, but he did not want to *inconvenience Uke*! As a result, Scott contorted himself in a way that actually hindered both participants from using proper form, and was therefore less safe for both. He described his correction of this problem as "pulling back" his attention from its near-exclusive focus on the attacker to a middle ground between the two. We could apply this discovery to his relationships. Scott needed to pull back from exclusive attention to what others think about him, assuming they think poorly of him, as did his parents and siblings.

Scott's pulling back to "middle ground" was a new experience. Previously there had been no middle ground, especially when it came to anger. There was either the explosive, world-ending anger that fuelled his teen years of property destruction and alcohol abuse, or its opposite, as when he erased his anger and vowed to unconditionally honor his parents. A middle ground of healthy assertion of his self and needs had not been an option, because he believed doing so could hurt, harm, or inconvenience others.

Arnold Modell (2007) describes metaphor as mapping or transferring meaning between dissimilar domains. He notes most metaphors are embodied in that they are generally developed from bodily feelings and sensations. Standing tall is not the only bodily metaphor for an assertive approach to the world. The more commonly used metaphor for assertiveness in a psychoanalytic context is the erect penis. Is the metaphorical link between assertion and erection innately any more meaningful than the link between assertion and posture? While both are useful, the latter is a simpler, more generalizable metaphor, and not just because it is applicable to all genders. The penis metaphor unnecessarily associates sexual arousal with assertion. The legacy of this historical association has been a denigration (as weak) or outright pathologizing (as deviant) of sexual arousal associated with a more passive sexual position, and hence psychoanalysis' past problematic stance on the sexuality of women and homosexual men. Metaphors of posture or bodily positioning, on the other hand, illustrate the link between assertion and aggression or anger, a more generalizable, intuitive association.

Modell argues that his broader definition of metaphor allows us to consider non-language-based examples, such as bodily metaphors. My work with Scott supports the usefulness of bodily metaphors. A strictly language-based definition of metaphor precludes thinking about the metaphoric aspects of non-verbal communication. When we consider meanings of relational enactments in analysis, we often attend to non-verbal metaphoric communication.

Scott was my first control case during my analytic training. We began our work face-to-face before I bought a couch. In an early period, I struggled with my anger about Scott missing sessions. I was reluctant to raise this matter because Scott was at the nadir of his functioning and I worried about hurting him. The result of my delay was that, when I did finally raise it, my anger was (try as I might) undisguisable. In response, something remarkable happened. Scott became anxious and inarticulate, then got out of his chair and lay down in a supine position on the floor, his head toward me. From this position, he could respond to my inquiry about the missed sessions more coherently.

Scott continued to lie on the floor for the next year and rarely missed appointments. He met my inquiries into the meaning of lying on the floor with such positive feedback that I delayed buying a couch for another year. His associations to this postural position were rich and varied, including that it was preferred for dealing with flares of back pain, the use of floor mats to practice Aikido break-fall techniques, and a memory of his father smiling down on him while Scott lay on a sack of grain, lost in thought. When I did eventually acquire a couch, he used it immediately and admitted he did find it more comfortable.

I resisted interpreting this postural enactment as an act of debasement or submission. While that possibility certainly crossed my mind, it seemed a simplistic interpretation, and Scott's life was full of people offering him simplistic advice for his complex problems. Returning to Modell's ideas about embodied metaphor, I note that analysts think metaphorically about wordless relational enactments before interpreting them to patients. That process affects analytic listening and can thus influence analysis in significant ways, even if the analyst has not yet put the enactment into spoken language.

As Scott's analysis continues, metaphors of posture and bodily interaction in Aikido continue to be helpful in interpreting his avoidant and self-defeating patterns as defensive processes developed to aid in affect regulation and maintenance of relational attachment. One of the metaphorical links I will make at an appropriate point will be about Scott's ability to practice relational Aikido on me. How does he disarm my analytic "attacks" without harming me and disrupting the relationship? I believe his "submissive" behavior (of which the lying down may be a part) can then be interpreted and be clinically useful.

In this treatment, bodily metaphors helped Scott return from the brink of total failure to live a more productive, satisfying life.

# References

Lakoff, G. & Johnson, M. (2003). *Metaphors We Live By*. Chicago: University of Chicago Press.

Modell, A.H. (2007). The body in psychoanalysis and the origin of fantasy. In J.P. Muller & J.G. Tillman (eds.), *The Embodied Subject: Minding the Body in Psychoanalysis*. Lanham, MD: Jason Aronson, pp. 1–15.

# 21

# THE FAILURE TO UNDERSTAND AS A TRANSITIONAL EXPERIENCE

*Ionas Sapountzis*

In *The History of the Siege of Lisbon*, José Saramago (1989) describes the sudden urge of an obsessive, hermetic proofreader to inexplicably insert his own word into the text he has been assigned to proofread. A mere "not" transforms the meaning of the entire paragraph and, in fact, the entire story. The intensity of the proofreader's urge is a total surprise to him, as is his inability to correct his momentary transgression by erasing the intruding word. It is as if failure to understand the source of this uncharacteristic impulse leaves him in a state of psychic numbness, unable to reflect and act, thus unable to undo what he has done. His act would have gone unnoticed had it not been for an astute female editor who, like a well trained analyst, does *not* dismiss the proofreader's act as momentary, inexplicable folly but, instead, invites him to pursue it and explore the possibility of a different account on how the Christians retook Lisbon from the Moors.

The story, in part, is a poignant metaphor of how historical narratives are constructed and how seemingly unshakable ethnic tales and longhead beliefs can shift if one is willing to deconstruct them and contemplate other possibilities. As the proofreader began to attend to possible meanings of his act, he constructed another, equally plausible narrative, one that had not been put forth until then; namely, that only a handful of crusaders took part in the siege, while the majority, unswayed by the plight of the Portuguese, simply sailed on, unwilling to risk their lives in assaulting a city that offered very little to loot.

Saramago's story is a powerful testament to how transformative a single word can be, especially if it jolts one's attention to what is "not" contemplated. It is a powerful metaphor of the space that can be created when one allows oneself to pause and attend to what is absent and what is not understood. Just as the proofreader became the author of his own thoughts instead of simply correcting and annotating the thoughts of others once he began to engage with the dissociated parts of his self, so patients are able to surprise (Winnicott, 1971a) themselves with the insights they create once they begin to attend to their experiences and disowned parts of themselves.

Most analysts have likely experienced of moments similar to the one the proof-reader had – moments when the personal becomes manifest through involuntary acts, incomplete statements, strange slips and omissions, and when analyst and patient are surprised by the insights that unfold, much like fellow travelers who, after an accidental turn off the road, encounter an unexpected vista in front of them. At such moments, analyst and patient "become aware of another experience of an entirely different phenomenological dimension" (Wilner, 2006, p. 15) that needs attention.

The literature is replete with accounts of how analysts make sense of such experiences and incorporate them into treatment. In earlier conceptualizations, analysts relied on a relatively linear process of observing and deconstructing patients' acts and statements to form understanding. Contemporary analysts attend to a wider, growing array of experiences and phenomena, including not only patient's statements, associations and inadvertent slips, but also the analyst's sub-jective feelings, unexpected fantasies and, even, sensations. The shift from a structured, linear model to a more intersubjective, experiential one, Wilner remarked, has brought forth a whole new constellation of foci that has expanded the analytic context and made analysts more attuned to even seemingly inchoate sensations and thoughts.

Over the past two decades, analysts have convincingly pointed to the heuristic, constructive value of random drifts and unexpected associations in enabling them to realize the intangibles in their patients' experiences and ways they engage with others (Ogden, 1997, 2004). Adding to the growing realization of how relative and context-bound the analyst's understanding is, Stern (1997, 2004) proposed that insight generated in treatment is not simply determined by the analyst's capacity to identify enactments and respond to dissociations, but also by unformulated experiences and unconscious identifications that are not part of analytic inquiry.

The ability to make sense of seemingly random data and generate links out of seemingly meaningless exchanges, coupled with the realization that a lot of what transpires in treatment may be outside the analyst's understanding, has increased analysts' appreciation and tolerance for the minute and bizarre. As a result, minute associations or seemingly trivial experiences are treated by most analysts as potentially valuable analytic objects. Yet the growing attention to the seemingly minute and random, coupled with growing awareness that the analyst's under-standing is dependent, to a large extent, on what patients project or, fail to project, cannot fully account for the fact that a lot of what transpires is first encountered in the sphere of the not understood, the not known, and that a lot of what analysts experience and understand emerges from the diffuse and formless.

Although analysts routinely encounter difficult treatment moments and find themselves unable to really understand and process what is going on, their diffi-culties and failures, once overcome, are always presented from the vantage point of the insight reached. This is an understandable, perhaps unavoidable, reaction since the underlying tenet in most psychoanalytic schools of thinking and, indeed, the underlying flow of the analytic encounter, is that of rendering the unknown

known, of moving from a state of not understanding and fragmentation to a state of growing understanding and relative integration.

What is rarely given the attention it deserves is the period before analysts are able to make associations and notice patterns that transform understanding of what their patients project and enact with them. In many cases, before analysts begin to formulate understanding and to pursue an idea, before they become able to link events and contemplate possibilities, there is a period, particularly with more troubled patients, where the emerged-to-be is not even remotely present. The patients' beta elements (Bion, 1962) may not even be experienced as elements by analysts. Before an act, a dream, a patient's sudden disclosure, or the analyst's own drifts and associations make something about the patient's psyche irrefutably present, there is often space created by absence of meaning and understanding, a diffuse, wordless experience that sets the stage from which unexpected and unbidden associations often emerge. Before analysts become conscious of their drifts and sensations and use them to understand what is projected and enacted, as Ogden (2004), Wilner (1987, 1998) and Jacobs (1993) have pointed out, there is often the sense of failing to grasp what is going on, of being involved in a treatment that feels incomprehensible and sometimes lifeless. It is these feelings, I would like to argue, these inarticulate sensations or beta elements that, if attended to, can help analysts locate their experiences and, in turn, understand their patients' psychic states.

The period before an analyst begins to make sense of what is going on is rarely experienced as productive or useful. Instances of not understanding, failing to grasp what is happening, are often experienced as personal failures, triggering paranoid and depressive anxieties and contributing to experiences of difference and futility.

The analyst's difficulties understanding what is going on may not be indicative of the analyst's limitations or level of patient pathology. They may indicate unconscious identification with what cannot be articulated or contemplated because the elements that are projected or enacted lie outside the sphere of their awareness. If the failure to understand what is happening is not treated as an intolerable experience that needs to be evacuated or denied through defensive acts that fall under Bion's (1963) $\psi$ column but, instead, is regarded as an integral part of how patients experience themselves and engage with others, then what is generated in the room may not feel as confusing and persecutory to analysts. Failure to understand may be a form of understanding, resonating with the inchoateness in the room and, also, with feelings of emptiness and confusion that patients generate in their encounters. In many cases, experiences of alienation and dis-identification in sessions can serve as valuable sources of information that can change the analysts' perspective on what is taking place. With some patients, it is in the space outside the realm of what can be immediately processed that analysts begin to develop an understanding about their patients. This understanding may be constructed not only from what is enacted and present but, also, from what is absent, from the void patients' acts generate that leaves analysts unsure as to what is going on.

In the case of Saramago's proofreader, before his inexplicable insertion of the word "not" jolted him out of his placid life and made him face the reverberations of an impulse he dared not explore, there was prolonged solitude and silence broken only by biweekly visits of his housekeeper. There were lonely walks in the old part of Lisbon, on which he was responding to a yearning he could not define, seeking answers to questions he could not formulate. This solitary, seemingly aimless search preceded and set the stage for his uncharacteristic act. His incomprehensible act could not have happened with the same suddenness, and would not have been left uncorrected, had he been conscious of the state he was in. Had he been aware of his turmoil, he would not have needed an act of disowned negation to express a core part of himself that had been, until then, denied.

In "Transitional objects and transitional phenomena," Winnicott (1971b) proposed that in the space between internal and external, "me" and "not-me," individuals are confronted with the reality of what is not there, what cannot be possessed. In the intermediate space between objectively and subjectively perceived reality, individuals come face to face with the limitations of their omnipotence.

From a Winnicottian perspective, a lot, if not most, of what happens between patient and analyst takes place in this intermediate area in which clear understanding is elusive. Participants have to fill the vacuum with their capacity to symbolize and create a transitional object which is often experienced as a new "possession" (Winnicott, 1971b, p. 3), an object that is created, even though it had always been there, "waiting to be created" (Winnicott, 1971d, p. 89).

The confusion and lack of understanding a therapist experiences points to a similar intermediate space in the analyst between what makes sense and what does not, what the analyst understands about the patient and the process, and what s/he does not comprehend. Analysts and patients who find themselves unable to understand what is going on are confronted, like the proofreader in Saramago's novel, with a reality outside the sphere of what they can grasp and possess. Much like Winnicott's transitional phenomena in which space between oneself and the other needs to be filled with a created object, the space between what is understood and what is not understood in treatment needs to be filled by the analyst's or patient's creative acts, whether through a statement, an association, or a dream.

If a patient can generate a creative moment through sharing a dream, an association, or an incident from his or her life, then the analyst's role is to process and expand the patient's act, rendering the trivial, seemingly mundane, meaningful and relevant. If the patient cannot offer such a moment and, instead, creates confusion and deadness, then, as Winnicott (1971c) argued, it is the analyst's task to create a playful encounter in order for analysis to begin. Ferro (2005) echoed Winnicott's thinking when he asserted that in treatments characterized by absence of alpha elements analysts must generate their own alpha elements so there can be "a thought in the process of constant expansion" (p. 68).

The analysts' ability to remain suspended between the understood and not understood without seeking to foreclose the experience, or to impose an external meaning to it, contributes to the creation of space in which thoughts and associations can emerge out of the confusing and bizarre. For patients who cannot create such space, who live in space filled with beta elements and cannot process their experience, potential space can often be located in the symptom itself, and in what the patients' incomprehensible acts and states of non-communication (Winnicott, 1963) evoke in the analyst. In the ripples (or vacuum) created by the patients' incomprehensible or bewildering acts, analysts can find, if they look for it, elements of the patients' selves that have been disowned or never owned. Attending to these acts, pursuing them, creates space that enables analysts and patients to engage with each other as perhaps never before, so that treatment, to paraphrase Winnicott (1971c, p. 54), can truly begin.

In the case of Saramago's proofreader, what contributed to his transformation was not the unformulated desire reflected in his impulsive act, or his belated realization of its implications, but his editor's urging him to pursue his act further and become engaged with what he could not yet understand and could not, until then, own.

Like the proofreader, a young woman[1] who, dressed like a teenage boy, hated her maiden name, and could not look at her vagina, left her therapist with little room for understanding. She adamantly refused any suggestion that she was transsexual or that she wished she were of opposite gender. She was "an orphan of the real" (Grotstein, 1981), living in a state of negation, determined to deny herself and what her mother-therapist could offer. Hating her name, she wished to be called Skyler, since that name was not associated with a gender. She wished she could fly in space as an astronaut. She lived in a place where there was no room to contemplate an unbearable, persecutory reality and untenable future. The only space she could create was through her wish to escape, to leave Mother Earth and be out of reach, therefore safe, in a sexless world with no attachments and relations. The intensity of her negation created a vacuum around her and within her that served to protect and insulate her. It also kept her forever grounded on the negative, without an escape, other than the wish to be someone else. Like her, the therapist also felt caught in states of not-me, feeling unsure of her skills and capacity to understand and engage, wishing she were someone else, a better, more experienced, therapist.

The jarring effect the patient's statements created, and the intensity with which she dismissed everything, left little room for understanding and play. It was necessary to let go of what could not be explored and formulated and, instead, acknowledge Skyler, and encourage him/her to take off, leave Mother Earth and report from space. Inviting the adolescent girl to focus not on what she knew, but could not tolerate, but on what she had not yet formed, inviting her to imagine what life would be like on other unknown, possibly sexless, planets, created a space for her to slowly begin articulating herself, not in the negative, but in the evocative potential, conveying what could be found when she allowed herself to imagine.

Just as playing and knowing takes place in time and space, so does the not understood occur in time (that feels disconnected from the here and now) and in space (where the "me" cannot be tolerated and needs to be "repudiated"

[Winnicott, 1971a, p. 41]). As Skyler began to imagine unknown galaxies and visit nameless constellations, she began to articulate repudiated aspects of her life. She began visiting her past, reporting parts of her story – trauma she had experienced living with an abusive, drug-addicted mother, and the intense ambivalence she felt for her.

Skyler's story did not emerge in the context of an exchange that was understood beforehand. It did not emerge out of the therapist's ability to stand in the space between me and not-me, as Bromberg (1998) advocates, for such a stance implies an awareness and understanding of different psychic states. Rather, it emerged out of the therapist's ability to attend to the repudiated and treat it as an integral part of the girl's "me." This stance created space for ideas and experiences to be articulated and explored. In the process of engaging the "not," the "me" began to emerge. She became able to articulate what she dared not until then. Much like the proofreader who, as long as he was unable to process the "not," could not articulate his own agency and desire, so did the girl's sense of herself begin to appear once she engaged with her desire to not be here, to take off for the unknown and report from there.

A little boy I saw several years ago had symptoms suggestive of a gender identity disorder. He busily confused himself and others by starting constructions that quickly became parodies of construction, drawing strange pictures that revealed his limitations, making statements that generated confusion and heightened his anxiety. His story began to emerge not through my ability to decipher his acts and statements, but in the transitional space created by his nonsensical language. His actions and expressions conveyed the "in-between" state he was in, an agent and non-agent, a creative child who could not create, a boy with intense presence that generated absences and left people wondering. That understanding felt strangely incomplete, just like his acts, leaving me unsure as to what else to make of our encounter and his expectations of me.

There were no evocative symbols, like the wish to be Skyler, nor sudden acts of negation, like the proofreader's "not," that revealed the split-off part of himself. His gender-related symptoms felt too reactive and spasmodic for me to be able to hold and engage with them. What was present, apart from the whirlwind of acts, were phi-pha-phu-pha statements he teasingly made between acts, such as moving pillows from one place to another, then putting them back a minute later, picking up sticks that he quickly abandoned in a pile, and opening containers of clay, mixing them with the decisiveness of one who had a project in mind only to abandon them, in an amorphous lump, soon after. "Hello phuma phuma!" he would say, as he moved toward one end of the room. Then, as he passed me again, "Phuma phuma you stink!" A bit later, as he was emptying clay or picking crayons, "Phi-pha-phu-pha, your face is ugly, phuma phuma!"

For the little boy caught in states between me and not-me, who sought refuge in frantic acts and "as-if" exchanges, the challenge became none other than treating these acts as expressions of an intermediate state that could not be expressed otherwise. Treating his phuma-phuma and phi-pha-phu-pha statements as statements that were very important, but should not be deciphered yet – just like the infant who does not need to be told that his beloved transitional object is not magical at all, just a teddy bear (Winnicott, 1971b) – and assuming the role of the big phuma phuma who met little phuma phuma in his phi-pha-phu-pha world, greeting him in the phi-pha-phu-pha vernacular, enabled me to become involved with him, preserving his desire to communicate in the illusionary, asymmetric language (Matte-Blanco, 1988) he devised. What felt important was to resist impulses to fill the space between real and not-real with meaning that would have exposed him and, instead, preserve his need to remain "hidden" (Winnicott, 1963, p. 186) so he could communicate while *not communicating* (p. 184).

Two or three months after the initial immersion into the phuma-phuma world, with no attempt at translation, since none was ever needed by either of us, the little boy did not seem as inclined to dart from statement to statement and activity to activity. He could speak more and more about feelings, themes of weirdness, what felt funny, and what he never liked. He was careful not to talk about himself – that came later – but articulated his thoughts in the transitional, through the hypothetical other and through his references to me, the other(s) he created to fill the space between his sense of himself and his fears about himself.

What I believe helped transform this boy's experience of treatment and of me was not the meaning of his acts and my understanding of it, but the transitional state of our encounter, our capacity to bridge the space between us with imaginary symbols and, in the process, create something shared. What felt important was the need to find the potential in his nonsensical expressions, and reflect them back as playful gestures that deserved to be acknowledged so he could feel engaged and begin, in turn, to engage.

The boy may have been easier to contain and play with than more dissociated or foreclosed patients because, in his unorthodox way, and through his provocative statements and acts, he was conveying his desire, inviting a playful response. This, of course, is also true in the cases of the proofreader and Skyler, both of whom created powerful ripples through acts of self-negation. One can argue this is the case with anyone, regardless of their state of retreat (Steiner, 1993) and foreclosure (McDougall, 1984), if one is willing to reverse perspectives (Bion, 1962) and treat the incomprehensible or bizarre, not only as a manifestation of the person's psychopathology, but also as a metaphor of his or her effort to generate a safe space and preserve, however precariously, him- or herself in the world. This act does not simply render meaning to what has not yet been formulated, because such an act implies that the therapist has a sense of what is going on. Rather it presupposes the will to imagine, play, and, especially, to insist on searching for the possible and creative in the discarded and disowned.

"Imagining" often requires analysts be able to not only remain "in doubt" (Ferro, 1999, p. 8) so that different meanings can emerge and other possibilities can be contemplated but, more important, that they are also able to engage with what is not known within, what they do not know about themselves, before they can become analysts to their patients (Searles, 1979). They have to contemplate what experiences of not understanding reveal about them and their own personal impasses, not as much an analytic third (Ogden, 1994) as an analytic first (Sapountzis, 2009), before they are able to engage (and play) with the dissociated and disowned in their patients' acts. Analysts need to treat their states of not understanding not as failures, but as *states of experiencing*, however diffuse and formless such states might be, from which other experiences will emerge. They can be manifestations not just of how infinite the space between patient and analyst is and how the essence of oneself is likely to remain "permanently unknown in fact, unfound" (Winnicott, 1963, p. 187), but also of the analysts' own "not-me" states, what they cannot process and what they have omitted (Levenson, 1995) in their lives.

The therapist's ability to look at states of not understanding as manifestations of something that cannot be articulated, is a beginning, an alpha element itself, from which other meanings and ideas will (always) emerge. This act facilitates creating space in which thoughts and sensations are expanded and the seemingly absurd and bizarre is transformed into something meaningful, like Skyler's wish to visit other galaxies and, through that, her own psychic constellation, like the boy's wish to escape and communicate in a language that made no sense, even to himself, ensuring his remaining hidden, in a state of "not communicating," a joy and a disaster (Winnicott, 1963, p. 186). For both these individuals, it was not simply a matter of moving them from a position of not knowing and not understanding to a new form of knowing and understanding, for no attempt was ever made to interpret their acts, but rather of facilitating an exchange for unformulated experiences (Stern, 1997) and suppressed desires (Lacan, 1988) to emerge, unfold, and become part of their lives.

It is interesting how intensely the three cases – one fictional, albeit with strong autobiographical elements,[2] and two nonfictional – experienced their respective states of "not-me," and how entangled and haunted they were by what they were not and what they feared they could never be. All three were caught up in acts of self-denial. These acts and statements contributed to their alienation and disconnection. Perhaps it cannot be otherwise, for any act of not-me is just that: a desperate act that serves to negate a reality that cannot be articulated and, therefore, cannot be faced. For such acts to be understood and engaged in treatment, they may need to first be located in the transitional space that can be found in any act of resignation, in any act that points to what is not understood and cannot be owned. It is in that space, the space that allows for different meanings and possibilities to emerge, that one can find what had been, until then, unspoken and discarded, what, to paraphrase Winnicott (1971d), is always there, waiting to be found.

## Notes

1  I am grateful to Dr. M.C. for sharing this case with me.
2  Saramago was also a proofreader, who became, like the character in his story, an author in his late forties.

# References

Bion, W.R. (1962). *Learning from Experience*. New York: Basic Books.

Bion, W.R. (1963). *Elements of Psychoanalysis*. London: Heinemann. Reprinted Northvale, NJ: Jason Aronson, 1979.

Bromberg, P. (1998). *Standing in the Spaces: Essays on Clinical Processes, Trauma and Dissociation*. Hillsdale, NJ: Analytic Press.

Ferro, A. (1999). *Psychoanalysis as Therapy and Storytelling*. New York: Routledge.

Ferro, A. (2005). *Seeds of Illness, Seeds of Recovery*. New York: Routledge.

Grotstein, J.S. (1981). Who is the dreamer who dreams the dream and who is the dreamer who understands it? In J.S. Grotstein (ed.), *Do I Dare to Disturb the Universe? A Memorial to W.R. Bion*. London: Karnac, pp. 357–416.

Jacobs, T. (1993). The inner experience of the analyst: their contributions to the analytic process. *International Journal of Psychoanalysis*, 74: 7–14.

Lacan, J. (1988). *The Seminar of Jacques Lacan*, Book 1, *Freud's Papers on Technique, 1953–1954*. New York: Norton.

Levenson, E.A. (1995). A monopedal presentation of interpersonal psychoanalysis. *Review of Interpersonal Psychoanalysis*, 1: 1–4.

Matte-Blanco, I. (1988). *Thinking, Feeling and Being*. New York: Routledge.

McDougall, J. (1984). The disaffected patient: reflections on affect and pathology. *Psychoanalytic Quarterly*, 53: 386–409.

Ogden, T.H. (1994), The analytic third – working with intersubjective clinical facts. *International. Journal of Psychoanalysis*, 75: 3–20.

Ogden, T.H. (1997). *Reverie and Interpretation: Sensing Something Human*. Northvale, NJ: Jason Aronson.

Ogden, T.H. (2004). The analytic third: implications for psychoanalytic theory and technique. *Psychoanalytic Quarterly*, 73: 167–195.

Sapountzis, I. (2009). Revisiting Searles' paper "The patient as a therapist to the therapist": the analyst's personal in the interpersonal. *Psychoanalytic Review*, 96: 665–684.

Saramago, J. (1989). *The History of the Siege of Lisbon*. New York: Harcourt Brace & Company.

Searles, H.F. (1979). The patient as a therapist to his analyst. In *Countertransference and Related Subjects: Selected Papers*. Madison CT: International Universities Press, 1999, pp. 380–459.

Steiner, J. (1993). *Psychic Retreats. Pathological Organizations in Psychotic, Neurotic and Borderline Patients*. London: Routledge.

Stern, D.B. (1997). *Unformulated Experience*. Hillsdale, NJ: Analytic Press.

Stern, D.B. (2004). The eye sees itself: dissociation, enactment and the achievement of conflict. *Contemporary Psychoanalysis*, 40: 197–237.

Wilner, W. (1987). Participatory experience: the participant observer paradox. *American Journal of Psychoanalysis*, 47: 342–357.

Wilner, W. (1998). The un-consciousing of awareness in psychoanalytic therapy. *Contemporary Psychoanalysis*, 35: 617–628.

Wilner, W. (2006). The analyst's embeddedness and the emergence of unconscious experience. *Contemporary Psychoanalysis*, 42: 13–29.

Winnicott, D.W. (1963). Communicating and not communicating leading to a study of certain opposites. In *The Maturational Process and the Facilitating Environment*. Madison CT: International Universities Press, 1965, pp. 179–192.

Winnicott, D.W. (1971a). Playing: a theoretical statement. In *Playing and Reality*. London: Routledge, pp. 38–52.

Winnicott, D.W. (1971b). Transitional objects and transitional phenomena. In *Playing and Reality*. London: Routledge, pp. 1–25.

Winnicott, D.W. (1971c). Playing: creative activity and the search of the self. In *Playing and Reality*. London: Routledge, pp. 53–65.

Winnicott, D.W. (1971d). The use of an object and relating through identifications. In *Playing and Reality*. New York: Basic Books, pp. 86–94.

Part VIII

# THE LONG SHADOW
# OF CHILDHOOD RELATIONAL
# TRAUMA

# 22

# THE BIG HIT

## How adult illness can recapitulate childhood trauma and fear of failure

*Judith E. Levene*

It is well known that childhood relational trauma can warp schemas of self and other so that the capacity for adult, spontaneous, creative gesture can be thwarted or suppressed. Early critical and punitive interactions with primary caregivers may set up shop in psychic structure as negative schemas of self and other, bad internal objects, or negative organizing principles. These schemas can grow tendrils, constricting creative potential. It becomes difficult to put oneself "out there" for fear of failure and the emotional correlate: shame. Thoughts of spontaneous, creative gestures bring anxieties about taking "a big hit."

What is less well known is the way emotional sequelae of adult physical illness can serve to overlay, entrench, and re-inscribe these same anxieties, renewing the fear of failure that may have previously been overcome. Bromberg (2011) suggests that people who have suffered developmental trauma are more vulnerable to adult onset trauma. Bucci (1997, 2002, 2007a, 2007b) explains how emotional experience can become de-linked from the memory at its source. Likewise, bodily experiences that carry emotional content may become associated to displaced meanings. In the experience described here, symptoms of physical illness became associated with fear of failure, "a big hit," originally attached to childhood trauma.

In my life, a near-miss car accident became the scaffolding for global transference associated with the fear of taking "a big hit," a fear previously ameliorated by analysis. With further work, it became apparent that anxieties about the "almost" accident had become associated with earlier experiences of life-threatening illness, undergirded by childhood trauma, displaced onto the incident with the car. Consciously, I had experienced little concern about the illness.

This chapter describes my traumatic response to a relatively benign occurrence that triggered panic and profound fear of failure. As described by Bucci, my trauma response had become dissociated from its true source, the deeper meaning obscured. Over time, in the context of a healing relationship, I was able to restore associational linkages to my experience. A parallel process with my patient,

Caren, suffering from her own traumatic reaction to illness superimposed on childhood trauma, helped us each to recover the "true" narrative sequences of our separate but convergent experience.

## The puzzle pieces

About six years ago, I was driving home from the university town where I taught. I approached a green light and began to make a right turn onto a major street. Out of my peripheral vision, I noticed two cars at high speed approaching the intersection from opposite directions. Cautiously, I stopped without proceeding through the intersection, although I was the only driver with a green light. Sure enough, both cars ran the red light, one turning left and the other heading straight on. I remember a serious crash with mangled metal, exploding glass, police arriving, an ambulance carrying away someone seriously injured. I was safely out of harm's way. The police asked me for a report. I gave them information that, in hindsight, was slightly incorrect. After collecting myself, I drove home, some 90 miles (145 km).

Several weeks later, I began what proved to be an obsessive rumination about that car accident. I was preoccupied with the cars whooshing through the red lights, with sounds and sight of the crash, with the blood of the person carried away on a stretcher into the ambulance. Over and over again, I imagined myself proceeding through the crosswalk on the green light, only to be sandwiched between the cars. These fantasies preoccupied me, intruding into consciousness. I suffered from bouts of anxiety, even panic. I could not sleep. It never occurred to me that I might be having a PTSD reaction. I struggled to name the emotional truth of this experience (Grand, 2000). I continued with my teaching and psychoanalytic practice. These thoughts intruded when I was not working. I was grateful for work's focus, realizing what a regulatory buffer it can provide from the vicissitudes of life.

Over the coming months, my fantasies and images became elaborated into memories of a serious illness in university that began to haunt me. I pieced together that I must have been born with a minor heart abnormality shared by many relatives on my father's side. At age 19, during third-year final exams, I developed a staph infection in my heart valve, about as likely as being struck by lightning. The illness was nearly fatal, something that has only recently reached my awareness. I spent ten weeks in hospital. I recall fantasies of floating, suspended in my hospital bed, plugged into the world through plastic tubing. As an interesting medical case, legions of medical students, residents and interns lined up to listen to my chest. I felt dehumanized, derealized. I remember knitting a sweater in my bed that summer. I felt like Madame Defarge from Dickens' *A Tale of Two Cities*, a *tricoteuse* knitting the names of royalists who would die in the French Revolution. Was I knitting my own name?

I was discharged mid-July in weakened condition, but with a strong need to "be in the world of the living." Despite concern from physicians, I returned to university in September, with a much-reduced load and a second-hand car so that I could drive to classes rather than walk. For years, I thought little about this illness.

I was told I would one day require surgery. I put that information out of mind and continued with life – undergraduate and master's degree, marriage to a cardiologist, babies (despite high-risk pregnancies because of my heart) and divorce. Although I was told the valve condition was worsening, I paid little notice, continued with work, doctoral studies, and other aspects of life. Finally I hit a wall – heart failure requiring open-heart surgery and valve repair. I tell this in a matter-of-fact manner, as if it happened to someone else. After one month off from teaching and practice, I returned to my life, surgery behind me, emotional dissociation in front – not an entirely negative development because I was able to function at a fairly high level.

Dissociation began to weaken five years later when I developed atrial fibrillation, an arrhythmia resulting from valve repair scar tissue. I was seized with sensations that my heart was rolling across my chest. Initially rare, these paroxysms were triggered by more and more subtle stimuli – fatigue, exercise, wine, countertransference, and once by laughing too hard. Despite cardiac medication, I sometimes landed in the ER for a medication infusion that restored my heart to sinus rhythm, a normal beat. After cardiac ablation to remove scar tissue that conducted abnormal beats, I was rid of the arrhythmia and medications. My heart was relatively normal in structure and function.

In my conscious mind, I was emotionally stable until the near-miss car accident. After that event, I began to worry I could no longer write, was no longer smart, characteristics I previously believed to be strengths. I began to think something had happened during surgery, perhaps anoxia causing cognitive damage. Although there was no medical basis for this notion, I developed this "idée fixe" to the extent that I stopped presenting and publishing for almost a decade. (This hypothesis reflects a fundamental human need to make meaning of chaotic experience to help contain anxiety.) Previously, I contributed approximately one refereed article plus two conference presentations per year, until the thought of "putting myself out there" that way brought waves of panic. I could not understand what was happening.

In the context of personal work with a respected colleague, I began to deconstruct the dissociated anxiety attached to the car accident, and to reassemble the trail of my associations into something resembling the narrative truth of my experience. It seems anxiety from my cardiac illness transferred to the "near-miss" car accident through a PTSD reaction. Both experiences were undergirded by childhood trauma, my relationships with an envious, thwarting mother who attacked my many early achievements. In this context, putting myself "out there" proved to be very dangerous, resulting in fear of a "big hit." Deconstruction and reassembly of my narrative in the context of a healing relationship ultimately brought renewed confidence and wellbeing.

## Trauma and cognitive science

Schemas of self and other based on childhood trauma may color illness experience. Wilma Bucci (1997, 2002, 2007a, 2007b), building on Piagetian theory and linking psychoanalysis and cognitive science, argues for an heuristic model that encompasses conscious and unconscious emotions, mental representations and processes. According to her, interactive experience forms linguistic, somatic, motoric, and emotional systems that cluster in relation to one another. These information chunks are contextualized within an interpersonal field. The mind is a multi-coded information processor, contextualized by another's mind. Bucci developed these ideas into "Multiple Code Theory," according to which chunks of coded information are built up through prototypical, repetitive, shared affective experiences with others. These schemas carry either declarative information symbolized in language, procedural information about information processing, or subsymbolic information. Subsymbolic systems involve automatic, rapid, emotionally driven schemas experienced as emotional or physical self-states. Subsymbolic schemas may link to symbolic thinking. These linkages can be defensively disrupted if emotional experience overwhelms the self, keeping emotional experience at the subsymbolic, non-language level, experienced as body memory. Donell Stern (1997, 2006, 2010) also described "unformulated experience": subsymbolic states that never fully develop to the symbolic level (words, images). Pathology may result from either disruption of symbolic thought, when emotional or physiological reactivity takes hold, or when symbolic thinking never adequately develop (Bucci, 1997; Davies & Frawley, 1994; Fonagy et al., 2002; Taylor et al., 1987).

In psychoanalytic treatment, emotional containment develops through holding (Slochower, 2004) that directly affects psychological and neurobiological processes. Psychoanalysis repairs disruptions, brings about greater reflective and symbolic capacity, and modifies emotionally laden schemas that regulate traumatic affect states. In the context of a healing relationship, new schemas of self and other develop in ways that are less harsh, more calming and supportive.

In examining the well-documented link between supportive relationships and amelioration of physical and mental illness, Schore (1994) describes the way containing social relationships mediate psychobiological systems at all levels. Emotionally regulating interactions potentiate changes in limbic activity, modulating intense emotional states that influence recovery from mental and physical illness. The supportive, validating aspects of psychotherapy and psychoanalysis work because interactive soothing directly affects the neurobiology of the orbitofrontal cortex that down-regulates intense emotions. The regulation of intense affect contributes to the development of new, calmer cognitive schemas of self and other by extending executive brain function to evaluate, sculpt, and inhibit transference-laden schemas (Solms & Turnbull, 2002) that trigger automatic reactions to emotional stimuli. In the process of calming, reflective capacity is enhanced to promote active inhibition of such spurious automatic transferential reactions.

## Reflection

My personal experience exemplifies the way an associational trail, originating in childhood trauma, can become unconsciously inscribed in the illness experience of a young adult, ultimately emerging at the time of a "near-miss" car accident. Using Bucci's formulation, it seems that affective aspects of traumatic early care-giving experience remained subsymbolic, manifesting in free-floating, high anxiety. (I was a very anxious child.) This sense of threat was exacerbated through my adolescent illness that came like a lightning bolt. Consciously, the emotional impact was dissociated. I simply soldiered on. This defensive dissociation began to break down during the crisis of the cardiac arrhythmia. I grew to expect danger at every turn, leading to the episode of the "near-miss" car accident, a concretization of the danger I feared.

According to Schore (1994), one situation is linked to another through arousal level similarity. Emotional memories (Le Doux, 2002) supplement current perceptions and are linked in the hippocampus (Solms & Turnbull, 2002). Linking is experienced as familiarity, albeit fallible familiarity.

Though I was safe from the danger of illness, I experienced the near-miss car accident through the schema of "the big hit." The sense of imminent, omnipresent danger generalized into a kind of global transference, slowing me to a crawl. The attribution of danger to academic accomplishment involved this spread of anxiety from prior experience of childhood trauma and subsequent illness.

## Parallel process with Caren

Through my experiences of childhood trauma and illness, I had much in common with my patient, Caren, whom I met fifteen years ago when she came for treatment as an adolescent during her first of two battles with cancer. The eldest of three girls, she described an idyllic early childhood highlighted by the year her family lived in Europe. Returning home, she had a rough time with peers, who seemed envious of her experience abroad, bullying her mercilessly. The following year, her father unexpectedly left the marriage. Caren had a vivid screen memory of standing on the front walk, tearfully entreating her father to stay, to no avail. This scene repeated itself with many men in her adult life.

After her parents' separation, Caren's mother took to bed in a depressive episode. As the eldest daughter, Caren assumed some of mother's roles, especially in relation to the younger girls. She became mother's confidante. She felt pride and efficacy in her acquired role, while "going it alone" with her emotional experience.

Pride soon yielded to burden. For hours, Caren rode the subway after school, trying to calm down from bullying, not wanting to go home to tell mother, for fear of upsetting her. We worked through some of these issues and others during this first period of treatment.

Caren returned to treatment in her thirties following a second bout with breast cancer. We lived through diagnosis, lumpectomy, chemo, radiation, and complete disruption of life and career. Despite a close-knit circle of friends and family, she frequently wanted to go it alone, refusing to allow others to accompany her to appointments. She experienced empowerment at these times, but also loneliness and disconnection as she painfully repeated childhood experiences of coping in isolation.

Work with Caren was moving and difficult. At times, parallels in our experience felt too close, especially the experience of life interrupted. Her terror about being struck down, yet again, was so close to my emotional home. There were times I struggled to contain my escalating anxiety as we worked to name and contain her experience. I deeply connected with the heady efficacy she experienced about going it alone. I also identified with the sense of disconnection and abandonment that came with her withdrawal from those who would support her, if only she would allow them. While understanding her fierce independence, I knew it was partially defensive and that Caren needed the comfort of connection.

I was moved by the way each of our struggles with childhood trauma shaped our emotional schemas of illness. Caren saw her illness through the failure of the other brought by her sense of abandonment while defensively "going it alone." I experienced my illness as a failure of self, decimated by "the big hit" through trauma, illness, and accident.

When I thought about sharing my illness story with Caren, I hesitated. While aware that self-disclosure has become commonplace among some analysts, I hesitated, in hindsight defensively so. I felt too vulnerable to give up my privileged position of OK-ness relative to Caren's vulnerability. I was not able to go to the place of my own life-and-death vulnerability. Part of me managed to see I was propping myself up through false complementarity – believing I was OK, but Caren was not. I was still too raw to be more open.

Consulting a colleague for personal work, I began to see that my mortality had been tested as much as Caren's. I became able to nudge my way into a calmer acceptance of what had been terrifying in my own life, grappling with the challenge of finding strength amidst the random meaninglessness of life's vicissitudes. I began to think about risking sharing this understanding with Caren.

Caren was surprised to hear that, as a young adult, I had fallen ill with a serious illness and that I had learned to live with the knowledge that I would eventually require open-heart surgery. It seemed important to know I had lived through and past that experience without giving up personal and professional goals. Later we talked about the meaning of my sharing. Caren said:

> I remember my parents' divorce and having ADHD and all the rest of it being very isolating. But cancer especially, is incredibly isolating. It is a chronic, never going away, no straight answers, completely random, we're going to kill you to save you from illness that is the pinnacle of isolation. I think most trauma is. You and I have these parallel stories on the illness front. In many ways, it's almost eerie. And especially being so young, there just wasn't anyone that I believed when they told me things. But when you told me that you had been ill as a child – dramatically, suddenly and as inexplicably as I had, and that you lived with many of the same issues, I felt less isolated. It also allowed in more of what you were

saying. I'm not sure it would be the same if you had just had cancer or if you had just been gravely ill as well. What I think makes me connect to you and trust you on this front is because the parallels in our experiences are so similar.

When I heard about your illness, I think I was more open, I didn't feel as foolish when I was having pity parties, and you picked up on things I'm not sure you would have without your own experiences – those things made huge differences. For example, I remember many sessions where you would just say, "It sucks! It just plain sucks!!" You knew there was nothing to say other than that because you knew that that is what it boiled down to. Any advice or counsel or psycho babble or whatever was going to fall on deaf ears at that point and what I just needed was not to hear that it was going to be OK. You validating the obvious was huge and I don't think would have been obvious to most. And many times where I knew that you recognized the despair I was feeling and I didn't have to articulate it yet again. There was just so much I did not have to explain because you already understood in a way that so few could. It meant we could deal with the issues in a much more streamlined way – I didn't spend half the session explaining what it was like to be in my situation. I know that I said many times: "You know what it's like." And you did in terms of the type of situation: obviously the details are different but the commonality of the experiences put a bridge in place that did not need to be painstakingly built by long hours of explanation on my part. On the flip side, I don't think that I missed out on anything by not having to explain every detail of my feelings and by being able to take for granted that you understood a lot without it being spelled out.

I do know that you did not initially tell me about your own illness until I had been seeing you for years. I don't know if my reaction would have been different if you had come out with that on our third session. But the bigger point is that you didn't. You knew when it was appropriate and it made a tremendous difference. And I do remember being stunned. I know that I had created a "story" about getting cancer at 18 and that I had come, after so many years, to believe that "story." Overall, it has helped a lot to know that I am not alone. I'm not the only one. I don't get a big medal. It's not personal. It's not about me not learning some lesson fast enough. It just is. And I have been able to let go of having to understand why faster; It happens and it doesn't just happen to me. You sitting in front of me was proof that crap happens to all of us and that despite what everyone in the outside world was telling me, I didn't have the market cornered on the worst crap around. It also inspired me. I obviously don't know where you are on the emotional roller coaster of the psychological healing, but I did know that you were doing it too, that you were living your life and that if you could, I could too.

Through our sharing, Caren began to locate a place of acceptance of her own narrative truth, allowing room for hope about the future. She appreciated my sharing because it allowed her to feel less isolated and more emotionally regulated. Part of my own movement toward greater self-acceptance came through understanding the process of comparison about my physical and emotional health and that of Caren. I realized that some of that comparison and competition may be a universal, but unacknowledged aspect of countertransference.

Much has happened in the years of our work since then. As Caren continued her recovery and re-entry into post-treatment life, she created ideas about new professional directions and began a promising love relationship. The mutuality of our sharing seemed to help her shift her emotional weight from one foot to the other in order to move forward. Sharing helped me feel calmer through developing an attitude of mentorship about my own illness narrative. With Caren's consent and encouragement, I have made progress by writing this chapter. I am overcoming my fear of "taking a big hit" through writing. This process of mutual healing feels profound.

## Conclusion

Illness narratives can derive their experiential coloration from transference based on early childhood trauma. The analysis of this transference, my own and Caren's, was central to our work. Equally important was sharing my own experience of illness with Caren. It helped her alter her personal illness narrative to feel more emotionally contained. To do this took time for me to establish some sense of regulation and agency about my own experience (Solms & Turnbull, 2002) and to ensure that sharing involved active consideration of the potential benefit for Caren. Through recognition of the competitive dimensions of the work, as well as the mutuality of our sharing, greater healing took place.

## References

Bromberg, B. (2011). *The Shadow of the Tsunami and the Growth of the Relational Mind.* New York: Routledge.

Bucci, W. (1997). *Psychoanalysis and Cognitive Science; A Multiple Code Theory.* New York: Guilford Press.

Bucci, W. (2002). The referential process, consciousness, and the sense of self. *Psychoanalytic Inquiry,* 22: 766–793.

Bucci, W. (2007a). Dissociation from the perspective of multiple code theory: Part I; Psychological roots and implications for psychoanalytic treatment. *Contemporary Psychoanalysis,* 43: 165–184.

Bucci, W. (2007b). Dissociation from the perspective of multiple code theory: Part II; The spectrum of dissociative processes in the psychoanalytic relationship. *Contemporary Psychoanalysis,* 43: 305–326.

Davies, J.M. & Frawley, M. (1994). *Treating the Adult Survivor of Childhood Sexual Abuse: A Psychoanalytic Perspective.* New York: Basic Books.

Fonagy, P., Gergely, G. & Jurist, E. (2002). *Affect regulation, Mentalization and the Development of the Self.* London: Karnac Books.

Grand, S. (2000). *The Reproduction of Evil: A Clinical and Cultural Perspective.* Hillsdale, NJ: Analytic Press.

Le Doux, J. (2002). *Synaptic Self: How Our Brains Become Who We Are.* New York: Penguin.

Schore, A.N. (1994). *Affect Regulation and the Origin of the Self.* Hillsdale, NJ: Lawrence Erlbaum.

Solms, M. & Turnbull, O. (2002). *The Brain and the Inner World. An Introduction to the Neuroscience of Subjective Experience.* New York: Other Press.

Slochower, J. (2004). *Holding in Psychoanalysis.* Hillsdale NJ: Analytic Press.

Stern, D.B. (1997). *Unformulated experience: From Dissociation to Imagination in Psychoanalysis.* Hillsdale, NJ: Analytic Press.

Stern, D.B. (2006). Opening what has been closed, relaxing what has been clenched: Dissociation and enactment over time in committed relationships. *Psychoanalytic Dialogues,* 16: 747–761.

Stern, D.B. (2010). *Partners in Thought: Working with Unformulated Experience, Dissociation, and Enactment.* New York: Routledge.

Taylor, G., Bagby, R. & Parker, D. (1987). *Disorders of Affect Regulation.* Cambridge: Cambridge University Press.

# 23

# THE MAN WHO MISTOOK
# HIS DAUGHTER FOR HIS EX-WIFE

*Brent Willock*

This chapter's title was inspired by Oliver Sacks' (1985) *The Man who Mistook his Wife for a Hat*. Whereas Sacks was concerned with neuropathology, my contribution focuses on complex sequelae of early relational failures. Since my case discussion involves incest from the perpetrator's perspective, this chapter could have borrowed a Rolling Stones title, "Sympathy for the Devil." Empathizing with my patient, some may perceive me as guilty by association. Anyone inclined to rush to such judgment will, I hope, endeavor instead to keep an open mind until they have heard Juan's story.

## Initial presentation

Referred to me at the University of Michigan Medical Center, Juan explained that when procreative efforts failed, he and Frida adopted Haitian twins, Erica and Ricardo. When their marriage failed, knowing she was the more talented parent, he did not contest custody. Being alone felt good. When the children were with him, he could attend to them fully, then relax. They were his reason for living, making him less self-centered. Frida congratulated him on what a terrific parent he had become. The couple got along better than ever. Recalling Frida's teaching him to love children, Juan wept.

Couple therapy with a social work colleague helped Juan through marital separation, until Erica disclosed his touching her inappropriately when he thought she was sleeping. Protective Services terminated access to the twins. Couple therapy ended.

While married, Juan was unaware of how much stress he experienced and expressed. Health issues and marital failure decimated his self-esteem. He now realizes Frida loved him. He had not understood that before, because there was no physical intimacy. For Juan, sex meant warmth, touch, love, comfort. Absence of sex signified those crucial ingredients were lacking.

Juan fell in love with Erica's beauty. He enjoyed putting his hand on her belly to soothe tummy aches. To his surprise, he became turned on. He knew this interest in

216

his prepubescent "Venus de Milo" (particularly her mons veneris) was wrong, but could not bring this situation to couple therapy as that would land him in jail.

The likelihood of Juan's conviction that he could fix his problem himself being fulfilled was small: "Perversions are more akin to dreaming than neurotic symptom-formation … If the pervert dramatizes and actually fulfills his body-dreams with a real person, he also cannot wake out of them" (Khan, 1979, p. 30).

Between sleepovers, Juan did not have sexual interest in Erica (nor other children). Observing her asleep, "Something overtook me." Since "there was no message in my head strong enough to pull me away," he slipped into the dissociative dream state Khan described.

Lacking younger siblings, Juan believed he never learned appropriate touching. In considering this pedagogical hypothesis, it may help to bear in mind Alizade's (2005) assertion that everyone has incestuous contact from birth on. Adults must "re-educate their own incestuous instincts, always present to some extent even if in a sublimated and partly repressed way" (p. 106). Childhood polymorphously perverse sexuality is "more or less firmly repressed—and therefore less likely to be re-awakened by the ups and downs of life" (Cournut-Janin's, 2005, p. 73). Unfortunately Juan's childhood sexuality was less solidly repressed, therefore more subject to returning in face of life's stresses.

Juan's most memorable childhood moments involved exploring the body of a young girl who lived near his relatives, not far from San Juan. Her breasts were the most incredible thing he had ever seen. To this day, he finds breasts amazingly attractive. With Erica, he became Juanito (Little Juan) once more, reliving that primal awakening to beauty and sexual delight. These experiences constituted his "first discovery of female bodies" (I would add the adjective "extrafamilial"). "The one chosen by the laws of exogamy is a recipient of part of the incestuous fantasy. This imaginary transgression opens up a whole universe of delight" (Alizade, 2005, p. 106).

Immediately incarcerated following his daughter's disclosure, Juan thought he would never see his children again. Society more readily forgives murder and would classify him as "not fixable," he believed. His sisters excommunicated him. His brothers wanted to kill him, but became distant instead. Recounting that his friend Carlos, who has a young daughter, stood by him, Juan cried. The family doctor was supportive, as was a psychiatrist prescribing anti-anxiety medication and, his group therapist (for deviants).

What could have interfered with Juan's ability to securely repress incestuous "polymorphously perverse sexuality"? Depressed around the time of his birth, his mother was hospitalized repeatedly for electroshock. For his first years, Juanito spent his days with grandparents. Mother became addicted to alcohol and tranquilizers. Returning from school, Juan would find her unconscious on the floor. He tried to help, but also pushed away to survive, seeking solace in nature. Children like Juanito have a chore "which can never be accomplished. Their task is first to deal with mother's mood" (Winnicott, 1948, p. 93). Juan felt he was a failure, not good enough, reminiscent of disorders in which self-hatred covers feelings of worthlessness and despair about failing to bring joy to caregivers

(Brandchaft et al., 2010). *"Primal failure and incurable defect* have been transgenerationally transmitted within an incompetent developmental system, becoming installed at the core of the child's being" (p. 174).

Juan's father was "cold though he had a warm heart." He slept separately from his wife. Hearing mother moaning in bed, Juan went to her. She wanted back rubs and hugs. Seeing her breasts, he was tempted to touch. The day he found an apartment, his parents separated. Having felt "loved but unloved," Juan feels he failed to acquire many essential tools.

Growing up in such a dysfunctional family, one can understand how important enlivening sex play with his Puerto Rican friend was, serving as a potent antidote to Juan's dismal home situation. Encountering similar dysphoria later in life, he reached for similar medicine. Having found "wrong love" with his daughter, he wanted to learn how to love. Tears rolled down his cheeks. Before, he never cried. He liked this new feeling.

Since this marriage constituted Juan's third romantic failure, he abandoned sexuality. With physical and psychological difficulties, he was no longer very excitable – until suddenly with Erica. To reduce this renewed sexual tension and get some touching, he purchased massages. He did not want a real relationship because: it takes energy; he never received enough love to know how love should be; he had no right to a relationship. Despairing and remorseful, he contemplated suicide. If self-neglect precipitated "medical suicide," he did not care, because "I'm not worth much."

## Interpretation

I suggested a core issue for Juan concerned separation. Contemporary losses (wife, children, job, health) resonated with ancient loneliness (Willock, Bohm, & Curtis, 2011) related to maternal "abandonment," reactivating separation anxiety from a time when loving, physical interaction was essential for survival. In an unconscious maneuver designed to protect himself from these rekindled terrors, Juan had shifted into a state dissociated from his ordinary adult self with its values, empathic capacity, and self-control. To escape retraumatization, he sought to undo loss, reestablishing life-sustaining contact with beautiful flesh. In that action-oriented, altered state, Erica represented his ex-wife and, at bottom, his mother. "The finding of an object is in fact a refinding of it" (Freud, 1905, p. 222).

These ideas made sense to Juan, kindling hope he may not simply be a "monster." He did not want to use such thoughts as excuses. Nonetheless, it comforted him to think this horror might not be entirely his fault. He felt he needed to educate Juanito. We decided to begin or, one might say, continue treatment.

## Developmental trauma

Following his wife's death, Stolorow (1999) felt "like a strange and alien being – not of this world ... deadened and broken, a shell of the man I had once been. An unbridgeable gulf seemed to open up, separating me forever from my friends"

(p. 465). Such alienation is common in trauma. In the chasm separating the over-whelmed individual from others, anguished "estrangement and solitude takes form" (p. 465). Juan would understand such reactions to loss. Sexual experiences with Erica seemed "not real, not him." This loss of self-feeling "can be disastrous, for the individual has lost touch with all that they value" (Modell, 2008, p. 1). We interpret present moments to anticipate the future. This process fails if the self, lacking feeling, is "unable to simulate or imagine the future consequences" (p. 1) of actions, locked in a present, dreamlike state, divorced from the future.

One shudders at the plight of psychologically less sophisticated persons than Stolorow. He understood how early development influences reactions to subsequent loss. Feelings become traumatic "when the attunement that the child needed from the surround to assist in the tolerance, containment, modulation, and integration of this affect was profoundly absent" (p. 465). Such knowledge helped him ponder and process contemporary distress in terms of earlier difficulties.

In contrast to the traumatogenic misattunement Stolorow described, good-enough mothers start with almost complete adaptation to infants needs (Winnicott, 1953). Over time, they adapt less, "according to the infant's growing ability to deal with her failure" (p. 94). Unable to manage her own affects, let alone anyone else's, Juan's mother could not provide "optimal failure" (Kohut, 1984, p. 69). Faced with her emotional unavailability, Juanito would have known the truth of Brandchaft et al.'s (2010) assertion that "Loss of the object foreshadows terrifying states of estrangement and encroaching nonexistence" (p. 174). He would deploy emergency defenses, seeking compensatory gratification wherever he could.

Early trauma precludes self-cohesion (Stolorow & Atwood, 1992) and derails mentalization (Sands, 2010). "Survival by dissociation alienates the pervert forever from relating either to his own true self, or another person" (Khan, 1979, p. 137). "Trauma introduced into the developmental process has a shattering and enduring impact not just on the victim's subsequent capacity for understanding himself but also on the ability of others in his surround to understand him. Trauma is thus invariably accompanied unconsciously by all but impenetrable feelings of isolation and aloneness" (Brandchaft et al., 2010, p. 226).

When a mother is away for more than a short time and understanding cannot be conveyed to the (possibly preverbal) child, "She is dead from the point of view of the child. This is what dead means" (Winnicott, 1971, p. 22). During Juan's mother's early hospitalizations and other absences, Juanito would have had to use potent magical defenses to survive intolerable loss, to sustain some feeling of aliveness.

Green (1983) characterized emotionally unavailable mothers, like Juan's, as "dead." Stern (2006) discussed mothers "in whose eyes and mind the baby is unable to find himself" (p. 759). Molesting Erica, Juan felt "lost, in a fog" (disconnected from loving mother's gaze). Referring to the *Star Trek* character, Data, one of Juan's sisters wondered if their mother, who spoke in a monotone and never reacted, had lost her emotion chip. With the twins, his mother manifested no joy. "That ended my relationship with her when my kids were on her knee and she was unrelated to them," Juan explained. "I was a proud father and wanted her feedback through her loving them."

## Problematic solutions

While Juan was not generally perverse, that literature throws light on his failure. To avoid catastrophic disillusionment and annihilation, perverts strive for intense eroticism (Khan, 1979). "This excited state has a distinctly manic quality, and displaces the pervert from his inner space to search for an external area of experience, where, through the instrumentality of another, this excitement can be processed and actualized" (p. 136).

Dissociative defenses disrupt psychosomatic unity, producing psychic deadness, countered by stimulation-seeking to create pseudovitality (Goldberg, 1995). With Erica, Juan used his senses (visual, tactile) to stimulate/simulate pulsating vitality.

Bion (1957) divided personality into psychotic and non-psychotic (neurotic) parts. Sanchez-Medina (2002) added a perverse component. This survival mechanism – attempting to dwell in a magical universe where no loss, death, or suffering exists – manifests vividly in severe character pathology (borderline, narcissistic, antisocial), but might be universal (Bonner, 2006). This adjustment to pain is a defense and curative technique (Glover, 1933). Individuals cannot likely cure themselves of this strategy. Basking in illusions of omnipotence, they have no shortcomings, nothing to heal. In the incestuous defense specifically, "children exist only as appendages to an ego that delights in its own grandiosity" (Tesone, 2005). At a deeper level, perverts harbor profoundly dejected mental states. Though they may appear reasonably adjusted and involved in relationships, they inhabit a parallel world of terror, "the hiding place of one's worst fears about oneself warehoused as horrid facts" (Bonner, 2006, p. 1550). Acting out is the guardian of ignorance (Kohon, 1999, p. 75).

What makes a person/relationship perverse is the incapacity/refusal to treat others as autonomous, Bonner believed. Perversion creates a dehumanized world ruled by intense feelings. Melding ecstasy and denigration, it conceals collapsed humanity and self-worth. Fantasized instant union trumps intersubjectivity. Molesting Erica was a knife going through butter, Juan declared. His drive (knife) was unopposed by ego, superego, or intersubjective constraints. Excitement obliterated alienation.

An interpreting subject only exists in the Depressive position (Ogden, 1986). Without subjectivity, the world simply is. The self is merely another object, "a knife going through butter." Reflective space is absent. Impinged upon by impulses, objects, fears, and excitements, one simply responds.

In breakdown, the typical relational mode is doer/done-to complementarity (Benjamin, 2000). Only one can be subject, determining action, getting his/her way. Analysts now concentrate on positive aspects of acting out, considered as potential communications, perhaps the only way patients can communicate something (Kohon, 1999). Bromberg (2006) noted the need to access not-me (one's personal "gorilla") via enactment. Negation and breakdown are not just regrettable but also necessary; manifestations of perverse complementarity are required to reveal personality parts needing treatment (Benjamin). Delinquency is a sign of hope, a cry for help (Winnicott, 1973).

Perverse patients can be difficult or impossible to reach, Bonner emphasized. Their defensively impaired capacity to feel pain and fear provides precarious protection from catastrophe. While analysts may believe insight and intersubjective vitality are solutions to these individuals' dilemma, these patients *know* the only alternative to perversion is annihilation (Bonner, 2006). They may refuse to venture beyond their characterological comfort zone.

## Regular and perverse sexuality

"There is no distinction between perverse and normal sexuality other than the fact that their dominating component instincts and consequently their sexual aims are different. In both ... a well organized tyranny has been established, but in each of the two a different family has seized the reins of power" (Freud, 1916, p. 322). Component instincts and aims are no longer every analyst's language, but Freud's other terms ("dominating ... tyranny ... power") resonate well with contemporary conceptualizations concerning doer/done-to relationships.

Only if the *postoedipal* (Benjamin, 1995; Davies, 2003) is reached and consolidated can one dwell securely in intersubjectivity. Otherwise, lustful experience attempts to: protect the self from and repair narcissistic injury; express dissociated aspects of self; reinforce defenses bolstering a flagging gendered self (Frommer, 2006). Eroticism disassembles psychic structure to access aspects of self and relationality that have been spoiled, damaged, lost, denied, or repudiated (Fonagy, 2008; Frommer, 2006).

Lust comes easily in cultures fostering narcissistic defenses, but intimacy requires vulnerability and recognizing others as kindred subjects (Wrye, 2006). Lustful subjectivities reach out for the other and/or in for the self, Frommer noted. Eroticism dependent on intersubjective meeting for bringing aspects of self alive may be precarious. Focus on bodily sensation and fantasy can be derailed by someone whose erotic sensibility requires intersubjective penetration, he remarked. Erica's sleeping enabled Juan to focus exclusively on his feelings.

Erotic heat often comes from objectifying self and/or other, engaging in fantasies and enactments pivoting on unequal power (Frommer). Preoccupation with one's experience and desire eclipses concern for others' experience. Movement between loving and lusting involves dimming the lights on tender, dependent feelings, allowing disavowed desires and affects to emerge. Objectification is often considered a breakdown product of failed mutuality. Dampening or deadening of desire in long-term relationships may not simply reflect failure to integrate lust with love, but failure to become sufficiently self-centered, Frommer remarked. After years without sexual intimacy, Juan found himself privileging lust over love, perversely, rendering his "success" a failure.

When marriage ended, Juan believes his worst mistake was giving up on sexual relationships. He felt he became like clergy vowing abstinence, then lusting after children. (His father and brothers may have been sexually assaulted by priests.) Closing his libidinal flow, it did not disappear, to Juan's surprise. Instead, it followed a regressive pathway, akin to how Freud (1900) imagined impulses that cannot be discharged during sleep reversing direction, hypercathecting perceptual processes, creating hallucinations (dreams). Molesting Erica, Juan entered a dream-state. He believes this regression revivified experiences with his childhood friend. I imagine it also resurrected older zones pertaining to mother's innumerable "deaths" that furnished the dysphoric substrate making Juanito's erotic awakening with his friend (and his ascension at the altar of his daughter) feel so fabulous.

## Further formulation

Juan's early traumatic experiences required the emergency protective reaction Winnicott (1954) called "freezing of the failure situation" (p. 281). Unconsciously, individuals hope to some day return to this zone "to bridge a gap in continuity of experience" (1953, p. 97). Meanwhile, their "life task is to keep dissociated and encapsulated the breakdown in the developmental process caused by failure of environmental (maternal) provision" (Khan, 1974, p. 35). Juan "succeeded" at this task for decades until, one night, encapsulation failed. Embodying confusion of languages of tenderness and passion (Ferenczi, 1949), his failure revealed his yearning to return to a place of developmental breakdown. In delusional space, gaps/failures are "healed."

When cumulative conflict and misunderstanding precipitated marital collapse, Juan may unconsciously have felt thrown back into the era of maternal emotional implosion. In that sensorimotor epoch (Piaget, 1955), he would have had a body-based mind. As symbolic space disintegrated, part object relations, subjective objects, primary process, sensation, and symbolic equation (Segal, 1981) filled the void. In that regressed state, Juan conflated his daughter's soft skin with Klein's (1962) life-saving, good breast. Mons Veneris = Venus de Milo = Mom. With combined positive and negative hallucinations, what is perceived trumps what is not seen (Venus's arms, daughter's inappropriateness as sexual object).

Symbolic equations lack contextual reference (Rose, 2000). Objects, experiences, even self, become things-in-themselves, things-by-themselves. To create space for thought, psychoanalysts provide context, transmuting equations into representations. Helping Juan consider current and early origins of his acting out provided context, facilitating shifting from thoughtless action toward reflective functioning.

Complementing Juan's need to reach the absent object would be infantile wishes to be contacted by mother. (He had no memories of her touching him.) Acting out with Erica, he played his mother, truly, madly, deeply loving her baby. He also played Juanito, now more attractive than alcohol, drugs, oblivion, or any other perverse good breast for mother. "The pervert lives through his actions … [and] knows himself only through his victim's actualization of his intentions … What is essential for him in fact happens to and is experienced only by the other. The pervert stays an onlooker to what he perpetuates as actions through the other" (Khan, 1979, pp. 208–209). Toucher, touched, and observer, Juan was the dreamer who dreams the dream, and the one who understands it (Grotstein, 2000).

## Continuing treatment

Wracked by guilt, remorse, and sadness for all he had ruined and lost (feelings characteristic of Klein's depressive position), only wish-fulfilling dreams provided relief. In them, Juan was thanked by Frida for things he did, money he contributed. Her milk of human kindness soothed his troubled breast. Four-fifths of his "sexual" dreams were about her. Usually the contact was hugging. He declared repeatedly that he would always be madly in love with Frida. Crying frequently, he sometimes forgave himself.

After two months, Juan exuberantly reported having a girlfriend. He no longer felt trapped in relationships. Never had he felt so sexual. Disclosing his crime, his paramour did not reject him.

At Juan's request, I wrote to the Court, sharing my understanding, explaining how remorseful he was, concurring with his psychiatrist that he was unlikely to reoffend. Though Juan was very willing to serve a prison sentence, I suggested his time would be better spent continuing treatment and longstanding volunteer activities. The sympathetic judge gave the minimum sentence, conveying expectations that Juan would learn, grow, and lead a good life.

Juan lamented being unable to contribute to his children's development. He knew he was missing important years. Watching television fathers and children, he sobbed. He liked these emotions, feeling he was coming alive.

I encouraged Juan to speak with his ex about what he had learned, seeing if it might be feasible to have supervised visits with his son (and, someday, Erica). Communication via lawyers proceeded slowly. Ricardo's therapist did not believe sex criminals were fixable. When Ricardo pleaded to see his father, Frida informed him of the crime, whereupon Ricardo declared he did not want to see dad for a decade. Meanwhile, he wanted a new father.

Juan thought he had not seen Erica as a child, but as an old soul (mother?). His only purpose was to repair damage he had done. The twins were on his mind before he slept and when he awoke. In dreams, he apologized and explained to them what had happened. "I do more work asleep than awake."

Taking his girlfriend for a drive, Juan announced she should fasten her seatbelt because he was taking the top off his new convertible. That night, he dreamed he was taking mother for a ride. She raised her top, displaying breasts, saying he could touch them. Juan associated to having touched Erica. His dreaming appropriately integrated day residues with archaic impulses.

A good dream "incorporates ... an unconscious wish and can ... be available for psychic experience to the ego when the person wakes up" (Khan, 1979, p. 35). It "is a measure of a psychic capacity ... the dream increment of ego-strength." When early satisfactions have been unreliable, inadequate, or inconsistent, the capacity to use "mnemic images of satisfaction" (p. 40) to mobilize dream-wishes is lacking or distorted. Analytic work depends on this capacity. Dream-work disturbed by ego-distortions, primitive defenses, or psychotic anxieties, results in tendencies to act out in intense, harmful ways, Khan noted. As Juan consolidated at a higher level, growth facilitating dream-work replaced destructive acting out.

Besides believing that the infant's relationship to the breast provides the template for all future loves (Freud, 1905), Freud also believed that "anyone who is to be really free and happy in love must have ... come to terms with the idea of incest with his mother or sister" (1912, p. 186). Treatment enabled Juan to transmute propensities to deep-freeze such longings, or enact them via symbolic equation, into more sophisticated, symbolic capacities (dreaming, talking, thinking) conducive to a rich, meaningful life.

Scott (1952) postulated a "wake wish" (p. 467). Jekels (1945) believed "the awakening function is inherent in all dreams and constitutes their quintessence, their fundamental task" (p. 183). The analyst is a "waker" (Lewin, 1955, p. 193). Although Bromberg (2006) does not mention these authors (cited by Khan, 1974), their thinking might have informed his *Awakening the Dreamer*. Juan hoped to wake up and find his mess was just a bad dream. During therapy, he awoke from his perverse "dream," becoming ever more capable of processing multilayered yearnings via productive dream-work.

## Further discussion

When things go well, infants' "id experience" is organized through interaction with mothers and becomes available for vital, authentic existence (Winnicott, 1960). When "id excitements" cannot be processed relationally, these failures present significant challenges to the ego, consuming energy and producing ego-distortions and symptoms.

Rather than being failures, Slavin and Kriegman (1992) believed symptoms signal the self that self-structure and worldview are alienated from genuine interests and engage others to renegotiate identity. With suffering neurotics, it is easy to see this formulation's merits. That is less easy when pathology assaults others. Neurosis and perversion are, however, opposite sides of one coin (Freud, 1905), different ways of handling similar frustrations.

When personality begins to form what Eigen (2004), following Winnicott (1989), called madness X, breakdown occurs. Movement toward and away from this most personal thing about the self occurs as individuals attempt to escape, taste, embrace, and work with it. Approaching one's madness makes one feel more real. Shutting it out makes one feel unreal. This structure contains psychic components that must be recognized. Its affective intensity is crucial for one's sense of being.

Similar to Winnicott, Jung (1912) noted that

> Man also has a shadow side to him, consisting not just of little weaknesses – and foibles, but of a positively demonic dynamism. The individual seldom knows anything of this; to him … it is incredible that he should ever in any circumstances go beyond himself … Having a dark suspicion of these grim possibilities, man turns a blind eye to the shadow-side of human nature
>
> (p. 30)

It behooves us to become more familiar with our shadowy madness, integrating its healthy aspects into our better selves.

Much sanity has a "symptomatic quality, being charged with fear or denial of madness" (Winnicott, 1945, p. 140). One should go through madness and emerge healed, Winnicott believed. Juan slid into his "like a knife through butter," emerging more sane, less dissociated, more alive and integrated. Hopefully his growth will benefit his children.

The ancient Chinese believed crisis represents danger/opportunity. Our society regards breakdown as affording little, if any, opportunity. This limiting attitude fails us. "Breakdown is not so much an illness as a first step towards health" (Winnicott, 1989, p. 126). "Failure in some cases is the beginning of everything. It is the essential thing" (Winnicott, in Hopkins, 2006, p. 169). Juan's story accords with this outlook. The lowest ebb signals possibilities for turnabout.

Understanding unconscious motivation opens new dimensions for ethical inquiry, making "compassionate accountability" possible (Rubin, 2004, p. 28). Elucidating self-centered drivenness and lessening irrational conscience, psychoanalysis improves conduct, Rubin asserted. Kierkegaard (1849) communicated a similarly compassionate, ethical perspective: "Sin is the intensification of despair" (p. 67). Juan fits these viewpoints.

Incest "has been taken into very little consideration by psychoanalysts during recent years" (Ambrosio, 2005, p. vii). We are beginning to redress that failure. We can learn a great deal working with these cases that involve so much personal, relational, intergenerational, community, and other sorts of failure.

## Epilogue

Hearing this chapter's title, a colleague wondered if I was writing about how her ex-husband treated their daughter post-divorce. No sexual violation occurred, but she believed he failed to differentiate between his daughter and her, punitively neglecting their child as a result. That comment points to the wide applicability of the concept of deep-rooted perceptual-relational failure that can wreak havoc, not only in severe cases but also in more seemingly normal, yet still problematic situations.

# References

Alizade, M. (2005). Incest: the damaged flesh. In G. Ambrosio (ed.), *On Incest: Psychoanalytic Perspectives*. London: Karnac, pp. 101–114.

Ambrosio, G. (2005). Foreword. In G. Ambrosio (ed.), *On Incest: Psychoanalytic Perspectives*. London: Karnac, pp. vii–viii.

Benjamin, J. (1995). *Like Subjects, Love Objects: Essays on Recognition and Sexual Difference*. New Haven, CN: Yale University Press.

Benjamin, J. (2000). Intersubjective distinctions: subjects and persons, recognitions and breakdowns: commentary on paper by Gerhardt, Sweetnam, and Borton. *Psychoanalytic Dialogues*, 10: 43–56.

Bion, W.R. (1957). Differentiation of the psychotic from the non-psychotic personalities. *International Journal of Psychoanalysis*, 38: 266–275.

Bonner, S. (2006). A servant's bargain: perversion as survival. *International Journal of Psychoanalysis*, 87: 1549–1567.

Brandchaft, B., Doctors, S. & Sorter, D. (2010). *Toward an Emancipatory Psychoanalysis: Brandchaft's Intersubjective Vision*. New York: Routledge.

Bromberg, P.M. (2006). *Awakening the Dreamer: Clinical Journeys*. Mahwah, NJ: Analytic Press.

Cournut-Janin, M. (2005). Incest: the crushed fantasy. In G. Ambrosio (ed.), *On Incest: Psychoanalytic Perspectives*. London: Karnac, pp. 65–80.

Davies, J.M. (2003). Reflections of oedipus, post-oedipus, and termination. *Psychoanalytic Dialogues*, 13: 65–75.

Eigen, M. (2004). *The Sensitive Self*. Middletown, CN: Wesleyan University Press.

Ferenczi, S. (1949). Confusion of the tongues between the adults and the child – (the language of tenderness and of passion). *International Journal of Psychoanalysis*, 30: 225–230.

Fonagy, P. (2008). A genuinely developmental theory of sexual enjoyment and its implications for psychoanalytical technique. *Journal of the American Psychoanalytic Association*, 56: 11–36.

Freud, S. (1900). The interpretation of dreams. In J. Strachey (ed. and trans.), *The Standard Edition of the Complete Psychological Works of Sigmund Freud* (vols. 4 and 5).

Freud, S. (1905). Three essays on the theory of sexuality. In J. Strachey (ed. and trans.), *The Standard Edition of the Complete Psychological Works of Sigmund Freud* (vol. 7, pp. 125–248).

Freud, S. (1912). On the universal tendency to debasement in the sphere of love (contributions to the psychology of love II). In J. Strachey (ed. and trans.), *The Standard Edition of the Complete Psychological Works of Sigmund Freud* (vol. 11, pp. 177–190).

Freud, S. (1916). Introductory lectures on psycho-analysis. In J. Strachey (ed. and trans.), *The Standard Edition of the Complete Psychological Works of Sigmund Freud* (vol. 15).

Frommer, M.S. (2006). On the subjectivity of lustful states of mind. *Psychoanalytic Dialogues*, 16: 639–664.

Glover, E. (1933). The relation of perversion-formation to the development of reality-sense. *International Journal of Psychoanalysis*, 14: 486–504.

Goldberg, P. (1995). "Successful" dissociation, pseudovitality, and inauthentic use of the senses. *Psychoanalytic Dialogues*, 5: 493–510.

Green, A. (1983). The dead mother. In A. Green, *On Private Madness*. London: Hogarth Press, 1986, pp. 142–173.

Grotstein, J.S. (2000). *Who Is the Dreamer Who Dreams the Dream? A Study of Psychic Presences*. Hillsdale, NJ: Analytic Press.

Hopkins, L. (2006). *False Self: The Life of Masud Khan*. New York: Other Press.

Jekels, L. (1945). A bioanalytical contribution to the problem of sleep and wakefulness. *Psychoanalytic Quarterly*, 14: 169–189.

Jung, C.G. (1966). On the psychology of the unconscious. In *Two Essays on Analytical Psychology*, 2nd ed., (trans. R.F.C. Hull). London: Routlege, pp. 3–122.

Khan, M. (1974). *The Privacy of the Self*. London: Hogarth Press.

Khan, M. (1979). *Alienation in Perversions*. London: Hogarth Press.

Kierkegaard, S. (1849). *The Sickness unto Death*, trans. Howard V. Hong & Edna H. Hong. Princeton: Princeton University Press, 1980.

Klein, M. (1962). *Envy and Gratitude: A Study of Unconscious Sources*. London: Tavistock Publications.

Kohon, G. (1999). *No Lost Certainties to be Discovered*. London: Karnac.

Kohut, H. (1984). *How Does Analysis Cure?* A. Goldberg & P. Stepansky (Eds). Chicago: University of Chicago Press.

Lewin, B.D. (1955). Dream psychology and the analytic situation. *Psychoanalytic Quarterly*, 24: 169–199.

Modell, A. (2008). Memory and self: a conversation with Arnold Modell. Interviewer: Gemma Ainslie. *The Round Robin: Newsletter of Section 1, Division of Psychoanalysis, American Psychological Association*, 23, 2/3, Fall.

Ogden, T.H. (1986). *The Matrix of the Mind: Object Relations and the Psychoanalytic Dialogue*. Northvale, NJ: Aronson.

Piaget, J. (1955). *The Language and Thought of the Child*, trans. Marjorie Gabain. New York: Meridian Books.

Rose, J. (2000). Symbols and their function in managing the anxiety of change. *International Journal of Psycho-Analysis*, 81: 453–470.

Rubin, J.B. (2004). *The Good Life: Psychoanalytic Reflections on Love, Ethics, Creativity, and Spirituality*. Albany, NY: State University of New York Press.

Sacks, O. (1985). *The Man who Mistook his Wife for a Hat and Other Clinical Tales*. New York: Summit Books.

Sanchez-Medina, A. (2002). Perverse thought. *International Journal of Psycho-Analysis*, 83: 1345–1359.

Sands, S.H. (2010). On the royal road together: the analytic function of dreams in activating dissociative unconscious communication. *Psychoanalytic Dialogues*, 20: 357–373.

Scott, W.M. (1952). Patients who sleep or look at the psycho-analyst during treatment. *International Journal of Psycho-Analysis*, 33: 465–469.

Segal, H. (1981). *The Work of Hanna Segal: A Kleinian Approach to Clinical Practice*. New York: Jason Aronson.

Slavin, M. & Kriegman, J. (1992). *The Adaptive Design of the Human Psyche: Psychoanalysis, Evolutionary Biology, and the Therapeutic Process*. New York: Guilford.

Stern, D.B. (2006). Opening what has been closed, relaxing what has been clenched: dissociation and enactment over time in committed relationships. *Psychoanalytic Dialogues*, 16: 747–761.

Stolorow, R.D. (1999). The phenomenology of trauma and the absolutisms of everyday life: a personal journey. *Psychoanalytic Psychology*, 16: 464–468.

Stolorow, R. & Atwood, G. (1992). *Contexts of Being: The Intersubjective Foundations of Psychological Life*. Hillsdale, NJ: The Analytic Press.

Tesone, J. (2005). Incest(s) and the negation of otherness. In G. Ambrosio, *On Incest: Psychoanalytic Perspectives*. London: Karnac, pp. 51–64.

Willock, B., Bohm, L.C. & Curtis, R.C. (eds.) (2011). *Loneliness and Longing: Psychoanalytic Reflections*. London: Routledge.

Winnicott, D.W. (1945). Primitive emotional development. *International Journal of Psycho-Analysis*, 26: 137–143.

Winnicott, D.W. (1948). Reparation in respect of mother's organized defence against depression. In *Through Paediatrics to Psychoanalysis*, 1975, pp. 91–96.

Winnicott, D.W. (1953). Transitional objects and transitional phenomena – a study of the first not-me possession. *International Journal of Psycho-Analysis*, 34: 89–97.

Winnicott, D.W. (1954). Metapsychological and clinical aspects of regression within the psycho-analytical set-up. In *Through Paediatrics to Psycho-analysis*, 1975. New York: Basic Books, pp. 278–284.

Winnicott, D.W. (1960). Ego distortion in terms of true and false self. In *The Maturational Processes and the Facilitating Environment*. Madison, CT: International Universities Press, pp. 140–152.

Winnicott, D.W. (1971). *Playing and Reality*. London: Tavistock Publications.

Winnicott, D.W. (1973). Delinquency as a sign of hope. In S.C. Feinstein & P.L. Giovacchine (eds.), *Adolescent Psychiatry*, vol. 2. New York: Basic Books.

Winnicott, D.W. (1989). *Psychoanalytic Explorations*, ed. Clare Winnicott, Ray Shepherd, & Madeleine Davis. Cambridge, MA: Harvard University Press.

Wrye, H.K. (2006). Sitting with Eros and Psyche on a Buddhist psychoanalyst's cushion. *Psychoanalytic Dialogues*, 16: 725–746.

# Part IX

# REFLECTIONS AND FINAL WORDS

# 24

# FAILURE AS A SPUR TO GROWTH

## Lori C. Bohm

> Failure is, in a sense, the highway to success, inasmuch as every discovery of what is false leads us to seek earnestly after what is true, and every fresh experience points out some form of error which we shall afterward carefully avoid.
>
> (John Keats)

When my daughter graduated from high school, a well-known actor/alumnus who was starring in a highly rated television series gave the commencement address. Instead of focusing upon his triumphs, he described the many auditions in which he had not secured roles, and what he learned from these experiences. He had an excellent piece of advice for graduates: one of the most important things one must do is to accept that failure is a part of life. The key is to learn to use failure as an inspiration for growth.

This is the message of many chapters in this book. Failure potentially spurs personal development, providing gateways to future success. Many of our authors focused on this theme, with patient, analyst, or both, being beneficiaries. Failing profoundly and using psychoanalytic therapy to understand these failures initiated the progress of Willock's, McIntosh's, Langan's, and Hyman's patients. Stern observed differences in mood and attitude between nursing home residents who came to terms with their "obsolescence," including failures of their minds and bodies, and those who could not use these changes to find new ways of feeling valued or appreciating life.

Failures of clinicians, when worked through and analyzed, provide chances for professional and personal growth. Hewitt's lessons from failures working with a chronically suicidal, self-defeating patient, and Sloane's development following his failure to become a Training Analyst at his Institute are chronicled in their chapters.

In several chapters, both patient and therapist benefit from failures in their work together, launching crucial opportunities for personal evolution. Clark describes enactments in which she sent her patient away early or failed to meet him at their appointed time. Treatment survived these failures which resonated with pivotal experiences in both patient's and analyst's lives, expanding both their repertoires. Becoming impatient, Bergman yelled at her traumatized patient, who promptly "quit." Via email, this patient processed her rage, communicating it to Bergman. Eventually she re-entered the therapy, having gained previously unavailable self-knowledge. Sapountzis describes therapists' initial failures to understand, which can ultimately be rich sources of therapeutic information if therapists can sit with this experience and continue to ponder its meaning.

Failure, despite the chaos it creates, may provide the sole pathway to living better. Discussing couples treatment, Ludlam points out that therapists must not perceive the goal as maintaining the relationship. Acknowledging failed marriage may be the only way both parties can fashion healthier, more satisfying lives. Borg's psychotic patient's decompensation and mandated treatment helped him come to terms with his myriad failures and unconscious identity based upon being a failure. Only then could he begin creating a new identity which included possible success.

Borg's patient's travails point out one of several scenarios in which it is particularly difficult for people to benefit from failure's lessons. Patients with identities defined by failing or by the fear of failing may be especially challenging to reach. Mendelsohn writes about two who found the Icarus myth particularly compelling. They identified with Icarus, who, excited by his new-found ability to fly, soared too close to the sun. His wings melted and he fell into the sea. Both patients had spent their lives getting in the way of their success. Only by deconstructing their personal versions of this myth were they able to live free of impending doom.

Perfectionism presents another barrier to using failure's lessons to create more satisfying, successful lives. One of my patients who suffered repeated suicidal depressions becomes obsessed with having a "perfect day". If anything happens that he deems short of perfect, the day is ruined, and he takes to bed. There are many people (several described by Benton) whose perfectionist standards destroy self-esteem and lead to perpetual self-recrimination and a sense of failure.

Shame-proneness may also prevent people from benefiting from failures. Simha-Alpern presented a case she considered a therapeutic failure due to the patient's extreme need to avoid shame. Trying to be perfect is one way but, as noted above, is ultimately self-defeating. Simha-Alpern suggests that shame results when children experience mothers as rejecting of their love, thus feeling unlovable (Fairbairn, 1944; Ogden, 2010). Shame-prone patients can be challenging to engage, as psychoanalytic treatment involves being able to feel safe enough to discuss shame-promoting experiences and work them through.

A major function of psychoanalytic therapy is to help patients learn to forgive themselves, tolerate, and hopefully embrace their humanness. Several chapters describe forgiveness both as clinically and personally salutary (Seiden) and as a theme in psychoanalytic theory more generally (Holloway, Loszak). O'Leary's development of Attribution Theory, a staple of social psychology, to include recognition of happenstance's role in poor outcomes, offers a path to forgiving oneself in face of failure.

There are times when psychoanalysis fails patients. Hewitt's brave description of her challenging work with a chronically suicidal man who ended treatment and died, likely by his own hand, depicts such a situation. Despite the widening scope (Grand, 1995; Stone, 1954) of psychoanalysis, there are some patients who seriously challenge the ability of most, if not all analysts, to help. Honest, soul-searching renderings of these cases are needed to help clinicians better assess who is less likely to benefit from psychoanalytic treatment. Grappling with what leads to therapeutic failures can specify more productive ways to approach these difficult patients.

There are rare examples in the literature that provide important lessons we can learn from treatment failures. I will consider a discussion of Ferenczi's treatment of "RN," Hans Strupp's review of an autobiography of a failed analysis, and Donnel Stern's (2011) paper on hard-to-engage patients. I will touch on Irwin Hirsch's work about universal countertransference vulnerabilities that may limit effectiveness, if not cause treatment failure, unless addressed. Finally, I will reconsider Winnicott's treatment of Masud Khan, asking whether it should be considered a failure.

It is well-known that Sandor Ferenczi conducted a lengthy, unorthodox treatment with a brilliant, but seriously disturbed woman, Elizabeth Severn (RN), that included attempted mutual analysis. Maroda (1998) reviewed this treatment, including excerpts from Ferenczi's clinical diaries describing his interventions. As RN's condition deteriorated, she became more demanding. Ferenczi responded by acceding to her demands, believing he needed to gratify at least some wishes of this severely traumatized woman. He often saw her four or five hours a day, seven days a week, including evenings. He allowed her to accompany him and his wife on vacation. When RN was financially strapped, he reduced her fee or saw her free. Ultimately, Ferenczi agreed to "mutual analysis" in which he felt entitled to express the hate he felt towards her. This aspect of mutual analysis seemed helpful. The patient became more trusting of Ferenczi because of his honesty. Boundary breakdown between patient and analyst finally proved to damage treatment. RN expected to be able to engage in a real love relationship with Ferenczi, which was not an option. The stress of mutual analysis wore on Ferenczi. They resumed traditional analysis, which did not work out well for several reasons, including Ferenczi's failing health.

In analyzing this treatment failure, Maroda asserts that "RN needed to feel Ferenczi's authentic presence" (1998, p. 122). Patients who suffered severe emotional neglect and abuse in childhood will inevitably find therapeutic relationships disappointing and frustrating, and feel neglected and possibly abused by the analyst. A crucial part of the analyst's authentic presence with such patients involves "expressing negative feelings, admitting weakness and asking for forgiveness" (p. 124). Although most analysts working with abused patients worry they will retraumatize them by revealing negative reactions to them, expressing the analyst's inevitable anger is therapeutic. Maroda suggests Ferenczi's error was not listening to himself. He should have acknowledged his true feelings about RN to her, paving the way for them to design a therapeutic arrangement that would work for both.

Unlike Ferenczi's treatment of RN, the failed treatments discussed by Strupp (1982) are not well known. His paper resulted from reading an unpublished book written in German by a former patient of two psychoanalysts. The patient wrote this book two years after her second analysis as part of an effort to come to terms with her analytic experience which she considered "a fiasco" (Strupp, 1982, p. 236). She was an analyst-in-training during both treatments. Ultimately pronounced unanalyzable, she was rejected for membership by the German Psychoanalytic Association. The book provides evidence that the author, like RN, prompted intensely negative feelings in her therapists, which they acted upon but did not acknowledge directly to her.

Strupp extracted several lessons from these failed treatments:

1   Therapists work with "powerful and potentially dangerous forces" by virtue of how important they become in their patients' lives. It is crucial that they be cognizant that they carry serious responsibility for patients' welfare, and respect the power they have been accorded by patients, using it wisely.
2   The possibility of unknowingly harming a patient always exists. Analysts must remain vigilant about this possibility.
3   Assuming an omniscient or omnipotent attitude is never justified.
4   Interpretations should never be used as weapons, as this patient thought they were. "A basic requirement for an interpretation must be its acceptability to the patient in the context surrounding it." Therapists are responsible for "clarifying and correcting misunderstandings" (p. 247).
5   Therapists must help patients deal with current life situations, including improving their sense of wellbeing and interpersonal relationships.
6   Therapy needs to be collaborative. The patient needs to feel accepted, supported, and that his or her positive qualities are recognized.

Consistent with his research findings (e.g., Strupp, Hadley, & Gomes-Schwartz, 1977), Strupp underscores the therapeutic alliance is central to the efficacy of psychoanalytic psychotherapy and psychoanalysis.

Strupp's article appeared thirty years ago, before Relational Psychoanalysis. Most contemporary analysts see the patient-analyst relationship as the heart of therapeutic work, in ways not captured by the notion of therapeutic alliance. The exigencies of the patient-analyst relatedness have become the focus of the psychoanalytic encounter. In that spirit, Stern (2011) dissects what he considered to be a treatment failure due to the analytic couple's inability to develop a workable relationship. He describes this patient as "hard-to-engage." Rather than using diagnosis to blame the patient, or invoking countertransference to blame the analyst for failure to create a viable process, he suggests patient and analyst were caught up in dissociative enactment that precluded engagement. Despite the fact that patient and analyst liked one another from the beginning, soon the patient's inability to access his desire and be curious about his inner life found an echo as Stern found it impossible to maintain curiosity about the patient. He suggests his patient's deadness and disinterest in his internal life (if there was one), smacks of fending off something unbearable. They parted amicably, with Stern suspending judgment about whether accessing whatever was unbearable would have produced a better outcome.

The interdigitation of the patient's familiar, maladaptive relational patterns with the therapist's needs can contribute to suboptimal outcomes. Hirsch (2008) discusses numerous examples of this in *Coasting in the Countertransference*. In these cases, therapists neglect to engage patients in ways that would disrupt comfortable, if static, patient-analyst equilibria. Reasons therapists might wittingly or unwittingly behave this way include concern over loss of income were the patient to leave, desire to avoid extreme discomfort, and loss of gratification of the analyst's desires, needs, and predilections. All are vulnerable to "using" patients to serve emotional needs. (One could argue that most, if not all, therapists gravitate to the profession due to emotional wounds.) Being in therapy ourselves does not guarantee we will not do this.

This last point brings to mind another famous treatment "failure" or partial failure: Winnicott's analysis of Masud Khan. In "The outrageous prince: Winnicott's uncure of Masud Khan," Dodi Goldman (2002) writes: "We sometimes unconsciously use our patients ... because of mutually resonating vulnerabilities. Perhaps the tragedy of Winnicott never having had offspring of his own is that he ended up investing part of his desire for a son in Khan. And, as we know, it is as disastrous to treat our patients as children as it is to treat our children as patients" (p. 13).

Goldman argues that, despite Khan's alcoholic self-destruction following Winnicott's death, his treatment was by no means a total failure. That treatment, which Khan said lasted fifteen years, was revealed in Winnicott's appointment diaries and clinical notebooks to have lasted only two and one half years. Khan had three analysts prior to Winnicott, two of whom died treating him. Goldman believes recognition Winnicott provided in their analytic work and subsequent supervision "held his worst tendencies more or less in check for decades" (p. 10) – when Khan was incredibly productive and added much to our literature.

Goldman's take on Khan's work with Winnicott reminds us that learning and growth occur even in treatments in which not all goals are achieved. One of the most helpful lessons of any treatment is that flawed analysts (like flawed parents) have something useful and beneficial to offer. Therapeutic "almost" failures may encourage us to become more modest about our work and ourselves as healers. As authors in this volume assert in widely varied voices, failure can spur growth, forgiveness, and greater self-acceptance for patient and therapist alike.

## References

Fairbairn, W.R.D. (1944). Endopsychic structure considered in terms of object relationships. *International Journal of Psychoanalysis*, 25: 70–92.

Goldman, D. (2002). The outrageous prince: the Uncure of Masud Khan. Madeleine Davis Memorial Lecture, Squiggle Foundation, London, July.

Grand, S. (1995). A classic revisited: clinical and theoretical reflections on Stone's widening scope of indications for psychoanalysis. *Journal of the American Psychoanalytic Association*, 43: 714–764.

Hirsch, I. (2008). *Coasting in the Countertransference*. New York: Analytic Press.

Keats, J. (1965). In C.N. Catrevas, J. Edwards, & R.E. Browns (eds.), *The New Dictionary of Thoughts: A Cyclopedia of Quotations*. Standard Book Company.

Maroda, K. (1998). Why mutual analysis failed: the case of Ferenzci and RN. *Contemporary Psychoanalysis*, 34: 115–132.

Ogden, T. (2010). Why read Fairbairn? *International Journal of Psychoanalysis*, 91: 101–118.

Stern, D.B. (2011). The hard-to-engage patient: a treatment failure. *Psychoanalytic Dialogues*, 21: 596–606.

Stone, L. (1954). The widening scope of indications for psychoanalysis. *Journal of the American Psychoanalytic Association*, 2: 567–594.

Strupp, H. (1982). Psychoanalytic failure – reflections on an autobiographical account. *Contemporary Psychoanalysis*, 18: 235–250.

Strupp, H., Hadley, S.W. and Gomes-Schwartz, B. (1977). *Psychotherapy for Better or for Worse: An Analysis of the Problem of Negative Effects*. New York: Jason Aronson.

# 25

# FAILURE'S PERVASIVE PRESENCE

## Brent Willock

"Why be a man when you can be a success?" Bertolt Brecht is said to have posed that unsettling question. I first encountered his provocative pensée in the 1960s. Immersing myself in our manuscript, this physician/playwright/political activist's challenge called again.

In the 1960s, many questioned longstanding social values, struggling with what it means, and could mean, to be human. In a successful film of the time, *The Graduate*, the most memorable line was spoken by a materially success-ful businessman. Endeavouring to influence a younger fellow, he shared, "Just one word – plastics!" Audiences roared. For a generation seeking authenticity and questioning the military-industrial complex's "business as usual" philoso-phy, this mantra seemed lacking. At that time, plastic was synonymous with inauthentic.

A generational divide was also in Freud's (1916) mind when he portrayed *Those Wrecked by Success*. Paralleling a theme in *The Graduate*, Freud discussed indi-viduals who believe their accomplishments constitute forbidden Oedipal victory needing punishment. Not only failure but also success can do us in. Brechtian "suc-cess" might ruin us differently. By unthinking accommodation to sociocultural pressures, we may succeed financially, but lose our souls, trading true self-potential for comparatively empty, false selves (Winnicott, 1955). Success can be failure.

In 1894, as Freud was launching his stellar career, Rudyard Kipling published *If*. It, too, is intergenerational: a father counsels a young man. The poem's best-known passages concern dangers of failure and success. "If you can meet with Triumph and Disaster / And treat those two impostors just the same," Kipling commences. Concluding, the speaker declares, "And – which is more – you'll be a Man, my son!" Like Brecht, Kipling favors character and attitude more than material success.

Why would people sacrifice their human potential for crass versions of suc-cess? They might strike such deals with the devil to flee failure. In Jung's terms, people might forge success Personas to mask failure anxiety. The Shadow of the abject falls upon the subject.

Success addiction manically attempts to keep the wolf of failure at bay. Many celebrities and other accomplished individuals suffer gravely on success's altar, numbing failure terror with drugs. Many perish from inability to treat those two impostors, triumph and disaster, similarly. Our authors offer non-chemical ways for coping with failure. Transcending tendencies to simply blame self or other, O'Leary recommends balanced attribution, underscoring the role of chance. "Luck has a lot to do with success ... and failure" (stated Leonard Cohen in 2009). Curtis and Frank emphasize failure's positive features. Recalling Edison failing 10,000 times before creating a viable lightbulb, Sharma (in Schachter, 2010) remarked: "Study any genius ... and you'll discover the same thing: They succeeded because they outfailed everyone around them" (p. B8).

When the stock market tumbled, my analysand remembered that melancholics fear impoverishment (Freud, 1917), noting he, too, is driven by failure anxiety. The possibility of losing his house felt worse than death. "I may be worthless but at least I have a degree and job, objective measures of being worth something. Money keeps bottomless fears about myself at bay. It allows me to hide or escape my failings." He likened himself to Michael Jackson and Howard Hughes, whose wealth not only protected them but also prevented them from coming to terms with their inner realities.

The "homelessmentallyill" (Borg, 2007) provide disturbing, contemporary images of failure. Begging and sleeping on streets, these suffering beings sometimes serve as containers for our worst fears (projective identification).

David Hochman (2011) asked spiritually minded physician Deepak Chopra, "Why do you think there are so many broken, psychologically damaged people out there? Many of them pick up your books for comfort and guidance. In that way, is your success a sign we've failed as a society?" Chopra's readers usually have accoutrements of success, but may sometimes feel spiritually empty.

## Developmental dangers

Failure haunts the life cycle. From birth to death, we expend enormous energy trying to cope with it, or banish it to the shadowy abyss. Consider Freud's (1926) sequence of early anxieties. All can be viewed in terms of failure. His first danger concerns object loss – a potentially catastrophic failure that can lead to failure-to-thrive and death (Spitz, 1945). Most babies have sufficient tastes of that experience to instill terror of complete caregiving failure.

Object loss frequently concerns *emotional* absence, as in Green's (2001) description of "dead" mothers. Offspring struggle to cheer these mothers up, but typically fail. A lifelong sense of inadequacy, despair, and failure may ensue. When my earlier-mentioned analysand was a child, he always interrupted play to go home to make sure his depressed mother was still there. In his sixties, after decades of struggle, he began to surmount a lifetime of despondency.

Freud's second developmental danger concerns loss of the object's love. Failure to secure caregiver devotion might be attributed to parental deficiencies. Alternatively, children may feel they deserve failing grades for being insufficiently endearing to attract and sustain parental love. These differing beliefs can reflect Klein's

Paranoid-Schizoid vs. Depressive organizing principles. In the former, blame is laid at the breast of the bad object. In the latter, infants assume their own badness underlies failure to secure parental love.

Freud's third developmental danger concerns loss of a valued body part (castration anxiety). Children's failures to accept subordinate familial positions provoke severe retaliation, at least in fantasy. Responsibility may be attributed by youngsters to themselves and/or unempathic/mean parents. O'Leary helps us consider that neither party is completely responsible since Oedipal conflicts are rooted in our existential condition.

Articulating early genital era fears, Freud viewed women as "failed men" (Chodorow, 2000). With Freud's emphasis on phallic competition, most men also seem destined to be failed men.

Freud's final developmental danger concerns loss of superego love. Failure to secure that internal object's blessing can fuel lifelong depressive conditions, anxiety disorders, and self-esteem problems.

Freud believed these early danger situations underlie all our inhibitions, symptoms, and anxieties. At the heart of what ails us, failure lies.

## Epigenetic oppositions

Erikson's (1950) expansion of Freud's framework created a life-cycle perspective that can be seen as failure-focused. In his model, life's first months are characterized by Trust vs. Mistrust. When families fail to create sufficiently loving atmospheres, fear of object loss and bad objects arise. Failure to establish trust in good object availability creates an enduring, insecure, hypervigilant, paranoid outlook, or a depressive sense of insufficiency, loss, and failure.

In Erikson's second stage – Autonomy vs. Shame and Doubt – failure to establish adequate sense of an independent, capable self can lead to life lacking in confidence, joy, and pride. One is plagued instead by feelings of uncertainty, inadequacy, and failure (including loss of the object's love).

The ensuing childhood era involves Initiative vs. Guilt. Failure to develop a feeling of being able to inaugurate action in a valued, non-harmful manner can lead to a guilt-ridden, inhibited, quasi-life. In Erikson's next stage – Industry vs. Inferiority – if one fails to find a way to become productively involved at home and school, one may feel forever below par. Between Initiative/Guilt (phallic) and Industry/Inferiority (latency), Blatt and Shichman (1983) inserted Mutuality vs. Alienation. Here, Oedipal resolution and cooperative peer play commence. A sense of "we" begins to compete with "I." Failure to become part of larger groups (family, peers, community) fosters enduring outsider feelings.

For Freud, successful adolescence results in solid genital character. Erikson places that achievement in psychosocial context: Identity vs. Identity Diffusion. Failure to establish a reasonably coherent, satisfying identity leads to a sense of not knowing who one is, what one's place is in the larger scheme. In the ensuing young adulthood stage, Intimacy vs. Isolation, failure in intimate relationships can lead to feeling profoundly unsuccessful. In midlife's challenge, Generativity vs. Stagnation, failure to create something valuable for the next generation, can feel like failure to go all the way. Some counter that feeling by wrapping themselves in objects supposedly indicative of success.

In the final life cycle stage, Integrity vs. Despair, if one believes one failed to live a worthwhile, authentic life, one may experience emptiness and meaninglessness. Kohut (1977) felt such reflection commenced in late middle age:

> We ask ourselves whether we have been true to our innermost design ... This was a time of utmost hopelessness for some, of utter lethargy ... which overtakes those who feel that they have failed and cannot remedy the failure in the time and with the energies still at their disposal. The suicides of this period are not the expression of a punitive superego but a remedial act – the wish to wipe out the unbearable ... mortification ... imposed by the ultimate recognition of a failure of all encompassing magnitude.
>
> (1977, p. 241)

As in earlier stages, one can mask this failure. It may, however, poke through the success Persona, wrecking havoc from behind the curtain of consciousness.

In later life, Leonard Cohen aspired to write a love song, an "anthem of forgiving, a manual for living with defeat" (*Old Ideas*, 2012). His yearning reflects needs arising as we review our failings in life's last stage. Cohen reinforces our authors' (Holloway, Loszak) messages concerning failing and forgiving. To fail is human, to forgive divine.

In Freud's and Erikson's models, while failure was not their focus, grappling with feared and actual failure is central to every stage they portray. Its omnipresence speaks to its importance.

## Necessary, beneficial, therapeutic failure

Many enter psychotherapy with a sense of failure. How do they get well, Winnicott (1963) asked?

> In the end the patient uses the analyst's failures, often quite small ones, perhaps manoeuvered by the patient, or the patient produces delusional transference elements ... and we have to put up with being misunderstood. The operative factor is that the patient now hates the analyst for the failure that originally came as an environmental factor, outside the infant's area of omnipotent control, but that is *now* staged in the transference. So in the end we succeed by failing – failing the patient's way.
>
> (1963, p. 258)

Other analysts endorsed Winnicott's perspective. Emphasizing "*the necessity of failure* in the clinical situation" (p. 276), Khan (1974) discussed one patient where

"I help her because I fail her … And what is even more important for her is that I accept my failures and am not devalued in my eyes by them" (p. 277). Slochower (2011) concurred: "There's no exit from our vulnerability to failing our patients" (p. 39). "It is the establishment of a reliable holding situation that allows the patient to stage a failure, or even a trauma, within the analytic setting and then integrate that experience" (Slochower, 1996, p. 169). Bromberg (2006) elaborated:

> The analyst's own repeated efforts to relieve his patient's distress must fail in order for the analyst to know the patient's experience for what it is. But knowing is not enough; the irreparable must somehow be repaired, and the only way the past-as-present can be repaired is within a relationship that repeats the failure of the past … All attempts by analysts to cure patients through the technical stance of trying to be the good object have failed … A patient needs a human being as a partner, a human being who can accept (eventually) his own limitations and failings, and, most important, a human being who can tolerate not having seen his failings when they are pointed out … The patient requires that the analyst fruitlessly try to help until he is forced to recognize himself as failing her in the same way she was failed by her primary objects … The repetition of the crisis is fundamentally the enactment and reenactment of a failed communication that has the potential to become a successful communication if the oppressiveness of the repetition eventually affects the analyst's communication with his own internal objects and draws the analyst's inner world into the enactment.
>
> (2006, pp. 94–96)

## Let me not fail to thank our authors and co-editors

"Born to Lose," Ray Charles crooned. We are also born to fail, bound to fail. Contributors to this volume help us understand, manage, and even grow from these experiences. If we ponder and discuss these matters, we will learn important lessons that will benefit us, and those with whom we work and otherwise relate. As a result, we may not have to lament, like the person Ray Charles channels, that we've lived our lives in vain and "every dream has only brought me pain."

W.H. Auden advised us to "Sing of human unsuccess" (1939) My co-editors and our authors have taken this famous poet's counsel to heart, blessing us with a symphony of thoughtful contributions. Their songs expand and enrich our psychic space with new ideas and tools for comprehending and dealing with this essential aspect of life.

## References

Auden, W.H. (1939). In memory of W.B. Yeats. In G. Roelofs (ed.), *The Major Poets: English and American*. New York: Harcourt, Brace and World.

Blatt, S.J. & Shichman, S. (1983). Two primary configurations of psychopathology. *Psychoanalysis and Contemporary Thought*, 6: 187–254.

Bromberg, P. (2006). *Awakening the Dreamer: Clinical Journeys*. Mahwah, NJ: Analytic Press.

Borg, M.B. (2007). Just some everyday examples of psychic serial killing: psychoanalysis, necessary ruthlessness, and disenfranchisement. In B. Willock, L.C. Bohm, & R.C. Curtis (eds.), *On Deaths and Endings: Psychoanalysts Reflections on Finality, Transformations and New Beginnings*. London: Routledge, pp. 180–196.

Chodorow, N. (2000). Reflections on The Reproduction of Mothering – twenty years later. *Studies in Gender and Sexuality*, 1: 337–348.

Hochman, D. (2011). Interview with Deepak Chopra. *Playboy* magazine, March.

Cohen, L. (2009). CBC Radio interview. *Q*, April 16.

Erikson, E.H. (1950). *Childhood and Society*. New York: Norton.

Freud, S. (1916). Some character-types met with in psycho-analytic work. In J. Strachey (ed. and trans.), *The Standard Edition of the Complete Psychological Works of Sigmund Freud* (vol. 14, pp. 309–333).

Freud, S. (1917). Mourning and Melancholia. In J. Strachey (ed. and trans.), *The Standard Edition of the Complete Psychological Works of Sigmund Freud* (vol. 14, pp. 237–258).

Freud, S. (1926). Inhibitions, symptoms and anxiety. In J. Strachey (ed. and trans.), *The Standard Edition of the Complete Psychological Works of Sigmund Freud* (vol. 20, pp. 77–178).

Green, Andre (2001). The dead mother. In *Life Narcissism, Death Narcissism*. London: Free Association Books.

Khan, M.R. (1974). *The Privacy of the Self: Papers on Psychoanalytic Theory and Technique*. London: Hogarth Press.

Kohut, H. (1977). *The Restoration of the Self*. New York: International Universities Press.

Schachter, H. (2010). Unraveling the traits of genius. *Globe and Mail*, December 13, p. B8.

Slochower, J. (1996). *Holding and Psychoanalysis: A relational Perspective*. Hillsdale, NJ: Analytic Press.

Slochower, J. (2011). Analytic idealizations and the disavowed: Winnicott, his patients, and us. *Psychoanalytic Dialogues*, 21: 3–21.

Spitz, R. (1945). Hospitalism – an inquiry into the genesis of psychiatric conditions in early childhood. *The Psychoanalytic Study of the Child*, 1: 53–74.

Winnicott, D.W. (1955). Metapsychological and clinical aspects of regression within the psycho-analytical set-up. *International Journal of Psycho-Analysis*, 36: 16–26.

Winnicott, D.W. (1963). Dependence in infant-care, in child-care, and in the psychoanalytic setting. In *Maturational Processes and the Facilitating Environment*. New York: International Universities Press, 1965, pp. 249–259.

# INDEX